AN INTRODUCTION TO THE
ENTERTAINMENT INDUSTRY

PETER LANG
New York • Washington, D.C./Baltimore • Bern
Frankfurt am Main • Berlin • Brussels • Vienna • Oxford

Andi Stein, Beth Bingham Evans

AN INTRODUCTION TO THE
ENTERTAINMENT INDUSTRY

PETER LANG
New York • Washington, D.C./Baltimore • Bern
Frankfurt am Main • Berlin • Brussels • Vienna • Oxford

Library of Congress Cataloging-in-Publication Data

Stein, Andi.
An introduction to the entertainment industry / Andi Stein, Beth Bingham Evans.
p. cm.
Includes bibliographical references and index.
1. Amusements. 2. Games. 3. Mass media.
I. Evans, Beth Bingham. II. Title.
GV1201.S812   793—dc22   2008035927
ISBN 978-1-4331-0341-4 (hardcover)
ISBN 978-1-4331-0340-7 (paperback)

Bibliographic information published by **Die Deutsche Bibliothek**.
Die Deutsche Bibliothek lists this publication in the "Deutsche
Nationalbibliografie"; detailed bibliographic data is available
on the Internet at http://dnb.ddb.de/.

Cover design by Clear Point Designs

© 2009 Andi Stein and Beth Bingham Evans
Peter Lang Publishing, Inc., New York
29 Broadway, 18th floor, New York, NY 10006
www.peterlang.com

Printed in the United States of America

Table of Contents

INTERACTIVE ENTERTAINMENT

COMMUNICATION AS ENTERTAINMENT

Figures

Acknowledgments

The authors would like to thank Genelle Belmas for contributing Chapter 13, Video Games, and Tom Clanin for contributing Chapter 14, Publishing. We would also like to thank our editor Mary Savigar and production manager Bernadette Shade for helping us make this book a reality. We are extremely grateful to all the people who agreed to be featured in the book's job profiles.

Introduction to the Entertainment Industry

BETH BINGHAM EVANS

Entertainment is big business. Whether it's a favorite television show, an artist at the top of the music charts, a best-selling book, or a hometown sports team, we love entertainment—and it shows. In 2007, total spending on entertainment in the United States, including advertising, was about $930 billion dollars.[1]

Competition for our attention and our money is fierce in the entertainment sector. Americans will spend an average of 3,601 hours in 2009 with traditional media.[2] The average American doesn't have much additional time in his or her day for more entertainment. We are saturated with entertainment options. So, for one segment of the entertainment market to grow, another segment must decline.

In the following chapters, we will examine the entertainment industry to understand how each segment operates. From television to publishing and from theme parks to shopping, one of the best ways to understand the industry is to know about its history, so we will take a look back and a look forward. We will discuss career options. We will analyze the challenges and trends facing each area of entertainment. All of this in an attempt to give you a competitive edge when you enter the workforce looking for your dream job in the field of entertainment.

Working in entertainment can be exciting, rewarding, glamorous, and also a lot of hard work. Entertainment industry executives understand the huge number of options available to consumers when it comes to entertainment. Because of that, those in the entertainment business take their work and their careers very seriously.

Grab a comfortable pair of shoes because we are going to be traveling long and fast through the world of entertainment. We start with electronic media including film, television, and radio and then make our way into arts and leisure entertainment including theater, music, museums, and theme parks. From there we journey to recreational entertainment including sports, travel, and shopping, and on to interactive entertainment, which encompasses gambling and video games. And finally, we wrap up with communications as entertainment with publishing and event planning.

Throughout our journey into the entertainment industry, we will introduce you to individuals who are working in different areas of the field. Each chapter will feature profiles of people currently working in the industry. We'll give you a glimpse of their daily work lives and show you how they got a foot in the door. We'll also talk about the job options that are available to you within the various segments of the entertainment industry. You'll learn about the different types of jobs that exist within the industry and discover that there is no single path to a career in entertainment. Instead, you'll be offered an overview of the job possibilities that exist and the opportunities you can take advantage of—such as internships—in order to be make these possibilities a reality.

At the end of each chapter, you'll find resources to help you jump-start your career in entertainment. These include lists of associations, trade publications, websites, and job-hunting resources related to the topics in each chapter.

So, get ready to learn about the many dimensions of the field of entertainment. As they say in the business: Lights! Camera! Action!

The Entertainment Industry as a Whole

Let's begin our journey into the world of entertainment by starting with a look at the industry as a whole.

Understanding Our Audience

In order to understand entertainment, we must first understand our audience. Everyone likes to be entertained, but not everyone is entertained by the same entertainment options. The Media Usage chart that follows in Figure 1 gives us a glimpse at how Americans spend their time with various entertainment options.

Figure 1: Media Usage in Hours per American 2000 to 2010

Media	2000	2001	2002	2003	2004	2005	2006	2007	2008	2009	2010
Usage	3,340	3,393	3,447	3,508	3,530	3,543	3,553	3,567	3,592	3,601	3,620
Television	1,502	1,553	1,572	1,615	1,620	1,659	1,673	1,686	1,704	1,713	1,733
Broadcast TV	812	777	744	729	711	679	684	672	666	657	650

Networks	717	680	646	629	612	576	579	567	558	546	538
Independents	95	97	98	100	100	101	105	105	108	110	112
Cable & Satellite	690	776	828	886	909	980	989	1,014	1,038	1,057	1,083
Basic	568	638	687	728	753	807	823	840	862	880	902
Premium	122	139	140	157	156	173	166	174	176	176	181
Broadcast/ Satellite Radio	784	792	825	834	821	805	794	786	785	778	776
Recorded Music	259	231	203	189	195	189	191	191	188	187	180
Newspapers	210	198	196	194	191	184	181	177	173	169	165
Consumer Magazines	135	127	125	122	125	124	122	121	122	120	119
Consumer Books	107	106	109	109	108	108	107	107	107	108	108
Videogames	65	66	71	76	78	73	75	78	80	84	86
Film/ Home Video	43	47	57	60	67	63	63	64	65	66	67
Box Office	12	13	14	13	13	12	12	12	12	12	12

Chart created with information provided by Veronis Suhler Stevenson, New York, NY/ Communications Industry Forecast annual report/U.S. Census Bureau.

The U.S. Census Bureau prepares many reports that chart population growth, industry growth, consumer spending, and much more. For more information, or to see some of the other reports available, you can visit the U.S. Census Bureau at www.census.gov and go to the most recent *Statistical Abstract*.

Television

Americans continue to have a love affair with television. It may seem hard to believe, but the average American adult spent more than two months, or 1,673 hours, in 2005 with television, mainly watching cable or satellite television. The number of hours Americans spent with network television continues to drop each year. We'll talk about this and other aspects of the business in our chapter on television.

Radio

The number of hours Americans spent with the radio on in 2005 was 805. It's the second-largest category after television. The amount of time with radio is significant and is expected to remain relatively constant through 2010. We sometimes overlook the power of radio, but from the numbers in Figure 1, it continues to be a significant entertainment

COLIN CAMPBELL

Freelance Writer / Producer / Director

Colin Campbell is a freelance writer/producer/director who works primarily at NBC News and The History Channel. Colin has also worked for E! Entertainment Television, Extra, and KCAL in Los Angeles. He attributes his success at staying busy as a freelancer to always working hard and always delivering what people are buying. "Know your limits," he said. "Over-promising won't help. No one likes to say 'no,' but if a project can't be done, say so."

Campbell graduated from Cal Poly San Luis Obispo with the goal of working in television news. He landed his first job at a local television station in San Luis Obispo. "I was sitting in the lobby of the television station at the right time," Campbell said. He was applying for a job when the morning show producer abruptly quit. The news director needed a replacement and fast. Campbell had worked at the station as an intern in college, and his boss remembered him as a hard worker and offered him the job.

"The nice thing about small market internships is they give students an opportunity to do everything. That's something you can't do in large television markets because of unions and other restrictions," Campbell said.

Campbell's big opportunity in Los Angeles came with the 1995 O.J. Simpson trial. With many writers and producers assigned to cover the trial, KCAL needed freelance news writers. He hasn't taken a staff job since.

Campbell enjoys the variety of producing the 5 P.M. news for NBC one week and working on an hour-long documentary about the Wild West for the History Channel the next month. "I end up knowing a little about a lot of things in news and a lot about one little thing for the History Channel," he said.

Surviving as a freelance journalist isn't easy, Campbell said. It's "a balancing act to make sure your plate is full but not too full." Over the past 10 years, the television news business has changed. More and more freelancers are being hired, and fewer staff jobs exist. Many of the people who freelance in the larger television markets belong to a labor union and receive health insurance and other benefits through the union.

Campbell believes anybody can learn to write well. He said there are some tricks, but they can be taught. "Practice is key and a willingness to be self-critical."

» » »

choice for Americans. Some of the reasons for the popularity of this medium will be discussed in the chapter on radio.

Recorded Music

Looking at the Media Usage chart in Figure 1, we see that Americans continue to spend less and less time with recorded music. This comes at a time when the recorded music industry is seeing sales slump and digital downloads skyrocket. The iPod has revolutionized the music industry as the portable device that dominates the market share. But what could be some of the other reasons why Americans are spending less time with recorded music? We'll explore that question and others in the chapter on music.

Video Games

The U.S. Census Bureau looked at the number of hours Americans spend with video games, and it has continued to rise since 2000 and is expected to continue rising through 2010. The average American spent 73 hours with video games in 2005. While the number is rising, it is still far below the number of hours spent with television, radio, and recorded music. The evolution of the video game industry is one of the topics addressed in the chapter on video games.

Film

Film continues to be a prominent segment in the entertainment industry as far as the amount of money spent making movies and the prestige of the film industry. However, Americans on average don't go to the movies very often. In 2005, the average American spent 12 hours going to see movies at the box office, which translates into approximately 5–6 movies a year for the average American. We spend significantly more time watching movies at home. These and other industry trends will be explained in the chapter on film.

Publishing

Compared to the amount of time we spend with television, Americans don't spend a lot of time reading. The number of hours spent with newspapers drops every year. Magazine and book reading remains relatively constant. In 2005, Americans on average spent 184 hours with newspapers, 124 hours reading magazines, and 108 hours reading books. Publishing trends will be further discussed in that chapter.

Additional Sources of Entertainment

While the Census Bureau's Media Usage chart covers some of the activities people turn to for entertainment, there are many other sources of entertainment not addressed in the chart that will be explored in this book.

Theater

One of the oldest entertainment options is theater. Long before most people could read, theater entertained the masses. Today, theatergoers can see shows on New York's Broadway, London's West End, and in a variety of regional and local theater houses to name just a few venues. Theater continues to be a vibrant place to work for both actors and for those who work behind the scenes. Some of the current challenges and trends facing the industry will be discussed in the chapter on theater.

Sports

Sports provide entertainment for both those who participate in them and those who watch them. Sports make up one of the largest segments of the entertainment industry. They appeal to people of all ages and consist of professional activities, such as baseball, football, basketball, hockey, and NASCAR, and mainly recreational activities like jogging, bowling, fishing, hiking, and bicycling. In the chapter on sports, we'll explore the diverse components that make up the sports industry and learn about the many job opportunities within it.

Theme Parks

Theme parks offer people hours of entertainment, as they allow visitors to escape into a simulated world. Thrill rides, shows, and interactive attractions are a standard part of today's theme park experience. According to the International Association of Amusement Parks and Attractions (IAAPA), in the United States alone, more than 335 million people visit theme parks every year, generating more than $11.5 billion.[3] In the theme parks chapter, we'll discuss what makes theme parks so popular and examine some of the issues currently impacting the industry.

Gambling and Casino Gaming

Gambling can provide hours of entertainment for those wanting to try their luck in hopes of hitting the jackpot. Gambling and casino gaming have expanded significantly throughout the United States and Asia over the last few decades, as more and more gaming locations have been legalized. Between 1995 and 2006, casino revenues more than doubled from $16 billion to $37.4 billion.[4] In the chapter on gambling and casino gaming, we'll show you why and how this has occurred.

Travel and Tourism

A greater focus on leisure time and a shift in demographics have led to increased interest in travel and tourism. Today's tourism industry includes airline and train travel, escorted bus tours, cruises, all-in-one vacation packages, and specialty travel. It also encompasses a trend toward upscale accommodations and gourmet dining. The Internet has made travel much more accessible for consumers who want to plan their own trips without relying heavily on travel agents. We'll explore more of these trends in the chapter on travel and tourism.

Museums

Museums can serve a dual purpose of both educating *and* entertaining. While museums once were places where people could learn about art, history, and science in a passive manner through the observation of artifacts, some of today's museums are much more hands-on and interactive. In the chapter on museums, we'll show you how the public's growing interest in interactivity has led many museums to focus on developing innovative exhibits that serve to educate their patrons while keeping them entertained.

Shopping

Shopping isn't merely shopping anymore—it's become a form of entertainment. Many developers are blowing the lids off traditional shopping malls and replacing the nondescript structures with outdoor venues that resemble downtown areas with lots of shopping and a dose of entertainment mixed in. You can dine, see a movie, hear a band, watch a fashion show, get an autograph, and watch a baseball game as well as do a little shopping. In the chapter on shopping, we'll explain the latest trends in malls and how entertainment and shopping really do go together.

Event Planning

Special events often provide a form of entertainment for the public and are therefore included in this book on the entertainment industry. Whether they are small social events, such as birthday or anniversary parties, or large-scale public events, such as the Academy Awards, special events are designed to keep those who attend them engaged and entertained. Event planning can be a fun and profitable career for those who are organized and detail oriented. In the event planning chapter, we'll discuss what it takes to put together big and small events and have them go off without a hitch.

What's Been Left Out?

Obviously, in a book like this, it's not possible to cover every single aspect of the entertainment industry. As a result, some readers may not find everything they thought they would find in this book. For example, some might argue that the Internet can be its own source of entertainment and therefore worth its own chapter. However, the authors felt this went beyond the parameters of this book. Instead, we've chosen to incorporate into the individual chapters some of the ways the Internet is being used in different segments of the entertainment industry.

Overall, we hope the topics covered in the upcoming chapters will provide you with a good overview of the many different aspects of the entertainment industry. And if you're interested in learning more about these or other entertainment-related topics, we encourage you to pursue additional reading and research that will enlighten you even further.

The information for this book was compiled in late 2008 when the United States was facing difficult economic times. As a result, some of the information discussed reflects the state of the economy at the time of the book's writing. In addition, all referenced website links were current when the book was written.

Issues and Trends within the Industry

Many key issues and trends are having an impact on today's entertainment industry. Here are some of the topics that will be explored further in this book.

Big Media Companies

The big media companies are getting bigger. Consolidation of media ownership in the 1980s and '90s has led to some big fish in the entertainment industry. Some of the biggest media companies are The Walt Disney Company, Time Warner, News Corp., General Electric, Sony Corp., and the Tribune Company. These companies have entertainment holdings that span film to television, radio to newspapers, sports to websites. The big media companies are no longer in the film business or television business—these companies are in the entertainment business—all of it. Students of entertainment are wise to understand how diverse some of these companies are. The *Columbia Journalism Review* keeps track of media ownership on its website, www.cjr.org/resources.

Vertical Integration

As the media companies get larger, they also have more vertical integration. That means that some of the big media companies control the entertainment product during production and delivery to the consumer. Time Warner is an example of a company with vertical integration. Time Warner owns Warner Bros. Television Production, The CW Television Network, and Warner Home Video. Time Warner has the ability to produce a television show, air the show on its CW television network stations, and eventually release the program as a series on DVD under the Warner Home Video label. Time Warner owns the content every step of the way from concept to delivery to consumer.

The advantage of vertical integration for the company is its ability to streamline costs. The disadvantage of vertical integration to the consumer is a monopoly of the market.

Horizontal Integration

Some of the big media companies are also utilizing horizontal integration to control more of the market share. Horizontal integration occurs when a media company owns assets that compete for the same demographic in the same entertainment sector.

MIKE FARREL

Freelance Recording Engineer

If you've been to Disneyland in Anaheim, CA, there's a good chance you've heard Mike Farrel's voice— as one of the creepy laughs in the graveyard of the Haunted Mansion attraction. That's just one of many jobs Farrel has completed over the years at Disneyland. As a freelance recording engineer, he has been called on to set up the sound system at the Tomorrowland Terrace and record voice-overs for the Happiest Place on Earth.

Farrel owns his own recording and sound company in Orange, CA. He's helped record albums for orchestras and punk bands. And if that isn't enough to keep him busy, he also tours with a country music band.

Music is Farrel's love, and he has built a successful career around music and recording. "There's nothing better than standing on stage, and everything comes together. The band can feel it, and the crowd can feel it," he said. As a musician, Farrel plays just about all brass instruments. He regularly tours with Boomer McClellan and the Rhythm Rangers band. Every year they perform in England.

As a recording engineer, Farrel feels just as comfortable recording one instrument in a small studio as he does setting up an entire sound system for an Easter sunrise Catholic mass. In fact, his recording and sound company was established and named after he set up the public address system for an outdoor mass. The company is called "Sound for the Masses."

Farrel majored in English as an undergraduate and has a master's degree in recording engineering. His advice for students trying to make a living in the creative field of music is to "go to school first." He said it's important to learn from people who know the technology and the history behind the music. "Don't assume you know because you are creative. You need a basis of knowledge. You need to know the core basics."

» » »

Clear Channel Communications is a company with horizontal integration. Clear Channel owns more than 1,000 radio stations across the country, and many of those stations are in the same market and play music that competes for the same demographic. In Los Angeles, Clear Channel owns radio stations KIIS-FM, KOST-FM, and KBIG-FM. All three stations play top 40 pop/rock music, and all three compete for a similar demographic. The advantage of horizontal integration for the company is primarily cost savings, and the disadvantage to the consumer is a monopoly with fewer voices controlling the content.

Synergy

Another concept that is being seen more frequently as the media companies get larger is synergy. "Synergy is all about marketing and the halo effect, which can enable one form of a product to morph into another," according to Al Lieberman and Patricia Esgate.[5] We see examples of synergy often in the entertainment industry. The original entertainment product—for example, a film or a television show—is a huge success and is morphed into merchandise, books, theatrical performances, home videos, etc.

Take the example of the movie *Beauty and the Beast* owned by the Walt Disney Company. The animated movie was a huge box office success. The *Beauty and the Beast* brand was turned into stuffed animals, princess costumes, books, straight-to-DVD sequels, and a successful theatrical production. The Walt Disney Company has become a master of synergy. More and more of the entertainment companies are using the idea of synergy to leverage a successful entertainment product, whether it be a film like *Beauty and the Beast* or a book like the Harry Potter novels.

Advanced Technology

Technology is changing faster than ever before. The entertainment industry is being challenged to change its traditional business models to meet the technological demands of its consumers. One example of changing technology affecting the content is in the music industry. The recorded music companies were slow to understand that consumers wanted to download music. None of the music labels offered pay online music websites during the late 1990s when Napster took off in popularity. Because there was no legal way to download music, the only alternative was to download illegally, violating copyrights. Instead of embracing the new technology, the music industry at first tried to fight it. Eventually the music labels understood and embraced this new way of delivery.

Technology changes are occurring in just about every area of the entertainment industry. DVDs, DVRs, VOD (video on demand), and MP3 players have vastly altered the way entertainment is delivered to the consumer. The entertainment industry is being forced to deal with the new technology, but the changes are difficult.

In some sectors of the entertainment industry, the business models that have been around for decades are becoming obsolete. The challenge now is to write a new operations manual and stay in business at the same time. One example is the television industry. Broadcast television is free to anyone who has a television set and an antenna and supports itself through paid advertising. The business model has been turned on its head because of the impact of DVRs and huge numbers of viewers fast-forwarding through the commercials.

Copyright Concerns

One of the biggest concerns throughout the entertainment industry is how to control content and protect copyrights. New technology is making it easier and faster to share files containing music, television, video games, etc. Now the big question for the entertainment industry is how to protect copyrighted material so that the company continues making a profit from the work it produces. Illegal downloading of music has decimated the music industry. Entertainment executives in other areas are worried the huge problems in the music industry will soon become their problems as well.

Power of Research

Many of the decisions in the entertainment industry are based on research. The earlier section of this chapter, "Understanding Our Audience" was based on the research done by the U.S. Census Bureau. The Media Usage chart provides useful information for the entertainment executive as well as students of entertainment. It doesn't happen often that a big decision in the entertainment industry is made solely on a gut feeling. More often than not the decision is based on research. Students of entertainment should understand how to do research and what its limitations are. If you are still in college, it might be helpful to take a research methods course. Understanding statistics is useful in this field as well as learning how to utilize research databases and search skills. Many university libraries offer courses and sessions on how to do research.

Obsessed with Entertainment

Americans have become obsessed with entertainment and celebrities. Television stars have replaced fashion models on the cover of magazines. Entertainment news programs are so popular that new websites, magazines, and television shows devoted to entertainment are popping up everywhere.

The entertainment industry is fun, glamorous, and exciting. The industry is also very competitive and a lot of hard work. The entertainment field needs smart, hard-working people who love the work they do. There are many opportunities to work in entertainment, but make sure you are going into the field because you love what you do. Life is too short to work hard and not be entertained at the same time.

ENDNOTES

1. "Introduction to the Entertainment and Media Industry," Plunkett Research, Ltd., 2 January 2008, www.plunkettresearchonline.com.
2. Veronis Suhler Stevenson, Media Usage and Consumer Spending: 2000 to 2010, www.census.gov/compendia/statab/cats/information_communications.html.

3. International Association of Amusement Parks and Attractions, www.iaapa.org.

4. American Gaming Association, www.americangaming.org.

5. Al Lieberman and Patricia Esgate, *The Entertainment Marketing Revolution*, Upper Saddle River, NJ: Prentice Hall, 2002: 15.

Electronic Media as Entertainment

2

Film BETH BINGHAM EVANS

One of the biggest gambles in the entertainment industry just might be making a big-budget studio film. According to the Motion Picture Association of America (MPAA), in 2007, the average cost to make and market a major studio film was $106.6 million.[1] Because there is so much money at stake, the risks are high. Just about everyone in Hollywood has had his or her fair share of flops and hits. Even huge box office draws like Julia Roberts and Will Smith have an occasional flop on their résumés.

But when it comes to a sure bet at the box office, Pixar Animation Studios has the golden touch. Nine animated movies in 13 years, and all nine were hits. The ninth hit for the studio was the film, *Wall-E*. The film cost an estimated $180 million to make and was number one at the box office in June 2008. During opening weekend, the animated movie about a lovable robot brought in $63 million at the box office.[2]

Opening weekend is crucial in determining a film's overall success. All nine of Pixar's films have opened at number one and have gone on to see tremendous financial success. Pixar's winning streak started with a $29.1 million box office opening for *Toy Story* in 1995. *Toy Story* went on to make an estimated $362 million at the worldwide box office.[3] Pixar's biggest hit was *Finding Nemo*, which raked in $70.3 million in its opening weekend in 2003 and has gone on to make almost $900 million worldwide.

Opening weekend sets the tone for a film's moneymaking ability. A strong opening weekend creates good buzz about the film. Usually, the better the buzz, the more potential the film has to make money at the box office domestically and in other areas, including international box office, pay-per-view television, DVD sales and rentals, network and cable television, and finally, re-release years after the original film debuted in theatres.

An example of a film franchise that has and will continue to make money is the *Star Wars* franchise. The seven films have made a combined $4.3 billion at the worldwide box office, and their appeal continues to be strong some 30 years after the first film was released.[4]

Figure 2: Pixar Animation Films

| Movie | Release Date | Box Office (in millions) | | |
		Opening Wknd	Domestic	Worldwide
Finding Nemo	5/03	70.3	339.7	866.6
The Incredibles	11/04	70.5	261.4	635.6
Ratatouille	6/07	47	206.4	620.4
Monsters, Inc.	11/01	62.6	255.9	529
Toy Story 2	11/99	57.4	245.9	485.8
Cars	6/06	60.1	244.1	461.8
A Bug's Life	11/98	33.3	162.8	356
Toy Story	11/95	29.1	191.8	362

For every success story, there is at least one story of failure. Combine two of the hottest stars in Hollywood with extensive exposure in the media as their off-screen romance blossomed; add $60 million dollars and a title no one was sure how to pronounce, and you get the movie *Gigli*.[5]

Gigli starred Ben Affleck and Jennifer Lopez at the height of the 2003 media circus surrounding their "Bennifer" romance, where the couple's every move and their now infamous called-off wedding made headlines. *Gigli* could not have gotten more exposure in the media and among fans.

But early screenings of the movie did not go well. The bad buzz that was generated could not be shaken no matter how big the stars of the film. The $60 million film went on to make just $5.6 million domestically at the box office. The headline for film critic Bruce Newman's summary of the film in the *San Jose Mercury* sums up the sentiment of film reviewers and filmgoers alike: "No Matter How You Say It, 'Gigli' Stinks."[6] The impact of the movie's failure was so severe that the company that produced the film, Revolution Studios, closed its doors after the release of *Gigli*.

Big budget movies are risky investment ventures. The MPAA reports that 6 out of 10 movies don't make back their initial investment in their domestic theatrical run.[7] But today movie studios are in a better position than maybe ever before to remain financially viable even if a movie tanks. The major media companies are diversified, and most of the entertainment giants now own television production, television channels, music companies, sports teams, tourist destinations, merchandising, publishing, etc. Just about every major media company has a major movie studio among its holdings.[8]

Figure 3: Top Movie Studios

Major Film Studio	Conglomerate
Walt Disney Pictures	Walt Disney Corp.
Touchstone Pictures	Walt Disney Corp.
Hollywood Pictures	Walt Disney Corp.
Pixar	Walt Disney Corp.
Paramount	Viacom
Dreamworks	Viacom
MGM/UA	An investor consortium including private investors, including Sony and Comcast
Sony Pictures Entertainment	Sony Corp.
Columbia Tristar	Sony Corp.
Universal	General Electric
Warner Bros.	Time Warner
20th Century Fox	News Corp.
Castle Rock Entertainment	Time Warner

Independent Film Studios

Fox Searchlight Pictures	News Corp.
Sony Pictures Classics	Sony Corp.
Miramax Films	Walt Disney Corp.

Films are important to a media conglomerate because a hit can create an entertainment asset that is sure to make money for years to come. Films such as *The Lion King*, and franchises such as Star Wars and James Bond are important to the bottom line of the film studio. One successful film can also spawn huge money in ancillary revenue sources. In other words, a successful film can translate into moneymaking ventures on many levels—the film itself, of course, but also merchandise, television shows, books, toys, magazines, etc. A media conglomerate's ownership of diverse entertainment businesses allows it to cross-promote. For instance, a successful film can spawn a television series; a best-selling novel can inspire a film.

Media conglomeration is only one of the many trends that have proliferated in the film industry in recent years. This chapter will examine some of the issues that those working in the film industry deal with on a day-to-day basis. It will look at the current challenges of the business as well as provide information on employment prospects for those interested in working in film.

History and Background

Early Years

Some of the first moving pictures were made from a camera called a Kinetograph in the late 1880s. The concept was based on adding pictures to Thomas Edison's phonograph. The first Kinetoscope parlor opened in a converted storefront in New York City and charged patrons 25 cents to watch a short film through the peep-show viewing device.[9]

The Lumiere brothers invented the first commercial viable projector, which was much lighter than the Kinetoscope. So, the Lumiere brothers' projector opened the way for the camera to be taken outside to film documentaries instead of circus or vaudeville acts that were brought in to perform before the Kinetoscope.[10]

Edwin S. Porter was a freelance projectionist who worked for the Edison Company and experimented with early filmmaking. His 1903 film, *The Great Train Robbery*, is considered the first narrative film to combine several camera angles together in the edit room. Viewers were able to watch continuous action from different perspectives.[11]

Longer films called features became popular around 1912, making motion pictures "respectable for the middle class by providing a format that was analogous to that of the legitimate theater."[12] By 1916, there were some 20,000 movie theaters across the United States. The stage was set for the studio "star system," which involved the creation and management of actors in an effort to promote the star, the film, and the studio. The studio "star system" would continue until the 1950s.[13]

Several locations were temporarily tried as a home for filmmaking including Jacksonville, FL, San Antonio, TX, and Santa Fe, NM. It turned out the studios found a small suburb in Southern California that appeared to be perfect. It was sunny just about every day and had a diverse topography including mountains, beaches, valleys, forests, lakes, and desert. This small town called Hollywood became the heart of the filmmaking industry.[14]

Golden Era for the Studios

In 1915, *The Birth of a Nation*, directed by D.W. Griffith, was the talk of the country and unleashed a wave of controversy. As the film was released, rioting erupted in several cities as audiences reacted to its racism. The film was banned in eight states.[15]

Prior to World War I, European filmmakers were far ahead of Americans in terms of production techniques and the number of films produced, but all that changed after the war. By 1919, 90% of all films screened in Europe, Africa, and Asia were American.[16]

Many of the big studios got their start during the 1920s. Paramount Pictures started in 1927; 20th Century Fox in 1925; Warner Bros. in 1923; and Columbia Pictures in 1924.[17]

Prior to 1927, all films were silent, but that changed with *The Jazz Singer*. Warner Bros. tried out a new system called the Vitaphone. Warner Bros. wasn't convinced that talking

MICHAEL BERENBAUM

Film Editor

By the age of 10, Michael Berenbaum, A.C.E. (American Cinema Editor), already knew what his career path would be. As long as he can remember, Berenbaum wanted to work in the film business. In high school, he shot his own films on Super-8. When it was time to go to college, he aimed high and was admitted to New York University's prestigious film program.

While in college, the dream became a reality. Berenbaum was interning with a movie studio and hanging out on the set of *The Cotton Club* when he was approached about a paying position as an apprentice sound editor on the film. Berenbaum's film career was off and running.

Fast forward 20 years, and Berenbaum is a successful film and television editor. He has worked with directors such as Joel Coen, Martin Scorsese, and actor Al Pacino, to name just a few.

"The most exciting thing is you never know who you will be working with. One day I got a call. Al Pacino wants to meet you," Berenbaum said. He ended up working with Pacino on the 2000 film *Chinese Coffee.* He has also worked on *Sex and the City,* both the feature film and the television series; *Goodfellas; Raising Arizona;* and *War, Inc.*

Berenbaum admitted that film editing is very competitive. He said the best way to make it in the business is to work hard and to understand the film business inside and out. "The most important thing is to have a real sense of history of film." He suggested, of course, that people who want to work in the industry see a lot of films.

To get started as a film editor, Berenbaum recommends editing student films. He said college can be a great place to network and meet other people passionate about filmmaking. It's a business all about relationships—you never know with whom you're going to work, so keep all working relationships positive.

Berenbaum gets most of his jobs today by word of mouth. Coincidentally, his brother, David Berenbaum, is a successful screenplay writer who wrote *Elf* and *The Haunted Mansion.* The two brothers collaborate occasionally.

» » »

films were the wave of the future; instead, the studio was looking for a money-making gim-mick. The gamble paid off—one year later every studio in Hollywood was making talking movies.[18] Color was introduced to filmmaking at about the same time.

The year 1939 saw the production of several well-known films that went on to become classics including *The Wizard of Oz* and *Gone with the Wind*.[19]

In 1941, during the height of the studio system, Orson Welles produced one of the most influential films ever made, *Citizen Kane*. The film's theme was controversial, and Welles also used an experimental technique in shooting it. What made the film unusual was the way Welles used flashbacks when friends and co-workers were remembering the life of the main character, Charles Foster Kane (based on newspaper baron William Randolph Hearst.) Although considered an important film now, in 1941 *Citizen Kane* was a box office failure.[20]

One of the darkest times for the film industry came in the late 1940s as the fear of com-munism spread to "witch-hunts" in the Hollywood studio system. The House Un-American Activities Committee, known as HUAC, turned its spotlight on the film industry. Some of the biggest names in Hollywood testified before HUAC. In November 1947 ten witnesses who worked in Hollywood were called and refused to testify and refused to name names. They were sentenced to prison. This group became known as the Hollywood Ten. Hollywood and the major film studios panicked. They didn't want more negative publicity, so they began a policy of blacklisting. No one who was even suspected of having communist ties was employable in Hollywood. Blacklisting ruined the lives of many talented artists.[21]

During the blacklisting period, studio executives were careful to green light only projects that were conservative in both story line and in look. Films during this time lacked creativity, and that, combined with financial difficulties, began the end of the Hollywood studio system. Another cause of the motion picture industry's financial problems was the fact that it had, for the first time, a true competitor, television. Americans loved the convenience of television and the ability to watch programs in their own homes.

End of the Studio System

In the United States, the 1960s were a time of intense conflict, and Hollywood was unresponsive when it came to turning out films that reflected the period's racial struggles. The studios believed that a film should appeal to the broadest audience possible, and studio executives wrongly believed that people wanted to see big-budget movies with safe themes.

Elizabeth Taylor and Richard Burton's $44 million epic *Cleopatra* in 1963 didn't do well at the box office, while the Julie Andrews musical, *The Sound of Music* in 1965 was an unexpected hit.[22]

The 1960s and '70s saw the film studios' profits declining as Hollywood ushered in one box-office disaster after another. This led to many of the studios being bought by big corporations. With big business in charge of filmmaking, the look of the movies produced during this time changed. Making movies was less about being an art form and more about profit.

The late 1960s saw the film industry trying to appeal to a younger demographic—and it worked. *Bonnie and Clyde* (1967), *2001: A Space Odyssey* (1968), and *M*A*S*H* (1970) attracted young people to movie theatres in record numbers.[23] As the themes of movies became more varied, there was a call for a way to determine if a movie was appropriate for children and teenagers. The Motion Picture Association of America started the ratings system in 1968.[24]

The cost of filmmaking skyrocketed in the 1970s reaching an average of $11 million a film.[25] Yet there were plenty of enormously profitable films made in the '70s including *The Godfather* (1972), *Jaws* (1975) and *Star Wars* (1977). This led to the film studios focusing their attention on just a handful of movies a year, hoping that at least one would be a blockbuster. The '70s also saw a large number of sequels produced as the new corporate managers lacked the judgment of filmmaking veterans who had come before them. The new executives in charge avoided risk and tended to rely on storylines that had worked in the past.

New technology changed filmmaking in the 1980s with computer-generated graphics and special effects. This decade also saw the film studios focus their attention on making their films available on videocassettes for the home viewing market.

Film Industry Today

The film industry remains vital and vibrant today. According to the Motion Picture Association of America, movie theaters continue to draw more people than either theme parks or major sports arenas combined in the United States. The domestic box office continued to grow in 2007, reaching $9.63 billion after a 5% gain over the previous year.[26] Much of that growth is attributed to sequels that did very well at the box office. *Spider-Man 3, Shrek the Third, Pirates of the Caribbean: At World's End,* and *Harry Potter & The Order of the Phoenix* all grossed more than $300 million dollars at the domestic box office.

The worldwide box office revenue also continues to climb. In 2007, a record was set at the worldwide box office with revenue hitting $26.72 billion, a 5% increase over the previous year.[27]

Climbing film costs are causing more and more films to be shot outside of the United States. The average cost to make and market a film rose 8% in 2007 over 2006.[28] With the average cost of a film in 2008 at $106 million, many film producers are looking for ways to save money. More and more movies are being shot overseas as foreign workers are typically less expensive than union workers in the United States.

Film studios are embracing Internet advertising when it comes time to create a "buzz" about the film. In 2007, the major studios spent 4% of their advertising and marketing budgets on Internet ads. Although still a small overall part of their budgets, Internet advertising has grown significantly over the past five years, increasing from under 1% in 2002.

Figure 4. Film Studio Contact Information

Disney 350 S. Buena Vista Street Burbank, CA 91521 (818) 567-5000 disney.go.com	Sony Pictures 10202 W. Washington Boulevard Culver City, CA 90232 www.sonypictures.com
MGM 2500 Broadway Street Santa Monica, CA 90404 (310) 449-3000 www.mgm.com	20th Century Fox 10201 W. Washington Boulevard Los Angeles, CA 90035 (310) 369-1000 www.foxmovies.com
New Line Cinema 116 N. Robertson Boulevard, Suite 200 Los Angeles, CA 90048 (310) 854-5811 www.newline.com	Universal Studios 100 Universal City Plaza Universal City, CA 92608 (818) 777-1000 www.universalstudios.com
Paramount/Dreamworks 555 Melrose Avenue Los Angeles, CA 90038 www.paramount.com	Warner Brothers 4000 Warner Boulevard Burbank, CA 91522 (818) 379-1850 www.warnerbros.com

How the Industry Operates

There are very few players in the business of big budget filmmaking and distribution. According to Tuna Amobi, the media and entertainment analyst of the *Industry Survey* from Standard and Poor's, "Six film distribution companies—Walt Disney, Viacom, Sony, News Corp's Fox Entertainment Group, Time Warner, and NBC Universal—typically account for at least 70% of domestic box office revenues."[29]

Typically, a big-budget film starts preproduction once a contract is signed by a major distributor, a production company, and a producer or director. The distributor usually pays for everything to make the movie from start to finish, and delivers it to the theaters. Occasionally, the producer of the movie may give theatrical rights to one distributor and home video rights to another. Most of the money is made on films after the domestic box office run. The owner of the film usually makes money when the film enters the home video and television markets.

Independent Films

Small budget films can also make a profit, and some can even go on to be blockbusters. The independent film market has continued to grow over the last two decades. Part of the growth is due to resources made available through programs like the Sundance

Institute, which was started by Robert Redford in 1981 in an effort to "create an environment designed to foster independence, discovery and new voices in American film."[30]

Since then, Sundance has become synonymous with the best in independent filmmaking. The annual Sundance Film Festival is the place to be and to be discovered if you are an independent filmmaker. A-list film director Steven Soderbergh (*Ocean's Eleven, Erin Brockovich, Traffic*) was discovered at Sundance with his film *Sex, Lies and Videotape* in 1989. The Sundance Festival attracts 50,000 people every winter in Park City, Utah.

My Big Fat Greek Wedding is one of the big success stories in the area of independent films. It was reportedly produced for $5 million dollars. The 2002 film took in sales of $241 million at the domestic box office, and as of the end of 2007, the movie's worldwide box office total of $368.7 million made it the 106th highest-grossing film of all time.[31]

The *Blair Witch Project* is another example of an independent film that went on to be a blockbuster. According to the Internet Movie Database, *The Blair Witch Project* is in the *Guinness Book of World Records* for "Top Budget: Box Office Ratio" (for a mainstream feature film). The 1999 film cost approximately a quarter of a million dollars to make and went on to earn more than $240 million at the box office. That's a ratio of approximately $1 spent for every $10,000 made.[32]

So, what is considered an independent film? Independent films are usually thought of as art films. They are produced for a much more narrow demographic. An independent film usually has a small budget. That makes sense since the smaller the budget, the less the risk that the film will not earn back its investment.

Independent films used to be defined as films financed outside the Hollywood studio system, but that isn't necessarily the case today, as many of the media conglomerates that own a major film studio also own a so-called small independent film studio. For instance, Disney owns both Touchstone and Miramax. The media conglomerates have caught on that the independent film market has the potential to make money. Every media executive hopes for a small, independent film that will have the success of *The Blair Witch Project* or *My Big Fat Greek Wedding*.

High-Concept Films

For every blockbuster, there are dozens of films that make little or no money. Most of these films aren't considered flops, but they certainly are not blockbusters either. Since the cost of a major film studio project is over $100 million, a lot is riding on whether or not the film makes a profit. Because of that, the film studios frequently use a "formulaic" approach to making movies called "high concept."[33]

High-concept films usually have well-known stars or a well-known director and a storyline that can be summed up in a clear, simple sentence. Also, the marketing materials usually consist of a single image and will likely have ties to merchandising. High-concept films can also be prequels, sequels, or be based around established music. The idea is that high-concept films are less of a risk to the studio because they have a built-in audience either for the star, the director, or the concept.

All of these films are considered high concept: *Saving Private Ryan, Sex and the City,* and *Harry Potter and the Sorcerer's Stone.* Each is considered high concept but for different reasons.

Steven Spielberg directed *Saving Private Ryan.* Spielberg is considered one of the most successful directors of all time. Not every film he touches turns to gold, but plenty do. Because of that, studios trust him to make movies that will receive critical acclaim as well as box office success.

Sex and the City was based on the successful HBO series of the same name. The movie already had a built-in audience who adored the characters of Carrie, Charlotte, Miranda, and Samantha.

Harry Potter and the Sorcerer's Stone was based on the best-selling children's book of the same title by J.K. Rowling. Moviegoers were not familiar with the young stars of the film or the director, but the film did have a built-in audience. The *Harry Potter* books were some of the best-selling books ever.

Not every high-concept film turns out well. It can be said that *Gigli* was a high-concept film based on the stars, Jennifer Lopez and Ben Affleck, but that didn't change the end results. Some films that appear to have tremendous potential just don't click with audiences. So, high-concept films might be less risky—but there's no sure thing in filmmaking.

Press Junkets / Publicity

Long before a film hits theaters, the marketing/publicity team is hard at work creating "buzz" about the film. Every studio assigns at least one public relations specialist during the filming of the movie to work with the media to create interest in the film early on. It's not uncommon for the unit publicist to escort television, radio, magazine, and newspaper reporters to the set to interview the stars and director and get pictures of the movie being shot.

Of course, these press opportunities are well organized and carefully controlled. The press will only be invited to see scenes that don't give away the plot and are usually only present during filming on days when the workload is not too rigorous. The last thing the unit publicist wants to do is have the media witness a meltdown by a major star or the director because filming isn't going smoothly.

Once the film is shot and postproduction is underway, the big job of creating an entire publicity campaign begins. Everything is orchestrated from the location and strategy of the press junket to the red carpet premiere at which media outlets get exclusive interviews with the stars. The idea is to give the media enough access to the film and the stars to put together a positive story but not enough access that the publicity department gives away control.

At the same time, the marketing department is working toward creating good "buzz" on the streets. That is usually done through test screenings of the movie to gauge the audience's reaction to the unfinished version. After seeing the film, the audience is asked to fill out a lengthy questionnaire or sit in on a focus group to get reaction to the plot, the characters, and the ending.

The marketing department might also schedule sneak previews of the film. This is usually done with movies that the studio feels confident will generate positive word of mouth among viewers. These sneak previews are often shown in a couple of select markets and are initiated just a few weeks prior to the opening of the film. The sneak previews frequently are concurrent with the big advertising push for the movie.

Usually a week or two before the red carpet premiere, the press is invited to the junket. Many of the junkets are held in Los Angeles near the headquarters of the movie studios, which is convenient for the studio publicists and the actors. The Four Seasons Hotel in Beverly Hills is a frequent location for press junkets. But sometimes the studio decides to go all out for the junket. Warner Bros. provided all-expenses paid trips to London for dozens of members of the media for the junket of *Harry Potter and the Sorcerer's Stone*. Invited media were wined and dined at several upscale London locations such as The Guildhall as well as put up in a five-star hotel for several days as part of the junket and premiere.

The concept behind the junket is to allow entertainment reporters a chance to view the film; interview the actors, directors, and producers; and publish a story. It works well for the studio because publicists can get all of the actors, directors, and producers together for one long weekend and give the media access to the key players of the film. The junket usually creates tremendous free exposure in the media for the film just a few days before it opens in theaters.

Junkets are common practice in the film business but are not without some controversy. Some people argue that it is unethical for reporters to accept these free trips because it taints their so-called objective coverage of the film. Junkets provide a service to media outlets by giving reporters access to major stars as well as providing a service to the film studio by generating free editorial coverage of the film.

Demographics

Just about everyone enjoys going to a theater and seeing a good movie. But some of us go to the movies much more frequently than others. According to the Motion Picture Association of America, the demographic that frequents the movies the most often is the 12–24 age group.[34] This 12–24 demographic is responsible for 38% of all movie theater admissions. Within this demographic, teenagers aged 16 and 17 attend the most movies.

The 25–39 demographic shows the next most frequent attendance at the movies, accounting for 29% of all movie theater admissions, followed by the 40–59 age group, accounting for 24%, and the 60+ demographic, accounting for 9% of admissions to movie theaters.

Figure 5: Percent of Admissions by Age Group

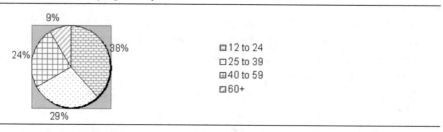

Source: MPAA Statistics for 2007

Whether you have children or are married also affects how often you go to the movies. In the 2007 Movie Attendance Study done by the MPAA, researchers found that moviegoers who live with children go the movies more often than those without children in the home.[35] Single people go to the movies more often than married couples. The study also found that frequent moviegoers make more than $50,000 a year. The research also looked at ethnicity among moviegoers. Caucasians go to the movies the most, followed by Hispanics and then African Americans.

Figure 6: Ethnicity of Moviegoers

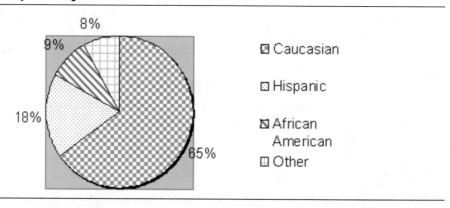

Source: MPAA Statistics for 2007

Release Schedule

There was little question about what date the fourth installment of the *Indiana Jones* series would be released. Memorial Day weekend had worked well for the first three *Indiana Jones* movies, so Paramount tried it again with the 2008 release of *Indiana Jones and the Kingdom of the Crystal Skull.*

Memorial Day weekend marks the customary launch of the summertime movie season, and it paid off for Harrison Ford and Steven Spielberg a fourth time. *Indiana Jones and the Kingdom of the Crystal Skull* scored the second-highest Memorial Day weekend opening ever. The only other movie to do better over the Memorial Day weekend was *Pirates of the Caribbean: At World's End.* The fourth "Indy" movie rang up ticket sales of $151 million over five days.[36]

Movie studio executives put a lot of time and consideration into when a movie should debut. Opening weekend is crucial for a film's potential moneymaking ability, so it's not surprising that a lot of research goes into deciding when a film should open.

A big-budget film typically opens "wide" during its debut weekend. That means it's seen across the country on at least 3,000 screens. Sometimes a studio or distributor decides that a film is better suited for a limited release. A limited release pattern usually involves opening on dozens or hundreds of screens in limited markets. It's not uncommon to see a smaller-budget film open in Los Angeles and New York with the hope that the audiences who see the film will like it and generate good buzz about the film. As the buzz builds, the studio then decides to release the film on additional screens in more cities.

Whether the release is going to be wide or limited, deciding when to open the film is a difficult decision. There are a few periods every year when it's pretty easy to predict the type of film that will open. For instance, romantic comedies usually open around Valentine's Day. Another good opening slot for a romantic comedy is the weekend of the Super Bowl. Since romantic comedies tend to appeal to women, it gives the wives of the football fans an alternative to watching the big game.

Big-budget/special-effects films tend to open in the summer because young people are out of school and are drawn to films with lots of action. Thanksgiving and Christmas holidays are usually the time when family-friendly fare is released. Academy Award contenders tend to be released late in the calendar year in an effort to remain fresh in the Academy members' minds when they vote for the Oscars.

But it seems that just as predictable as some of the release dates are, there are always surprises. The third weekend of August used to be considered a dumping ground for flops: The belief was that kids were getting ready to go back to school and weren't interested in movies. That was until *The 40-Year-Old Virgin* was released August 19, 2007. The racy comedy turned out to be a hit. Now the end of August is considered a perfect time to release a crazy comedy that takes kids' minds off returning to school.

Challenges and Trends

Piracy

The biggest challenge in the motion picture industry is piracy. The MPAA commissioned a study on the impact of piracy worldwide and found that "The major U.S. motion picture studios lost $6.1 billion in 2005 to piracy worldwide…80% of the losses resulted from piracy overseas, 20% from piracy in the U.S."[37]

Piracy rates were the highest in China, Russia, and Thailand. The majority of losses were due to purchasing or acquiring illegally produced VHS/DVDs. The other losses were due to Internet piracy, which is defined as obtaining movies by either downloading them from the Internet without paying or acquiring a hard copy of an illegally downloaded movie. The MPAA study also found that the typical worldwide pirate is a male between the ages of 16–24 who lives in an urban area.

Many people believe the key to fighting movie piracy is education. The Motion Picture Association of America implemented a program to help raise awareness about copyright theft and is providing educators with resources to introduce the topic of protecting copyrights in school and universities around the world.

Attendance

Another challenge of the motion picture industry is finding ways to continue to attract people to theaters. The number of people who go to the movies has remained relatively constant over the past 10 years. Numbers for 2007 were up but just slightly. With so many different entertainment options available, movie studios are going to have to find ways to keep people going to the movies.

Runaway Production

More and more movie and television productions are moving out of Hollywood. The reason—to save money. Several years ago the concern was productions being shot outside the United States in such locations as Canada. Some film producers have even gone as far as India or Romania to avoid high labor costs and restrictive regulations in California. But as the dollar lost value against foreign currency in mid-2008, the concern was less about runaway productions moving overseas and more about productions relocating to other places within the United States.

Georgia, New York, Mississippi, and Michigan legislators have increased incentives and offered tax credits to producers willing to shoot in their states. The television show *Ugly Betty* moved from Los Angeles to New York to save money. In May 2008, just one month after Michigan lawmakers approved the tax-credit program for producers, 100 scripts had been submitted to the Michigan Film Office for consideration, including a Clint Eastwood film.

Figure 7: Production Company Contact Information

Castle Rock Entertainment
335 N. Maple Drive, Suite 135
Beverly Hills, CA 90210
(310) 285-2300
www.lone-starmovie.com

Lucasfilm
P.O. Box 29901
San Francisco, CA 94129
www.lucasfilm.com

Imagine Entertainment 9465 Wilshire Boulevard, 7th Floor Beverly Hills, CA 90212 (310) 858-2000 www.imagine-entertainment.com	Pixar 1200 Park Avenue Emeryville, CA 94608 (510) 752-3000
Jerry Bruckheimer Films 1631 Tenth Street Santa Monica, CA 90404 (310) 664-6262 www.jbfilms.com	

Employment Opportunities

The number of people employed in the movie industry has remained relatively steady over the past 10 years. In 2006, 357,000 people were employed directly in the motion picture and video production business.[38] Many people in the filmmaking business work on a freelance, contract, or part-time basis, usually working from project to project.

The workforce is much younger than in most industries, with 57% of employees being under the age of 35. One reason why this is the case is because working on a film can be physically and mentally demanding. The industry is very cutthroat, and making movies usually requires working long hours on location and making changes to schedules at a moment's notice. Most of the employment is based in Los Angeles or New York.

Jobs in the film industry can be classified according the three phases of filmmaking: preproduction, production, and postproduction.

Preproduction

Preproduction is the planning phase, which can include formulating the idea for the movie and writing the script, budgeting, casting, location scouting, set and costume design, set construction, and scheduling.

Some of the job titles typically associated with the preproduction phase are producers, directors, screenwriters, art directors, costume designers, set decorators, electricians, painters, and carpenters. It's not uncommon for people who work in preproduction to move back and forth between film, television, and theater.

Production

Production is the actual shooting of the film. This is the shortest phase of filmmaking but usually the most expensive and labor intensive. Jobs in production include actors, cinematographers, camera operators, lighting specialists, sound engineers, multimedia artists and animators, production assistants, and grips (stagehands).

Postproduction

Postproduction involves everything after the film is shot including editing, music scoring, sound effects, graphics, and computer-generated effects. Postproduction employs people who can work with digital media in several capacities: film and video editing, audio recording engineers, and sound effects specialists. Jobs in postproduction also include marketing, advertising, promotions, accounting, law, and sales.

The number of jobs in the film industry is expected to increase just slightly. The U.S. government's Bureau of Labor Statistics estimates that in the next 10 years the number of people employed in the movie business will increase almost 11%.[39]

Future Outlook

New Media/Impact of Technology

Technology is changing the film industry. More advanced technological changes in special effects and filmmaking are driving up the cost of making a film. Audiences want to see sophisticated storytelling techniques, but at what point will filmmaking become too expensive to make a profit? Will the high cost of making a movie have a chilling effect on the number of films produced each year?

Technology is also changing the way that producers market a film. According to the Motion Picture Association of America, Internet research plays a significant role in getting people to the movies and will continue to do so. Studies show that 73% of U.S. moviegoers use the Internet to learn about a movie before going to see it. Also, people who go online to research a movie are more likely to see it on opening weekend. They go to the movies more often and even see some movies more than once in the theater.[40]

Summary

The motion picture industry remains strong and vibrant more than 100 years after Thomas Edison's first invention allowed viewers to witness action on film. The number of people employed in the industry is expected to remain relatively constant. The number of people who go to the movies is also expected to remain constant. Changes in the industry will likely come in special effects/graphics and in the number of productions shot outside of Hollywood, where labor and expenses make a film cheaper to produce.

The biggest threat to the film industry is piracy. The big studios are working to stem the growing number of people who buy pirated films. The two biggest priorities in the

JULIE DEY

Senior Publicist, Paramount Pictures
www.paramount.com

As a broadcast journalism major in college, Julie Dey dreamed of working as a television news reporter. But when her professors at California State University, Fullerton, told her she would have to move to a small city and wouldn't make much money at first, Dey changed her mind. She always wanted to be in front of a camera, but once she had her Communications degree in hand, she set out on a different path.

Dey's first job out of college was working as a coordinator for Feld Entertainment, which produces live-action entertainment such as Ringling Bros. and Barnum & Bailey Circus and Disney on Ice productions. She traveled a lot and was promoted very quickly. "I was willing to do anything. I worked as many hours as possible," she said.

Just a few years after graduating from college, Dey landed a job in publicity at Dreamworks SKG. When the studio merged with Paramount Pictures in 2005, Dey's career hit the fast track. During the summer of 2008, she worked on several big-budget films: *Indiana Jones and the Kingdom of the Crystal Skull, Kung Fu Panda,* and *Iron Man.*

"I love seeing people really enjoy our product," Dey said. "It's a fast-paced atmosphere. Every day is different. I'm out of the office a lot—I work two weekends a month and one or two nights a week."

But Dey doesn't mind the long hours. The pay is good, and she has her sights set on her boss's job. "I'd like to be a vice president by the time I'm 30. It might take a little longer than that, but I'm willing to work hard to earn it."

She has plenty of advice for others wanting to follow in her footsteps. "Take the initiative. When I'm hiring an assistant, I am looking for someone who is prompt, detail-oriented, has done research on my company, asks thoughtful questions, and is very eager."

» » »

fight against piracy are taking legal action against people who violate copyrights and educating people about copyright theft.

The studios are looking closely at what the music industry is doing to prevent illegal copies of copyrighted material. But the music industry, thus far, cannot stop piracy from creating huge losses. Film executives are worried that these losses just might continue.

The film industry is an important part of the entertainment landscape. Hugely popular films become embedded in popular culture, and some of the most quoted lines today are straight out of movies. "May the force be with you," as you go forth and embark on a career in film.

ADDITIONAL RESOURCES

Associations / Organizations

Adams Media Research
www.adamsmediaresearch.com
Provides market data and financial analysis of the film business.

DEG: the Digital Entertainment Group
www.dvdinformation.com
An industry-funded corporation that advocates and promotes benefits associated with DVDs and provides
   information related to the DVD format.

E! Entertainment Online
www.eonline.com
Provides news and gossip about the entertainment industry.

Forrester Research Inc.
www.forrester.com
Reports on and analyzes technological change, including that related to the entertainment industry.

Independent Film & Television Alliance
www.ifta-online.org
Trade group for small companies that develop, finance, produce, and/or distribute movies and TV programs worldwide.

Motion Picture Association of America (MPAA)
www.mpaa.org
An advocacy group made up primarily of larger movie companies. Publishes annual statistical information on the movie industry.

National Association of Theater Owners
www.natoonline.org

Nielsen EDI
www.entdata.com
Provides information on the movie industry, including box office results.

ShowBiz Data Inc.
www.showbizdata.com.
Provides news and data related to the movie industry.

Women in Film
www.wif.org
A nonprofit organization dedicated to helping women achieve their highest potential in the entertainment
business.

Job-Hunting Resources

The Biz: thebiz.variety.com
Cinema Spot: www.cinemaspot.com/industry/employment.htm
Filmaking Careers: www.filmmaking-careers.com

Books

Dzyak, Brian. *What I Really Want to Do on Set in Hollywood: A Guide to Real Jobs in the Film Industry.*
Los Angeles: Lone Eagle, 2008.
Greenspon, Jaq. *Careers for Film Buffs and Other Hollywood Types.* New York: McGraw-Hill, 2003.
Gregory, Georgina, Ros J. Healy, and Ewa Mazierska. *Careers in Media and Film: The Essential Guide.*
Thousand Oaks, CA: Sage Publications, 2008.
Yager, Fred, and Jan Yager. *Career Opportunities in the Film Industry.* New York: Facts on File, 2003.

Magazines and Trade Publications

Boxoffice Magazine: www.boxoffice.com
The Hollywood Reporter: www.hollywoodreporter.com
Variety: www.variety.com

Miscellaneous

IMAX
2525 Speakman Drive
Mississauga, ON L5K 1
Canada
(905) 403-6500

TiVo
2160 Gold Street
Alviso, CA 95002
(408) 519-9100

ENDNOTES

1. Motion Picture Association of America, www.mpaa.org.

2. Box Office Charts, Box Office Mojo, www.boxofficemojo.com.

3. Ibid.

4. Internet Movie Database, www.imdb.com.

5. Ibid.

6. Bruce Newman, "No Matter How You Say It, 'Gigli' Stinks," *San Jose Mercury News*, 1 August 2003.

7. Motion Picture Association of America, www.mpaa.org.

8. "Who Owns What," *Columbia Journalism Review*, www.cjr.org.

9. Anthony R. Fellow, *American Media History*, Belmont, CA: Thomson Wadsworth, 2005: 221.

10. "History of the Motion Picture: Early Years, 1830–1910: Edison and Lumiere Brothers," *Encyclopedia Britannica Online*, www.britannica.com.

11. Ibid.

12. "History of the Motion Picture: The Silent Years," *Encyclopedia Britannica Online*, www.britannica.com.

13. Ibid.

14. Ibid.

15. Ibid.

16. Ibid.

17. "History of the Motion Picture: The pre-World War II Sound Era," *Encyclopedia Britannica Online*, www.britannica.com.

18. Fellow, 233.

19. "History of the Motion Picture: The War Years and post-World War II Trends," *Encyclopedia Britannica Online*, www.britannica.com.

20. Ibid.

21. Fellow, 240.

22. "History of the Motion Picture: The War Years and post-World War II Trends," *Encyclopedia Britannica Online*, www.britannica.com.

23. Ibid.

24. Ibid.

25. Ibid.

26. Motion Picture Association of America, www.mpaa.org.

27. Ibid.

28. Motion Picture Association of America, www.mpaa.org.

29. Tuna N. Amobi, "Movies and Home Entertainment," *Standard and Poor's Industry Survey*, 3 July 2008, www.netadvantage.standardandpoors.com.

30. Sundance Film Festival, www.sundance.org.

31. Internet Movie Database, www.imdb.com.

32. Ibid.

33. See Al Lieberman and Patricia Esgate, *The Entertainment Marketing Revolution*, Upper Saddle River, NJ: Prentice Hall, 2002: 46.

34. Motion Picture Association of America, www.mpaa.org.

35. Ibid.

36. Josh Friedman, "Studios Relying on Same-weekend Strategy for Movie Openings," *Los Angeles Times*, 27 May 2008.

37. Motion Picture Association of America, www.mpaa.org.

38. Bureau of Labor Statistics, www.bls.gov.

39. Ibid.

40. Motion Picture Association of America, www.mpaa.org.

3

Television

BETH BINGHAM EVANS

The television show *American Idol* entered its seventh season in 2008 with no sign of its star fading. The show continued to be at the top of the ratings charts and the darling of the Fox Television Network. The premiere of *American Idol* season 7 attracted 33 million viewers in the United States, according to Nielsen Media Research.[1] The near-record ratings for the Fox network proved that *American Idol* continued to be one of the hottest U.S. television shows for seven seasons in a row. That success makes *American Idol* one of the most successful franchises in television history. Success translates into money in the entertainment business.

As early as the fourth season, it became apparent that *American Idol* was a money-making machine for the Fox network and not just in terms of television advertising revenue. Fox made more than $400 million in *American Idol's* fourth TV season alone. According to David Lieberman's article in *USA Today,* "Fox sold about 10 minutes of advertising per hour, and each 30-second spot cost an average of $600,000."[2] That's big money for a television show.

Additionally by the fourth season, approximately $100 million had been made in album sales by the *Idol*-related singers. Then, add in the approximately $215 million consumers spent on *American Idol* branded merchandise, and you have a franchise that is successful in several different areas of entertainment and could continue making money for years to come. But success isn't limited to the United States. *American Idol* aired in 85 countries, while a similar version of the show aired in another 33.

American Idol has been a smash hit for the Fox network, which is owned by News Corp. The first season saw ratings increase by 70%.[3] The second season averaged more than 21 million viewers.[4] And in its seventh season, more than 33 million people watched the finale, making it one of the most popular shows during the 2007/2008 television season. All of this is quite remarkable considering the show almost didn't make it on the air in the United States.

Back in 2001, the creator of *American Idol* had a show on the air in Great Britain called *Pop Idol*. But when the show was pitched in the United States, television network executives showed no interest until Rupert Murdoch's daughter, who was living and working in London, told her dad about the popularity of *Pop Idol*. Murdoch, as the head of the Fox Network, decided to take a chance on the show. And the rest is history.

American Idol is successful for several reasons. It's interactive. Viewers are given the opportunity to call in or text message for their favorite performer. It's cross-promoted. Fans can buy show merchandise including karaoke machines, video games, and CDs of the contestants' music. And it's real—real people competing for real fame and fortune.

But for every success story like *American Idol,* there are thousands of television shows that fail. This chapter will analyze the television business to understand how it works, who the players are, employment opportunities, and challenges and trends for the future.

History and Background

Early Television

Television is one of the most influential media of our time. That really isn't all that surprising since broadcast television is free when you purchase a television set. Couple that with the fact that television penetration in the United States is 98.2%,[5] and you end up with a powerful entertainment medium.

It's hard to believe that just seven decades ago people didn't have the option to turn on the tube and plop down on the couch after a long day at work to be informed, entertained, or educated.

Commercial television made its public debut in 1939 at the World's Fair in New York City.[6] President Franklin Roosevelt opened the Fair with a live broadcast from NBC's experimental station in New York City. About 200 television sets throughout the region picked up the live signal. While this was the "official" debut, several experimental stations had been sending out television programs over the airwaves for a dozen years.

After the World's Fair debut, NBC began regular television programming, which included sitcoms, vaudeville shows, dramas, and live music. Audiences were mesmerized by the fact that they could see an actor or singer perform live while they were sitting several miles away watching the television set. As magical as television was, people at that time were not rushing out to buy television sets. The cost of a television was $125 to $600, which was a lot of money back then, approximately one to two months' salary.[7] World War II would further delay the development of television as factory production in this country was geared toward the war effort, not building television sets.

In 1941, the Federal Communications Commission (FCC) called together a committee of engineers to recommend a television standard for the United States. The committee was called the National Television System Committee or NTSC. The NTSC decided on the 525-line system, which has been phased out with the new standards for HDTV. That's why the television standard in this country was called NTSC. Many other parts of the world use a standard called PAL.

Television Gains in Popularity

On May 7, 1945, World War II ended in Europe, and television became popular almost overnight. The focus for American factories turned from the war effort to making consumer products like television sets. Electronics stores couldn't keep TV sets in stock. Americans had money to spend and were ready to buy after enduring rationing during the war. Advertisers saw the potential of reaching prosperous Americans and turned to television to place their ads. It was a perfect situation for television and the networks. Advertisers at that time usually sponsored an entire television program. There was no such thing as 30-second ad spots back then.

By 1948, four television networks were on the air: NBC, CBS, ABC, and DuMont (DuMont went out of business in 1955.)[8] Each network began a full prime-time schedule seven days a week. Most of the original television programming got its start in radio. Shows like *The Adventurers of Ozzie and Harriet, Dragnet*, and *Texaco Star Theater with Milton Berle* made the transition from radio to television in the 1940s and 1950s.

The transition to television was relatively easy. Instead of showing up at the radio station, the actors now gathered at the television studio and worked in front of the camera. The days in front of the camera were longer, but work was done in pretty much the same way the actors had performed for the microphone for radio.

By 1949, television had become very popular, with 49 stations broadcasting throughout the United States. A year later the number of television stations had doubled to 98.[9] Television was on its way to becoming one of the most popular and influential entertainment media in this country.

The move to color television took place in 1951. A one-hour show featuring Ed Sullivan was CBS's first color broadcast.[10] However, very few people witnessed the transition to color, as out of the more than 10 million television sets in the United States, only about two dozen were capable of receiving a color signal.

One of the most popular shows of the time was *I Love Lucy*, which premiered on CBS in 1951. The show was a hit from the start. The episode in season three in which Lucy gave birth to Little Ricky earned a 92% share of the television audience. That means 92% of all television sets in use that night were tuned to *I Love Lucy*.

I Love Lucy marked the move of the television production capital of the country from New York City to Hollywood. CBS wanted Lucille Ball and Desi Arnaz to broadcast live from New York, but Lucy and Desi didn't want to leave their home in Los Angeles, so they convinced network executives to shoot the show on the West Coast.

The innovative show was the first television show to use three cameras simultaneously during filming. Most other television shows were shot live before a single camera, and the footage was later edited into a finished product. This style of shooting a sitcom remains in place today as most television sitcoms are shot with three, four, or five cameras.

In the 1960s, television proved to be a powerful tool for politicians, with the Richard Nixon/Jack Kennedy presidential debate. The power of television was evident on September 26, 1960, when an estimated 75 million viewers watched Kennedy beat Nixon. Kennedy understood the power of the television image. He wore makeup and had wardrobe consultants pick his suit and tie for television. Nixon didn't think he needed such aids. Also, Nixon had been sick and had lost weight, and on camera, he appeared thin and tired looking. Those who watched the debate thought Kennedy had won. Those who heard the debate on radio thought Nixon had won. Politics would never be the same.

By 1964, 90% of households in this country had a television set. Americans rocked to the sound of the Beatles on the *Ed Sullivan Show* and cried as news coverage of President Kennedy's assassination shook the country.

War came into American living rooms on a nightly basis for the first time in history during the Vietnam War. Each of the networks sent news reporters to the front lines during the mid-1960s. The nightly reports from Vietnam had a profound impact on viewers.

The decade of the 1970s saw some very controversial topics discussed on television. Television news had become a popular source of information for many Americans, and news coverage focused on racism and civil rights. Racism also permeated entertainment programming as well. Norman Lear's *All in the Family* debuted in 1971, showing that a sitcom that ventured into what had been taboo subject matter could be successful. Archie Bunker kept the audience entertained as the show took viewers through story lines dealing with ethics, sex, politics, and racism.

Some of the networks' made-for-TV movies also dealt with subjects previously considered taboo on television. Movies tackled issues like homosexuality, incest, battered-wife syndrome, and other sensitive topics.

In 1978, *Dallas* became the first of the truly successful nighttime soap operas and topped the ratings chart week after week. Spin-offs also became popular during the 1970s. Supporting characters on successful programs were spun off from the original show to start their own show. Some of the successful spin-offs were *Laverne and Shirley* from *Happy Days* and *Rhoda* and *Phyllis* from *The Mary Tyler Moore Show*.

More Channels, More Choices

By 1980, television penetration in the United States was 98%.[11] The 1980s also saw cable television starting to attract more of the viewing audience. More and more cable television channels gave viewers many more choices than the three broadcast networks,

ABC, CBS, and NBC, provided. In 1985, the start-up of a new broadcast network, Fox Television, by media mogul Rupert Murdoch, further split the viewing audience.

The Cosby Show aired on NBC in the mid-1980s and was a hit from the start. It was one of the first shows to portray a minority family in a non-stereotypical fashion. Bill Cosby starred as the head of a middle-class family; he was a physician, his wife, an attorney. Considered a step forward in showing minority role models on television, *The Cosby Show* came at a time when television viewing was at its peak. In 1986, Americans were watching more than ever before: Television sets were turned on an average of 7 hours and 10 minutes per day per home.[12]

The 1990s saw television station ownership being consolidated as big media companies bought more and more media and entertainment assets. It was not uncommon for media giants to own a broadcast television network or two, multiple cable channels, newspapers, dozens of magazines, theme parks, film and television studios, major league sports teams, and music labels. The Walt Disney Co., News Corp., Time Warner, General Electric, Liberty Media, Sony, and Vivendi/Universal, to name some of the largest, were buying up more and more media outlets.

The 1990s also saw the expansion of satellite television. Direct-to-Home satellite receivers were developed to bring television signals into the homes of people who lived in rural areas of the United States. Small receiving dishes picked up the television signal from a satellite in orbit around the earth. Two companies continue to dominate the satellite industry: DirecTV and Dish Network.

Two New Networks

In January 1995, broadcast television saw the start-up of two new networks, the WB Television Network and the UPN Network. Both networks, although owned by different companies, were a reaction to the success of Fox. The two new broadcast networks were trying to offer alternative programming to what the big three networks were offering, but neither really became successful. The WB's first programs were inexpensive sitcoms targeted at an ethnic audience. None of the early shows clicked with viewers. A few years after its launch, the WB began to focus on programming that appealed to teens. It was much more successful with shows like *Buffy the Vampire Slayer* and *Dawson's Creek* and became number one with teenage audiences.

UPN, United Paramount Network, took a slightly different approach in its programming, first gaining attention through *Star Trek: Voyager.* But it would be shows like *America's Next Top Model* and *Everybody Hates Chris* that put it on the map. UPN found success with a demographic that was both young and African American.

Despite a few hit shows for each network, both the WB and UPN struggled. In January 2006 the two networks announced they were shutting down to start a joint venture called the CW Network, a partnership between CBS and Warner Bros. The CW launched in the fall of 2006, taking the most successful shows from each of the previous networks with it.

Television Loves Reality

The beginning of the twenty-first century saw a shift to reality programming. *Survivor* debuted in 2000 and was a huge hit from the start. The reality craze was underway. It wasn't long before dozens of reality shows were on the air and at the top of the ratings chart.

Cable Television

Cable has given viewers many more choices when it comes to television programming. The beginning of cable television can be traced back to 1948. The owner of an appliance store in Mahanoy City, PA, was having trouble selling television sets because it was difficult to get a broadcast signal in the area. The store owner installed an antenna on the top of a mountain near his store and ran a wire from the antenna to his shop. The television signal in his store was excellent. He offered a deal to his customers. He would run a wire from his store to their homes if they bought a television set. Other similar systems were built across the country.

The 1980s saw an explosion in new cable channels starting up. In 1980, CNN went on the air. The Cable News Network provided television viewers with all news all the time. MTV was launched in 1981. By the mid-80s, cable channels like VH1, Movie Channel, and TBS were on the air, giving viewers alternatives to the network programming. Today, the average cable subscriber has access to hundreds of channels including many music and pay cable movie channels. Cable television is more popular than broadcast television. In 2005, Americans watched 980 hours of cable programming and 679 hours of broadcast television.[13]

Digital and High-Definition Television

Television went digital on February 17, 2009. On that day, full power television stations in the United States were required by the Federal Communications Commission to stop broadcasting on their analog channels and covert to digital programming. The move to digital freed up broadcast spectrum space for other uses, including additional television stations and public safety communications. Television viewers benefited from an improved picture and sound quality. Many television stations actually began broadcasting in digital long before the mandated transition. After the digital transition, consumers were able to continue watching television on older analog television sets by using a digital-to-analog converter box.

Television Today

Television is still very popular today. The average American spent 1,659 hours with television in 2005. That's 15 times as much time as the average American spends reading books.[14]

ASHLEY ADAMS

Director of Production, Michael Hoff Productions
www.mhptv.com

Ashley Adams is a television show producer specializing in nonfiction television. In her 13 years in the business, she has produced shows for National Geographic Television, A&E, E! Entertainment Television, HGTV (Home and Garden Television), and DIY (Do It Yourself Television). Adams is the Director of Production for Michael Hoff Productions in the San Francisco Bay Area. She moved from show producer to management at the company in January 2005.

Adams has produced, written, and directed some of the most popular shows on cable television. Her credits include numerous episodes of the Emmy-nominated E! *True Hollywood Story,* such as "Jon Benet Ramsey," "Diana: Legacy of a Princess," and "William Shatner," as well as National Geographic's *Critical Decisions: Oklahoma Tornado,* and A&E's *Investigative Reports: Inside the FBI.*

Adams grew up in Connecticut and received a degree in English from the University of London. She got her start in television production by working as an intern for National Geographic Television in Washington, DC. After her summer as an unpaid intern, she was offered a position as a production assistant.

"The advice I give to young people wanting to get started in the television business is, don't be afraid to start at the bottom and work your way up," she said. "It's the way I started, and just about everyone in the business started as a production assistant or a creative assistant. Managers in the business expect you to pay your dues. Also, it's a great way to learn the idiosyncrasies of the television business."

One of the aspects of her job that she enjoys the most is traveling around the world to interview people for the shows she produces. "The job is always different; every day is something new. There's no time to get bored," Adams said. She admitted the hardest part of her job is finishing her shows on time and on budget. "It always seems like I could use a little more money or a little more time to make the show exactly the way I'd like it."

» » »

How the Television Industry Operates

In order to understand the relationship between the television studios that produce the content for television and the television stations themselves, it's important to know the structure of the business.

Network Television

The networks today are ABC, CBS, NBC, FOX, and CW. All of the networks send their signal into homes via broadcast television, and all of these networks are owned by a media conglomerate. Disney owns ABC. General Electric owns NBC. News Corporation owns Fox. Viacom owns CBS. Time Warner and Viacom own CW.

O&Os

Owned and operated television stations are owned by the network (ultimately the media conglomerate that owns the network) and operated by the network. The ABC Network (parent company is Disney) owns 10 stations in the country including WABC (New York), KABC (Los Angeles), KGO (San Francisco), WLS (Chicago), and additional stations in Flint, Fresno, Houston, Philadelphia, Raleigh/Durham, and Toledo.[15] O&Os are usually found in the largest television markets in the country. These stations air the programming of the network and also some local programming, which usually consists of local news and local sports.

Network Affiliates

The network does not own network affiliate television stations. Oftentimes other media giants own large groups of network affiliate stations. Gannett owns 22 television stations in addition to more than 100 newspapers. Clear Channel owns more than three dozen television stations in addition to some 1,000 radio stations.[16]

Network affiliates are located in all 210 television markets. Network affiliate stations enter into an exclusive contract with the network to air the network's prime-time programming, network news programs, late night talk shows, and some daytime soap operas. These contracts ensure that only one station in the market airs each network's programming. For instance, only one affiliate in a market will air CBS' programming. When an affiliate airs the network's programs, it also airs the network's commercials. The contract does allow the affiliates a few minutes each hour to sell local ads. In exchange for airing the network's programming and commercials, the affiliate stations are compensated by the network. Each of the major networks spends millions of dollars on affiliate compensation.

Independents

Independent television stations do not have a relationship with the networks and do not air network programming. They rely on local original programming like news or syndicated programming to fill their schedules. Syndicated programs may be reruns of hit shows that usually air a year or two after they appeared on the networks. This type of syndication is referred to as off-network or off-net syndication. The independent stations might also buy first-run syndicated shows.

First-run syndicated shows are produced exclusively for the syndication market and sold in individual television markets rather than to networks. First-run syndicated shows do not air on the network first. Such shows are usually talk shows like *Oprah,* game shows like *Jeopardy,* or magazine shows like *Entertainment Tonight.* First-run syndicated shows may air on network affiliates or O&Os, but they are sold separately in each individual market and not as a package to the entire network.

Public Television

The public broadcasting system is made up of more than 300 PBS television stations across the country, including stations like KCET in Los Angeles, WGBH in Boston, and WNET in New York City. PBS is a nonprofit corporation that supports its member television stations through programming and funding. On November 7, 1967, President Lyndon Johnson signed the Public Broadcasting Act, which created the Corporation for Public Broadcasting. The idea behind public broadcasting was to provide alternate voices and television programs to improve the democratic process in this country. PBS aims to provide educational, public affairs, and arts programming. Successful programs on PBS over the years have included *Sesame Street* and *Masterpiece Theatre.* Government funding helps pay for the programming and operation of the stations. PBS stations also receive money when corporations underwrite programming. In exchange for donating money for a specific program, a company will receive on-air mention before and/or after the program. PBS stations also ask viewers to donate money to help support the quality programming they watch.

Ratings

Television shows (and often television executives' careers) live or die depending on the ratings. The goal of most television programming is to achieve the highest ratings possible. The relationship between ratings and programming is quite simple—the higher the rating, the more the television station can charge for a commercial. PBS also desires high ratings because the higher the rating, the more viewers might donate to the station, and the more a company will pay to sponsor a program.

But ratings are more than a simple number at the end of the day. Entire departments at television stations across the country evaluate and scrutinize the ratings numbers that come into the station in hopes of learning what television audiences want and when they want to watch it. Nielsen Media Research provides television stations with detailed information about audiences including changes in viewing habits, demographics of the viewer, and detailed ratings numbers that show changes in viewing every 15 minutes.

What the Ratings Mean

The premiere of the fifth season of *American Idol* did well in the ratings for the 2005/2006 television season with a 15.3% rating and 34% share in the adults 18–49 demographic, according to Nielsen Media Research.[17] But what do those numbers really mean? The rating percentage refers to the percentage of television homes watching *American Idol*. A rating of 15.3 points means that 15.3% of American's TV homes (or 35.5 million viewers) are watching the program.

The share is also a research tool to help network executives estimate how popular their program is with viewers. Share is probably a better measurement of how well a show does against its competition. Share refers to the percentage of television homes with sets turned on that are watching a particular program. In this case, *American Idol* had a 34% share. That means that 34% of the people who were watching television at that time were watching *American Idol*.

As impressive as *American Idol's* ratings numbers are, they are much smaller than those of other network programs from the 1970s and the 1980s before cable television diluted the viewing audience. The highest-rated show in television history (since Nielsen began generating research in 1961) was the *M*A*S*H* two-hour series finale with an impressive 60.2% rating and 77% share on February 28, 1983. The second-highest rated television show was *Dallas's* "Who Shot J.R.?" episode with a 53.3% rating and a 76% share on November 21, 1980.[18] *American Idol* is still considered a hit even though it received a little more than a quarter of the ratings *Dallas* received.

Sweeps

National ratings are calculated every day. Ratings in all the smaller individual cities are calculated just four times a year. Those ratings periods are called sweeps and occur in February, May, July, and November. These are the time periods when the networks and local stations pull out all the stops in an effort to get the most people watching their programming.

During sweeps, it's not uncommon to see a major Hollywood film actor make a guest appearance on a sitcom or a local television news team report the findings of an undercover report on food safety at popular restaurants. The purpose of these sweeps stunts is to boost ratings. That's because the ratings numbers during the sweeps period determine the amount of money a station can charge for advertising over the next quarter until another sweeps period arrives.

Ratings also help media buyers at advertising agencies decide where to spend a client's television money because Nielsen Media also provides the television executives with very detailed information about the demographics of the television audience. Ultimately, the ratings numbers help television executives decide which programs to keep on the air and which shows to cancel.

During sweeps, Nielsen Media measures television audiences in all 210 of the television markets. Television markets are also referred to as DMAs—Designed Market Areas. These DMAs are determined by the number of television households reached by the broadcast signal of the television stations in that market. It's not uncommon for entry-level television news producers and reporters to start their careers in a relatively small market; for instance, a DMA of 160 (Sioux City, IA) is a good starting market—the goal being to move up in market size until you reach a major market (DMAs from 1–20). New York City is DMA #1, Los Angeles DMA #2, Chicago DMA #3, Philadelphia DMA #4, Boston DMA #5.[19]

New Shows

Every fall the networks unveil their new shows for the season. Competition for these new shows is fierce. Thousands of ideas for new shows are pitched to the networks, and a few dozen are developed into pilots. Of those shows that are produced into pilots, fewer than half will end up on the fall schedule. And of those new shows that make it on the air, fewer than 20% will be around for a second season. Once a television show is successful for two or three years, the owner of the show might try to sell it in the lucrative syndication market. A show like *Seinfeld* or *Friends* is a huge moneymaker in the off-network syndication market.

Federal Communications Commission (FCC)

The Federal Communications Commission (FCC) is the independent federal government agency whose job is to oversee the broadcast industry. Five commissioners are appointed by the U.S. president and confirmed by the Senate. The term for a commissioner is five years.

The FCC was established through the Communications Act of 1934 as a way to protect the public airwaves. The FCC is responsible for allocating broadcast licenses, renewing licenses, setting media ownership guidelines, and enforcing complaints of indecency on television. However, the FCC is not in the business of telling stations what they can and cannot air—that would be prior restraint, which is unconstitutional under the First Amendment. However, the FCC will investigate incidents of broadcast indecency if viewers send complaints to the agency.

Challenges and Trends

The television industry is changing probably faster than ever before. The trends in the industry create multiple challenges for the next generation of people employed in the television industry. Success in the industry will require those working in the field to embrace changes in technology, content, and delivery.

Reality Shows

Reality shows became a mainstay on network television after the success of *Survivor* in 2000. Copycat programs showed up on competing networks and cable channels. It appeared that no topic was off limits from programs like *The Swan,* where young women are transformed from an ugly duckling to a beautiful swan through extensive plastic surgery, or *The Bachelor,* where young women compete for love and ultimately a diamond ring and a marriage proposal.

These reality shows have dominated the ratings. Writers, producers, and actors argue that the reality show genre takes work away from those who make a living on scripted, fictional television. Another concern about the reality genre is whether there is much potential for success in the syndication market since most of us already know the outcome of the past season's episodes.

Time Shifting

Back in the 1980s, videocassette recorders first gave television viewers the opportunity to shift the time in which they watched a television program. VCRs allowed viewers to record a show and watch it at a different day or time. Today, viewers have many digital options that allow the recording of a television show. Digital video recording (DVR) devices such as TiVos are giving viewers the potential to store hours and hours of programming to watch when they find it convenient. The DVRs also give viewers the option to skip over commercials. Broadcast television relies on commercials to support itself. In other words, without the commercials there would be no free television. So, the industry has adapted to make sure viewers see the products even if the viewers don't watch the commercials.

An emerging trend in the industry is in-show product placement. Product placement is not a new idea. For decades companies sent products to television producers in hopes the producers would decide to include the product in an episode of their show. But, the newest idea is for a company to pay the producers to place its product in the middle of the storyline. For instance, on NBC's *The Biggest Loser,* weight-loss contestants struggle to break the lock on a Jell-O branded refrigerator. Or on the hit *America's Next Top Model,* aspiring models compete to see who can do the best job of applying Cover Girl makeup in a timed contest.

Critics of in-show product placement have primarily been writers and producers. They argue in-show product placement is erasing the line between content and advertising and detracts from the art of storytelling, which could lead to less quality programming. Network television executives who support the practice insist it's a way to add to the bottom line when ratings are declining and people aren't watching commercials.

Consolidation

Another challenge the industry is facing is the growing influence of the media conglomerates. Companies like Disney, Time Warner, and Viacom own television broadcast networks, cable networks, film studios, television production companies, and, in the case of Time Warner, extensive cable services to get the product to the consumer. Independent producers worry the media giants have too much power and might not need to turn to outside producers for content. Critics worry that network television's vertical integration limits the number of voices and viewpoints in television programming.

Ratings Shift from Network to Cable

Americans aren't watching fewer total hours of television, but we are watching fewer hours of network television and more hours of cable programming. In the 1980s, network television had 80% of the viewing audience during prime time. That number had dropped to below 50% by 1997 and continues to drop each year. Meanwhile, the number of people watching cable programming during prime time continues to increase. Every year, more and more cable channels are introduced, further fragmenting the viewing audience. Advertisers like cable television because it is becoming a niche market, enabling advertisers to better reach a specific demographic.

DVD Sales

Selling television shows on DVD is becoming big business. It used to be if you went into a video rental store, films lined the shelves of the store. Nowadays, films compete for shelf space with television shows. DVD sales and rentals of television shows are generating a lot of money for the television studios that own the shows. Some of the shows for sale are vintage programs like *I Love Lucy* or *Welcome Back, Kotter,* but many new television shows enter the syndication market and the DVD sales market at the same time. TV series on DVD are now the fastest growing area of the overall DVD business. DVD revenue has become a key component tied to a television show's profitability.

Television on the Go

Television sets are getting bigger and smaller. It's not uncommon to see a 60-inch television set as the cornerstone of the home theater experience. It's also not uncommon to see someone watching the latest episode of *Desperate Housewives* on a 2.5-inch iPod screen.

The video iPod and other portable devices are changing the way television programmers reach their audience. No longer are the television networks insisting that people sit down on the couch at 8 P.M. on Sunday to watch the latest edition of a hit show. Now they can download the television show on their iPods and watch the next day aboard a plane bound for Hawaii. This is changing the financial model that has governed television since the beginning. Viewers are charged a fee to download the television episode from the Internet. Buyers can now view where they want and when they want. It's television on the go.

Employment Opportunities

Television is an exciting field and, regardless of changes in the industry, continues to be an attractive area of the entertainment business in which to work. The cable networks have given many people getting started in the industry a chance to hone their skills before moving up to the executive offices or to the networks. The 24-hour cable news networks have provided many jobs in reporting and anchoring as well as behind-the-scenes experience in producing or engineering. The Internet is a growing area of television in terms of marketing, news, and delivery of television shows.

Despite the networks' shrinking audience share, there continue to be many opportunities in the industry. Some of those jobs are in cable, others in marketing and promotion, and still others in new technology. At the network level, thousands of people continue to work in an effort to develop and foster the next hit show—hoping to match or exceed the success of *American Idol*.

Working in the television industry can be demanding. Television producers work hard when a show is in production. Reporters are oftentimes required to work long hours, weekends, and holidays when a major story breaks. Engineers can expect to be called to the station in the middle of the night if a vital piece of equipment fails.

Salaries in the television industry can be low to start because of the number of people competing for entry-level positions, but as people move up in rank or to higher markets, money follows. The television industry is a demanding field but can be very rewarding if you consider that your work has the potential to be seen by the 112 million U.S. households that currently have television.

Future Outlook

Television News

According to a study prepared by Nielsen Media Research in September 2002, 57% of Americans get most of their news about the world from television.[20] Yet, television newsrooms' staffs are getting smaller. Part of this is due to media consolidation in some of the larger television markets. For instance, when Viacom purchased a second major television station in the Los Angeles market, the newsrooms of KCBS and KCAL were merged, resulting in a single news director and a single assignment desk for both stations. Several other positions were also consolidated into one job.

Television news has never been exceptionally good at explaining the "why" behind many stories that dominate the newscast. Increasingly we are seeing television newscasts filled with news "that sells." Some of that news is consumer news, and a large portion of local news is about entertainment and celebrities.

GEORGE KIRIYAMA

Reporter, NBC11 Bay Area News
www.NBC11.com

George Kiriyama admits it's a crazy business, but he loves every minute of it. Kiriyama is a television news reporter in the San Francisco area. In his 12 years in the business, he has moved four times. His first on-air job as a reporter was in Midland, TX. Then, he moved to Grand Rapids/Kalamazoo, MI. After four years there, he moved to Kansas City, MO, and eventually made his way back to California, landing in the Bay Area.

Kiriyama got his start in television news after graduating with a degree in Communications by working on the assignment desk of KCAL in Los Angeles. But in order to land a job on-air, he knew he had to move to a small market. "I grew up in Southern California, so moving to a small town in West Texas was a culture shock. I had no friends or family in Midland, TX. I was homesick the first three months, but you learn to overcome all of that because you have a passion for what you do," he said.

Kiriyama recommends that others wanting to follow in his footsteps should realize the business is a lot less glamorous and a lot more hard work than it looks. "Make sure you have the passion, the drive, and the fire in your heart for news. If you don't, you'll be eaten alive by people who do," he said.

He also said news people have to stay informed. "Read newspapers, magazines, and news websites. Watch local news as well as the networks. Listen to local news radio and NPR. You need to stay on top of everything if you want to survive in this crazy business we call news."

Kiriyama loves what he does. He said the best part is meeting new people and telling their stories. "Informing, educating, and empowering the public is a responsibility I take seriously," he said.

The most memorable story Kiriyama has covered in his career was one in which he met a family who lost everything to Hurricane Katrina. The father, mother, and three children moved to Kansas City to start over. Kiriyama remembers that after his story aired, the phone lines at the station lit up. Dozens of people called in because they wanted to help. One man offered his lakefront home to the family rent-free for a year. Others threw the family a big party. Donations for the family poured in—everything from clothes to school supplies and toys for the kids.

Kiriyama recalled visiting the family again after his story aired, and the parents just cried. "They were overwhelmed by the generosity. You can't forget a story like that one."

» » »

Twenty-four-hour cable news channels are changing the business of television news, creating more competition and more pressure to be the first to report a story. It's becoming more common for correspondents to go "on-the-air" with the latest details of a story before there is time to double-check the facts.

Network broadcast news is undergoing a major change as well. The three anchors who were the face of network news for almost three decades are gone. ABC's Peter Jennings died of lung cancer in 2005, and CBS's Dan Rather and NBC's Tom Brokaw have retired. Network news executives are now in the process of reinventing the newscast in an effort to appeal to a wider demographic, including young people who traditionally turn to other sources for information.

Spanish-Language Television

Spanish-language media have grown rapidly in this country. Spanish-language television networks are increasing their programming, buying more television stations, and seeing significant ratings increases. There are two U.S. Spanish-language networks: Univision owns 50 stations and has 43 affiliates; Telemundo owns 15 stations and has 32 affiliates. Both Univision and Telemundo are supplying their stations and affiliates with news, dramas, and talk shows.

The Spanish-language audience is attractive to advertisers. First of all, Hispanics watch much more television than the national average—over four hours more per week. The audience also has more of the desirable youth demographic than other audience. In 2003, Nielsen Media Company estimated that 65% of the Hispanic population is under 35, compared to 45% for non-Hispanics. Experts predict Spanish-language media will continue to grow in coming years.

Summary

Americans were first introduced to television in the early part of the twentieth century. Many of them saw television for the first time during an experimental broadcast during the 1939 World's Fair in New York City. Viewers were fascinated by what they saw, but the industry wouldn't significantly grow until the end of World War II. During the 1950s, television's popularity skyrocketed as Americans watched some of their favorite shows make the transition from radio to television.

The 1980s saw network television at its height in terms of ratings and audience share, but soon cable television would begin to chip away at the networks' dominance. Cable television continues to offer viewers many different options.

Consolidation by big media companies in the 1990s continues to change the landscape of television and the entertainment industry. Media giants, like Disney and Time Warner, have achieved significant vertical integration in the market and own the network stations to air the programming.

Despite all the changes in the industry, the growth of the television industry is strong. Network programs are finding a new life after syndication in the DVD market. Viewers are finding ways to watch their favorite shows while on the go through technological advances such as the video iPod. And hit shows like *American Idol* are finding growth throughout the entertainment industry as successful brands to be leveraged into music, merchandise, and live events such as concerts.

ADDITIONAL RESOURCES

Associations and Organizations

Academy of Television, Arts and Sciences
www.emmys.org
5220 Lankershim Boulevard
North Hollywood, CA 91601
(818) 754–2800

American Federation of Television & Radio Artists
www.aftra.org
New York National Office
260 Madison Avenue
New York, NY 10016–2401
(212) 532–0800

Los Angeles National Office
5757 Wilshire Boulevard, 9th Floor
Los Angeles, CA 90036–3689
(323) 634–8100

American Women in Radio and Television
www.awrt.org
8405 Greensboro Drive, Suite 800
McLean, VA 22102
(703) 506–3290

NAB
National Association of Broadcasters
www.nab.org
1771 N. Street, NW
Washington, DC 20036
(202) 429–5300

NATPE
National Association of Television Program Executives
www.natpe.org
5757 Wilshire Boulevard, Penthouse 10
Los Angeles, CA 90036–3681
(310) 453–4440

RTNDA
www.rtnda.org
Radio Television News Directors Association
1015 I Street, NW, 7th Floor
Washington, DC 20004
(202) 659–6510

Books

Blumenthal, Howard J., and Oliver R. Goodenough. *The Business of Television.* New York: Billboard Books, 2006.

McDowell, Walter S. *Broadcast Television: A Complete Guide to the Industry.* New York: Peter Lang Publishing, 2006.

Noronha, Shonan. *Opportunities in Television and Video Careers.* New York: McGraw-Hill, 2003.

Taylor, T. Allen, and James Robert Parish. *Career Opportunities in Television and Cable.* New York: Checkmark Books, 2006.

Magazines and Trade Publications

Broadcasting & Cable: www.broadcastingcable.com
Communicator: www.rtnda.org
Entertainment Weekly: www.ew.com
TV Guide: www.tvguide.com
Variety: www.variety.com
Hollywood Reporter: www.hollywoodreporter.com

Websites

TVSpy: A Vault Service
Shoptalk (Broadcasting Industry Information):
www.tvspy.com

Television Networks

ABC
www.abc.go.com
7 W. 66th Street
New York, NY 10023

CBS
www.cbs.com
51 W. 52nd Street
New York, NY 10019

Fox
www.fox.com
205 E. 67th Street
New York, NY 10021

NBC
www.nbc.com
30 Rockefeller Plaza
New York, NY 10112

PBS
www.pbs.org
1320 Braddock Place
Alexandria, VA 22314

ENDNOTES

1. Nielsen Media Research, www.nielsen.com.
2. David Lieberman, "American Idol Zooms from Hit Show to Massive Business," *USA Today,* 30 March 2005, A1.
3. Nielsen Media Research, www.nielsen.com.
4. Ibid.
5. Ibid.
6. Anthony R. Fellow, *American Media History,* Belmont, CA: Wadsworth Thompson, 2005: 282.
7. Ibid.
8. Erik Barnouw, *Tube of Plenty: The Evolution of American Television,* Oxford, England: Oxford University Press, 1990: 99–103.
9. Fellow, 283.
10. Ibid., 285.
11. "Media Trends Track," Television Bureau of Advertising, www.tvb.org.
12. Nielsen Media Research, www.nielsen.com.
13. Veronis Suhler Stevenson, *Media Usage and Consumer Spending: 2000 to 2010,* www.census.gov/compendia/statab/cats/information_communications.html.
14. Ibid.
15. "Who Owns What," *Columbia Journalism Review,* www.cjr.org/tools/owners.
16. Ibid.
17. Nielsen Media Research, www.nielsen.com.
18. Ibid.
19. Ibid.
20. Ibid.

4

Radio   BETH BINGHAM EVANS

Shock jock Howard Stern's decision to go where the Federal Communications Commission (FCC) couldn't reach him was billed as a huge boost to the satellite radio industry. Stern bolted from traditional radio to Sirius satellite radio in 2004. Stern's famously foul mouth wasn't popular with the FCC. His show on traditional radio had been fined $2 million over the years for obscene or indecent material. When Stern moved to Sirius satellite radio, where the FCC would have no jurisdiction over the content of his show, it was expected millions of fans would follow. And millions did. His show was so successful that Stern received a bonus in January 2007 of $220 million in company stock. The bonus, combined with his original five-year $500 million contract, meant that Stern's paycheck just one year after he moved to satellite radio was more than $700 million.

All of this sounded as if Sirius was a company on its way to huge success. But in reality neither Sirius nor the only other satellite radio company, XM, was making a profit. In July 2008, the FCC voted in favor of the two companies merging. The merger ended a 16-month drama that had been closely watched by Washington, the radio industry, and Wall Street. Groups opposing the merger called it a monopoly and argued it would hurt consumers. Satellite radio executives said the merger would cut costs by hundreds of million of dollars and lead to greater choice in programming for subscribers.

In the end, Howard Stern helped increase the number of people who paid for satellite radio, but it would take much more than one popular shock jock to keep the satellite industry in business. Maybe satellite radio was just ahead of its time. Or maybe radio listeners just weren't ready to pay for something that they had been getting free for more than 100 years. This chapter will discuss the potential for satellite radio and other trends in the radio industry as well as the employment opportunities in the field.

History and Background

Early Radio

The beginning of radio dates back to the 1880s. Scottish physicist James Maxwell studied electricity and magnetism and eventually came up with a theory of electromagnetic radio waves that would be the basis for radio. Maxwell's theory was put to the test in 1887 when German physicist Heinrich Hertz proved it by producing radio waves through an oscillator, which included two coils of wire. Hertz was able to transmit radio waves from one coil to the other.

Just before the turn of the century, Italian Guglielmo Marconi put together everything he had read about Hertz's experiments and developed the first wireless telegraph. Marconi was finally able to use Morse code to send signals that traveled over two thousand miles from England to Newfoundland.

Reginald Fessenden developed the theory needed to change the Morse code that Marconi was sending to actual voice communication. He was the first to send his voice via radio waves. According to Anthony R. Fellow, on December 23, 1900, near Washington, DC, Fessenden said, "'One-two-three-four, is it snowing where you are, Mr. Thiessen? If it is, would you telegraph back to me?' From a mile away, Mr. Thiessen indeed confirmed that it was snowing."[1] Radio was born.

Radio's Golden Age

The first radio network, the National Broadcasting Company (NBC), was founded in 1926. NBC's first broadcast was a music special from the luxurious grand ballroom of the Waldorf-Astoria Hotel in New York. The venture into radio broadcasting was so successful that NBC executives eventually divided NBC into two networks, NBC-Blue and NBC-Red, in an effort to offer affiliates more choices in programming. Eventually, NBC-Blue would become the American Broadcasting Company (ABC). William S. Paley founded the Columbia Broadcasting System (CBS) in 1927.

Radio had entered its Golden Age, which ran from approximately 1930 until 1950. Radio stations sprang up all across the United States. Advertisers discovered the potential to reach hundreds or even thousands of listeners through the power of radio. Americans tuned in to catch their favorite programs, which included dramas, soap operas, and live big band musical performances. There was something for every member of the family. Boys loved *Jack Armstrong, the All-American Boy*. Girls loved *Little Orphan Annie*. Mom enjoyed *Just Plain Bill*. The whole family laughed over the antics of *Amos 'n Andy*. While other nights, the family was glued to the set listening to *The Adventures of Sherlock Holmes*.

Probably the most famous radio broadcast took place on Halloween eve of 1938. Orson Welles's broadcast of *War of the Worlds* ended up panicking millions of Americans who were listening to the fictional account of Martians invading the Earth. Listeners who had missed the introduction that declared the broadcast a piece of fiction found themselves terrified by the events described in the radio drama.

People loaded up their cars and drove out of town, hoping to avoid the invasion. Other people called the police, and eventually the military was alerted. Welles was surprised by the reaction and insisted he never meant to panic anyone. This broadcast illustrated the power of the radio medium.

Radio was also used extensively for news coverage. Radio's ability to report stories live was perfect for breaking news stories. Regular radio programming was interrupted for several days in 1932 as news anchors reported the latest on the kidnapping of the Lindbergh baby.[2]

In 1937, listeners gathered around their radios to hear reports of the *Hindenburg* disaster. The largest audience in radio history was riveted to the set listening to President Franklin D. Roosevelt on December 9, 1941. An audience estimated at 90 million people heard the president address Congress two days after the attack on Pearl Harbor.[3]

Radio Regulation

Radio was so popular during the 1920s that radio stations popped up all across the country. Broadcasters were given a frequency, but there was no law or government body to regulate transmission power, hours of operation, or any consequence for changing frequency. So, the airwaves became jumbled. Station after station sprang up, and if another station's frequency interfered with the signal, the station just increased its power or switched frequencies. Interference became so bad; it was difficult for listeners to find their favorite stations or shows. The Radio Act of 1927 helped solve some of these problems. The Radio Act set up the Federal Radio Commission (FRC), which would later become the Federal Communications Commission (FCC) to cover television as well. The FRC was in charge of regulating the airwaves and granted licenses to broadcasters who would serve the public interest. It was also in charge of regulating transmission power and had the authority to fine broadcasters who violated the terms of their license.

Television Threatens Radio

Americans loved radio, but they would love television even more. As television became popular in the late 1940s and '50s, radio seemed doomed. A 1948 issue of *Time* Magazine predicted that TV "will eventually (maybe sooner) make radio as obsolete as the horse— and empty all the nation's movie houses."[4] Of course, that didn't happen. But radio was threatened and had to find a way to reinvent itself.

The popular programming that filled the radio airwaves was a natural for television. Soap operas, vaudeville shows, dramas, and live concerts all migrated to television. Viewers loved being able to hear and see their favorite shows. Radio had to act fast. Radio stations were going off the air, and those that did manage to stay on the air saw advertising revenues plummet. Radio turned to recorded music to remain viable.

Three events helped turn radio to a primarily recorded music format. The first event was the introduction of the 45-RPM vinyl single in 1949. The single "brought an easily handled, nearly unbreakable, inexpensive, high-fidelity recording into the marketplace," according to Albert N. Greco.[5]

The second event was the introduction of the top-40 format. A disc jockey by the name of Todd Storz came up with the idea of a "closed play list with a limited number of selections and a rotation that played the most popular songs more often."[6] Today, just about every commercial radio station that plays music uses a similar music format to determine which songs to play and how often. The last event was rock 'n' roll, which became incredibly popular in the 1950s. As more and more radio stations started playing this music, they attracted the listeners who did not like the predominately middle-of-the-road music formats that were common before rock. More demand for rock 'n' roll on the radio created more demand for rock music on records. So both the radio industry and the recorded music industry prospered.

Threat of Satellite Radio

When satellite radio was first introduced in 2001, it was billed as the next big thing in radio. It was expected that subscribers would flock to satellite radio, where they had to pay a subscription fee to avoid commercials and get more choices when it came to music formats. But satellite radio was slow to get going. In 2004, when Howard Stern moved to Sirius Satellite Radio, the two satellite companies were losing hundreds of millions of dollars. Sirius was the underdog with about 300,000 subscribers prior to Howard Stern. Launched in 2002, Sirius boasted of 61 music channels, 43 sports, news, and entertainment channels, and 10 channels for traffic and weather. In 2003, Sirius had a net loss of $226.2 million.[7]

The other satellite radio company, XM, was launched in November, 2001, and offered its customers 68 music channels, 32 channels for news, talk, and entertainment, and another 21 channels just for traffic and weather. In 2003, XM posted a net loss of $584 million. In 2004, XM had 1.5 million subscribers but was still losing money.[8]

Traditional or terrestrial radio was so worried about satellite radio that the powerful lobby group, the National Association of Broadcasters (NAB), pushed through legislation that severely limited satellite radio. The new legislation required that satellite radio operators pay royalties to recording artists even though traditional radio doesn't have this requirement. The FCC also requires satellite radio to be subscription based; satellite radio is forbidden from offering free advertising-supported stations.[9]

In February 2007, the two satellite companies announced they wanted to merge. The $13 billion merger finally took place 16 months later when the FCC voted 3–2 in favor of it.

Radio Today

Radio continues to be a steady source of entertainment. Statistics show that the average American spent 805 hours a year listening to the radio in 2005.[10] Radio is second in usage hours to television and ahead of all other forms of media and entertainment. It is sometimes easy to overlook the amount of time people spend with radio since they are oftentimes listening while doing something else such as working, driving, cooking, waiting in a doctor's office, or relaxing at home.

The growth areas of radio today are in digital radio and traditional radio stations via a personal computer. These trends will be discussed in depth in the next section.

Challenges and Trends

Demographics

Radio continues to be an attractive medium for advertisers. According to Arbitron, radio reaches more than 235 million listeners in the United States during a week's time.[11] Ninety-six percent of adults between the ages of 18 and 49 with a college degree and an annual household income above $50,000 tune into radio every week.[12] Many companies want their ads heard by radio's primarily college-educated, full-time-employed demographic.

Other notable demographic information about radio listeners includes the fact that fewer young people between the ages of 12 and 17 are listening to radio. Among minorities, radio reaches 94% of African Americans in a week's period and 96% of Hispanics between the ages of 25 and 54.[13]

Radio Consolidation

The Telecommunications Act of 1996 cleared the way for big media companies to buy almost as many radio stations as they wanted. Thousands of radio stations changed hands. Media companies like Clear Channel Communications bought up dozens of radio stations. In 2007, Clear Channel owned an estimated 1,100 stations in approximately 230 cities.[14]

Critics of consolidation in the radio industry argue that listeners lose when there are only a few big players in the business. One company might own multiple stations in the same market. These big players have consolidated jobs, so one program director might oversee multiple stations. That has led to fewer jobs in the radio industry. It has also eliminated diversity of opinion and programming. For the music industry, it has become more difficult to get a new record on the air as fewer programming directors are making decisions about which songs to play. As the number of songs that get the opportunity to be added to a play list have shrunk, it's difficult to get the radio exposure that can help boost sales.

Relationship with Music Industry

The majority of radio stations play recorded music. Yet there is a love/hate relationship between radio and the recorded music industry. From the radio executive's perspective, music attracts an audience, which then allows the radio sales team to sell advertising. So, the radio industry is using music to sell ads, and the labels are not among the top advertisers on radio.[15]

From the recorded music executive's perspective, "Radio airplay still accounts for a significant percentage of the exposure of record buyers to new music," according to Albert N. Greco.[16] So, music labels give radio stations free CDs in hopes that the program directors will include the music in their play lists. Even though a lot of people are exposed to new music on the radio, that trend is changing. Young buyers are learning about music from alternative sources such as video games, television shows, social networking sites, and movies.[17]

Radio Formats

The most popular format among radio stations across the United States is country music. In June 2008, 2,037 stations reported that their format was country music. The second most popular format is news/talk. According to insideradio.com, 2,032 radio stations listed news or talk as their format.[18] When discussing radio formats, it is interesting to notice how many different types of formats there are. Radio has been excellent at carving out a distinct niche based on listeners' needs and wants. That in turn has helped advertisers target their messages to narrow demographic audiences.

Figure 8: U.S. Radio Formats: June 2008

Format	Number of Stations
Country	2,037
News/Talk	2,032
Religion (Teaching, Variety)	1,262
Spanish	933
Contemporary Christian	928
Oldies	737
Variety	685
Adult Contemporary	680
Sports	595
Classic Hits	527
Classic Rock	482

Hot AC	385
Alternative Rock	263
Soft Adult Contemporary	227
Classical	179
Modern Rock	172
Urban AC	166
R&B	158
Jazz	141
Ethnic	136
Pre-Teen	56
R&B Adult/Oldies	39
Gospel	38
Easy Listening	25
Rhythmic AC	25
Modern AC	21

Source: Insideradio.com

Web Streaming/Podcasting

One of the growing trends in broadcast radio is streaming real-time programming from a website to listeners all around the world. This makes it possible to increase the number of listeners outside the broadcast reach of the station. Radio listenership via website grew to 29 million listeners each week in 2007, up from 20 million in 2004, according to Arbitron.[19]

Streaming programming via the Internet also gives listeners more than just a radio experience: It becomes a multimedia experience. The radio station can offer so much more than just audio. It can post ads, program schedules, contests, blogs, interactive elements, and announcer biographies all on the website.

Another advantage of a website is the ability to share music with friends. "Social FM is one site which provides users with social distribution channels for listening on PCs or over mobile devices. In late 2007, the site launched social music applications with Facebook users," according to Plunkett Research.[20] These radio stations offer the music legally to listeners. The music files are temporary and can be listened to at the computer user's convenience. The files cannot be permanently downloaded.

Internet radio without the ability to broadcast over the air has become a popular way to break into the industry for some organizations that can't get a broadcast license or don't have the money to start a broadcast radio station, to get into the radio industry. California State University, Fullerton, in Orange County started Titan Internet Radio after the university was unable to secure a broadcast license. Titan Internet Radio is run by students, and all the on-air personalities are students. It has been a terrific way to introduce Communications and Radio/TV/Film students to the business of radio.

HD Radio

Another area of radio that is being watched very closely is high-definition digital radio. HD technology gives listeners a better radio signal while increasing the number of broadcast radio channels available. In early 2007, the top 100 radio markets in the United States were offering listeners high-definition stations.[21]

High-definition allows radio operators to create additional stations using the same bandwidth. So, a broadcaster that typically offers a country music format on its main channel could also offer a country/pop station on one of its high-definition channels and another station that plays music from new country artists on its other high-definition channel.

The drawback to HD is that the receivers are much more expensive than those of traditional radio: They can cost several hundred dollars. Some new cars are being equipped with HD receivers. Digital radio is just getting a foothold but could eventually become the standard of radio just as high-definition has become the standard for television in the United States.

National Public Radio

Some of the best in-depth broadcast news coverage is available on National Public Radio (NPR). Programs like *All Things Considered* or *Morning Edition* are popular news/talk shows that report on everything from the fate of gorillas in Congo forests to the fact that all of the players on the 2008 U.S. Olympic Ping-Pong team were Chinese, a fact that was of great significance because the Olympics were held in Beijing.

National Public Radio was founded in 1970 and has become a primary source of news for millions of Americans. In 2008, NPR was heard on more than 860 independent public radio stations.

NPR began three years after national leaders established the Public Broadcasting Act of 1967. The Public Broadcasting Act created federal funding to support public radio and television in an effort to offer Americans programming that dealt with arts and public affairs. Today, public radio supports itself through government funding, sponsorships of programming by corporations, and pledges by listeners.

Many public radio stations across the country are located on campuses of colleges and universities, but most of them are run by professionals not by students. KPCC is located on the campus of Pasadena Community College in Southern California. KPCC employs professionals to run the station and to host the programming. Students have limited access to the station, mostly working as interns or assistants.

Crisis Response

One of the things that radio probably does better than any other mass media is alert an audience to an emergency or crisis. Television and the World Wide Web also can report live breaking news; however, radio is still the most portable and abundant news source when people are away from home. Listeners have relied on radio to provide the latest

ANTHEA RAYMOND

Freelance Radio Producer

One look at Anthea Raymond's daily schedule, and most people would be exhausted. Raymond is busy, and she loves the frenetic pace. This radio producer/college educator works four jobs. She is a news producer for National Public Radio's *News and Notes,* a substitute host for NPR's *Morning Edition,* a writer/producer for all-news radio station KNX in Los Angeles, and an instructor at a local community college.

Raymond said she works hard, but she also works hard at taking care of herself. She is careful to make sure she gets enough sleep and exercise and doesn't let the work or the Los Angeles traffic get her too stressed out.

Raymond's busy work schedule isn't all that unusual for radio producers/writers. She said more and more of the industry is turning to freelancers to produce the programming that goes on the air.

"One of the future trends is that there will be more freelance work," she said. The key to thriving in the freelance environment is to "be persistent, very fast, and able to communicate your ideas effectively." Another trend she sees in broadcasting is the need for people with some background in technology. She thinks there will always be work for news people who write well, but some experience with new technology is a plus.

Raymond graduated from Wellesley College and took a job right out of school as a reporter/ producer for Bloomberg News Radio in New York. She moved to California eight years later when she was offered a management job at a National Public Radio station.

She meets lots of interns at the radio stations and noted that they can turn the volunteer work into a paying job. "Internships are high-pressure environments. Be agreeable and willing to work hard. You also need to be able to improvise without a lot of direction."

Raymond also has a law degree from UCLA and loves to teach broadcasting and communications courses. She said it's her way of giving back to the industry that she loves.

» » »

information during times of war, fires, hurricanes, and the national crisis on September 11, 2001. People are accustomed to turning to radio when there is an emergency, and it is likely that radio will continue to be the place they turn to find out the very latest breaking news.

Employment Opportunities

With more than 10,000 commercial radio stations in the United States, there are many jobs in the radio industry. Many broadcasters get their start in radio because radio executives are often more willing to hire a beginner than their counterparts in television. Radio stations are located all across the country, so people wanting to work in radio aren't necessarily forced to relocate.

One of the most promising areas for people to get started in radio is in the general administration of a radio station, which includes the station manager, business manager, community service director, music director, promotion/community relations director, producer, announcer/deejay, and programming director.

Station Manager

The station manager is the boss of the station. At smaller stations the station manager is often also the owner. The station manager has control over operations, programming, sales, engineering, and all personnel.

Business Manager

The business manager handles all the bookkeeping and financial records. This person usually has a background in accounting or management.

Community Service Director

The community service director is in charge of planning all the station's public service programs. This person usually writes and produces the programming and is responsible for executing the programming to the standards set by the FCC for public service. This position exists primarily in large radio stations.

Music Director

Music format stations need someone to catalog and organize all the CDs. The job requires the music director to be familiar with the type of music played at the station. Some music directors select the music to be aired.

Promotion / Community Relations Director

At some of the largest stations, the job of promotions/community relations director is divided into two positions. One person handles the promotions for the stations, and the other handles all public relations. The promotion/community relations director is concerned with image building and works with the local community. Job tasks might include station tours, writing press releases, speaking to community groups, and pitching story ideas to the press. A background in advertising or public relations is good preparation for this job.

Producer

Producers are in charge of content for a particular show. Producers typically plan and organize the theme of the show, book guests or interviews, work with the announcer, and might write introductions or questions for an interview. The producer is involved in every phase of the show from initial concept through airing of the show. Producers usually work the day before the show airs getting the show ready. They may prepare an outline or a rough script of the show. The producer is almost always working during the show along with the announcer. Producers often start in small radio stations and work their way up to larger stations. It's not uncommon for a producer to have little or no experience at the small radio station level.

Announcer / Deejay

Announcers and deejays are on-air personalities who introduce music, programs, or recordings. They may host a music show, a talk show, or an interview show. The announcer usually has a unique personal style that gives the show a distinct tone. In smaller radio stations, it's not uncommon for the announcer to also operate some of the studio control equipment. Usually announcers start in small radio stations and move up to bigger stations with the goal of moving to a large station, where the announcer will make the most money. Sometimes the announcer may also be the producer for a show.

Programming Director

The programming director is responsible for everything that is broadcast on the air. A program director usually has extensive experience in radio and is familiar with music trends, music formats, radio demographics, the station's advertisers, and the FCC's public service requirements for broadcasters. This position requires planning the program schedule with an understanding of the audience, competition, advertisers, and budget.

News Department

Stations with an all-news format certainly have a news department. At music-format stations usually the news department is just a couple of people who decide which stories to air, write the copy, and deliver the news on the air. At all news stations, the news department usually includes a news director, reporters, sportscasters, meteorologists, and traffic reporters.

Sales

Every commercial radio station has a sales staff. Commercials are sold to pay for the station's costs. Account executives are in charge of selling airtime. They are expected to know the audience and match an advertiser with the right time period to reach the right audience. Account executives can be paid very well. A degree in marketing or advertising is usually a good background.

Future Outlook

Radio remains a strong entertainment medium a century after it was conceived. Radio doesn't always get the same exposure or respect as television or film but remains a stable entertainment medium with potential for the future. Radio is considered a mature medium, which means there is very little broadcast spectrum space available in the United States for new stations. It is also considered mature because most people already listen to radio, and there isn't much potential to attract many new listeners.

The potential growth areas are in satellite radio and in Internet radio or streaming live broadcasts via a website. Stations can reach new demographics and increase the number of people listening.

Radio may not make headlines on a regular basis, but it continues to be an attractive medium for advertisers to reach their targeted audiences. It is attractive to advertisers because the audience that listens to radio the most is well educated and makes a good living. That makes sense because most people listen to radio in the car on the way to work or at the workplace.

Summary

Radio has been around since the 1900s. It has made us laugh, informed us during national disasters, and kept us company on the drive to work. Radio's golden age was 1930 to 1950—a time of tremendous growth in the industry. It was a time when families would gather around the set to listen to their favorite dramas or sitcoms. It was also a time when advertisers flocked to the medium because they realized the potential in reaching large numbers of consumers.

Radio was forced to reinvent itself when television came into the picture. Most of early radio's programming was better suited to television. So, radio became primarily a medium

JENNIFER BAUMAN

Radio Reporter, KFWB-980 AM

www.kfwb.com

After more than 20 years as a reporter, Jennifer Bauman still gets excited about going to work every day. "I love the variety. I love telling stories. I like meeting new people," Bauman said about her job as a reporter for all-news radio station KFWB in Los Angeles. Bauman is one of two reporters assigned to the Orange County bureau.

A typical day for this Huntington Beach, CA, resident includes arriving at work at 2 P.M. and getting caught up on the stories currently underway in Orange County. She typically files multiple versions of several stories every night. She also writes and produces a couple of stories for the early morning shift and a story or two each week for the Saturday and Sunday shows.

Bauman might report from two or three different locations in one evening before heading home around midnight. It's a hectic schedule, but she thrives in the fast-paced environment.

Bauman got her start in broadcasting by volunteering at a small Christian radio station in Long Beach. She worked hard, and eventually she was on the payroll. But the pay wasn't enough to make ends meet, so she drove a limousine on her days off to cover the bills. Eventually, she was able to quit the side job when she landed at Money Radio as a news anchor.

She moved easily to television with an anchor job at the Financial News Network and then the Orange County Newschannel, a 24-hour regional cable television network. Along the way, she also freelanced as a print writer/reporter for the *Orange County Register* and several other newspapers.

Bauman said the job of a reporter might seem glamorous, but the reality is, it's a lot of hard work. "If you don't love the business, you won't succeed. It's too hard. It's tough."

Bauman frequently mentors young people trying to get started in the business. She advises college students to do an internship to see if you like the business and the work before you invest a lot time and energy in a job. "Do your best to get into the door (of a station). Start small. And don't think you'll start at the top. You probably won't get Katie Couric's job right away."

» » »

to play recorded music. The popularity of rock 'n' roll in the 1950s also helped radio gain listeners who were enamored of this new music style.

The Telecommunications Act of 1996 cleared the way for big media companies like Clear Channel Communications to own hundreds of radio stations, with many stations broadcasting in the same city. Critics say media consolidation has led to fewer voices and opinions in the radio industry.

The biggest growth areas for radio in the early twenty-first century are satellite radio, high-definition radio, and streaming radio via the Internet. The industry will be watching these areas very closely, but it is expected that traditional radio will continue to be an important entertainment medium for a long time. Radio is like an old friend, someone who has been there through the difficult times and the good times and will continue to be there for years to come.

ADDITIONAL RESOURCES

Associations and Organizations

College Broadcasters Inc.: www.askcbi.org
UPS—Hershey Square Center
1152 Mae Street
Hummelstown, PA 17036
(713) 348–2935

National Association of Broadcasters: www.nab.org
1771 N Street, NW
Washington, DC 20036
(202) 429–5300

Radio Advertising Bureau: www.rab.com
125 West 55th Street, 21st Floor
New York, NY 10019
(800) 252–7234

RTNDA: www.rtnda.org
Radio Television News Directors Association
1025 F Street NW, 7th Floor
Washington, DC 20006
(202) 659–6510

Job-Hunting Resources

National Association of Broadcasters Career Center:
broadcastcareerlink.nabef.org

American Women in Radio and Television: www.awrt.org
8405 Greensboro Drive, Suite 800

McLean, VA 22102
(703) 506–3290

American Federation of Television & Radio Artists: www.aftra.org
New York National Office
260 Madison Avenue
New York, NY 10016–2401
(212) 532–0800

Los Angeles National Office
5757 Wilshire Boulevard, 9ᵗʰ Floor
Los Angeles, CA 90036–3689
(323) 634–8100

Books

Broady, Jack. *ON-AIR: The Guidebook to Starting a Career as a Radio Personality.* BVI, 2007.

Diamond, Bob, and Jay Frost. *Selling Air: How to Jump-Start Your Career in Radio Sales.* iUniverse, Inc., 2008.

Richter, William A. *Radio: A Complete Guide to the Industry.* New York: Peter Lang Publishing, 2006.

Schneider, Chris. *Starting Your Career in Broadcasting: Working on and off the Air in Radio and Television.* New York: Allworth Press, 2007.

Magazines and Trade Publications

Broadcast & Cable: www.broadcastingcable.com

Radio Business Report: www.rbr.com

Radio Magazine: radiomagonline.com

Radio Station World: www.radiostationworld.com

Talkers Magazine: www.talkers.com

ENDNOTES

1. Anthony R. Fellow, *American Media History,* Belmont, CA: Wadsworth Thompson, 2005: 249.
2. Ibid, 263.
3. Leonard Mogel, *Careers in Communications and Entertainment,* New York: Simon & Schuster, 2000: 179.
4. "The Infant Grows Up," *Time,* May 24, 1948.
5. Albert N. Greco, *The Media and Entertainment Industries,* Needham Heights, MA: Allyn & Bacon, 2000: 131.
6. Ibid.
7. John O'Dell, "Satellite Radio Eager to Receive Howard Stern Fans," *Los Angeles Times,* 24 March 2004, C1.
8. Ibid.
9. "Satellite Radio Fails to Earn a Profit/Traditional Radio Faces Challenges," Plunkett Research, Ltd., www.plunkettresearchonline.com.

10. Veronis Suhler Stevenson, *Media Usage and Consumer Spending: 2000 to 2010*, www.census.gov/compendia/statab/cats/information_communications.html.

11. Arbitron, www.arbitron.com.

12. Ibid.

13. Ibid.

14. "Who Owns What?" *Columbia Journalism Review*, www.cjr.org.

15. Greco, 128.

16. Ibid.

17. Russ Crupnick, "Consumer Profiles & Retail Experience," National Association of Recording Merchandisers, www.narm.com.

18. "Monthly Chart of Format, June 2007-June 2008," www.insideradio.com.

19. Arbitron, www.arbitron.com.

20. "Radio Via IP Grows/the Era of Digital Radio Begins," Plunkett Research Ltd., www.plunkettresearchonline.com.

21. Ibid.

Arts and Leisure Entertainment

5

Theater   ANDI STEIN

No one in the 2008 Tony Awards audience appeared to be particularly surprised by the fact that Tracy Letts' play, *August: Osage County* took home five of Broadway's highest honors, including the award for Best Play. As the show had opened to rave reviews by New York theater critics and had already won a Pulitzer Prize, the fact that it had picked up a few more awards was almost a given.

What was a surprise, however, was the history behind the award-winning play about a dysfunctional Oklahoma family. Unlike many productions that are specifically created for the Broadway stage, *August: Osage County* had started out as a regional theater production at the Steppenwolf Theatre Company in Chicago. And while the theater-going public may have been nonplussed by the play's tremendous Broadway success, its cast members—most of whom had come to New York City from Steppenwolf specifically to appear in the production—seemed stunned by the accolades and national recognition of their work.

As Deanna Dunagan, who won the Tony award for leading actress in a play explained during her acceptance speech, "When we started rehearsals in Chicago a year ago, none of us dreamed we would be here. I certainly didn't—I never even thought about it."[1]

The story behind *August: Osage County* is a testament to the power of live theater and the impact it continues to have on the entertainment industry. In an age where so much entertainment comes in an electronic form, the experience of seeing a performance live in a theater still provides the public with a sense of excitement and enjoyment that can't be replicated electronically.

Live theater has been used to entertain the public since Greek and Roman times, and while the format of the theatrical performance has evolved over the years, the concept remains the same. From the development of early Greek tragedies to the popularity of the Shakespearean stage to the creation of the all-singing, all-dancing Broadway musical, theater has long provided a form of amusement that allows the audience to make a direct connection with the performers entertaining them.

Today, live theater can be found in a variety of venues. New York's Broadway is perhaps the most well known of these within the United States—a place where people go specifically to see an assortment of plays and musicals, all being performed simultaneously within a few blocks of each other. London's West End is the British counterpart to Broadway, with hundreds of theatergoers flocking to see imports from Broadway as well as original works for the stage written by English playwrights.

In addition, countless regional theaters like the Steppenwolf Theatre Company offer audiences an opportunity to see great drama performed within smaller communities, making the theatrical experience affordable and accessible to those not within easy range of New York or London. Colleges and universities, high schools, and children's repertory companies present the public with even more opportunities to enjoy the experience of live theater by putting on scaled-down versions of hits from the Broadway stage.

Working in the theater can offer a vast array of opportunities for performers, directors, producers, playwrights, costume and stage designers, to name just a few. It can also present career options for those interested in management, marketing, promotion, and fundraising.

This chapter will examine the history of live theater and how it has evolved into what we know today. It will discuss some of the challenges involved in launching a theatrical production and the trends that are influencing what's being performed onstage. Finally, it will explore career options for those interested in working in theater.

History and Background

Early Beginnings

While live theater can be traced to ancient Egyptian times, it is the Greeks who are given most of the credit for the development of what we know today as traditional theatrical performances and venues. Early Greek theaters were constructed outdoors and designed with a flat, round base in the center surrounded by a semi-circle of seats carved out of the surrounding hillside.

Performances consisted of a primary "thespian," or actor, named for a Greek citizen called Thespis of Attica. This actor addressed a "chorus" or group of other performers who responded to him. Some of the early Greek performances consisted of tragedies and comedies penned by writers such as Sophocles, Euripides, and Aristophanes, who lived during the fifth century B.C.[2]

The Romans built upon the work of the Greeks by adding elements of music and dance to theatrical performances. The Romans also further developed the physical theater space by adding backdrops to the stage and building stand-alone structures where plays could be performed.

Influence of the Church

The growth of theater was stunted by the Catholic Church during the Dark Ages because it was deemed irreverent by church officials. However, this trend was eventually reversed, according to Robert L. Lee.

> Sometime around the ninth century, the church began using elements of drama and theater as additions to its celebration of the Mass. These small playlets were called *tropes,* and were probably developed in order to make it easier for the congregation to learn and appreciate the message of the church.[3]

These church-sponsored tropes led to the creation of religious pageants called mystery cycles and later morality plays designed to educate audiences about ethical issues.[4]

European and Elizabethan Theater

Theater began to flourish across Europe during the Renaissance. Theatrical performances became popular in Spain in the late 1500s, while in Italy, an improvisational theater called "commedia dell arte" was created. In the meantime, Elizabethan theater was developing in England with the performance of works by playwrights Christopher Marlowe, Ben Jonson, and, the most famous of all, William Shakespeare.

Shakespeare (1564–1616) wrote 37 plays, which were performed at London's Globe Theater. This theater featured an open-air stage and incorporated a balcony into the traditional theater setting. No women were allowed to perform on stage at the time, so elaborate costumes were created to disguise men playing female roles.

Author Lee characterizes the impact Shakespeare had on theater:

> Shakespeare was the Steven Spielberg or Francis Ford Coppola of his day. He wrote plays to be enjoyed by all kinds of people, and none of them considered him a *classic,* to be approached with awe and reverence. It's true that our language has changed since Shakespeare wrote, but the basic facts of human nature—and the masterful way Shakespeare exposes them to our view—haven't changed a bit.[5]

Growth and Development

Between the seventeenth and nineteenth centuries, theater productions became more structured and sophisticated, as did their performance venues. The square, box-like staging used today was developed in Europe during this period. A movement toward realism and naturalism led to changes in staging, costumes, and scenic design. Playwrights such as Henrik Ibsen, Anton Chekhov, and George Bernard Shaw began emerging in Norway, Russia, and Ireland, respectively, giving rise to an increase in performance venues in these countries.

While the Western world had created its own brand of theater, Asian theater culture was developing as well. In China, the popularity of Peking Opera in the eighteenth century eventually led to the performance of spoken drama by the early twentieth century. Two forms of theatrical performance—No and Kabuki—flourished in Japan, beginning in the fourteenth century, while in other Asian countries such as India and Indonesia, theatrical performances using shadow puppets became extremely popular.

Early U.S. Theater

By the twentieth century, theater in the United States began to come into its own, breaking away from its European roots, thanks to the efforts of a new generation of American playwrights such as Eugene O'Neill, Tennessee Williams, Thornton Wilder, Arthur Miller, Lillian Hellman, and Edward Albee. The early part of the twentieth century saw the birth of burlesque and then vaudeville, a mixture of song, dance, and slapstick comedy. This eventually led to the creation of musical theater.

According to Milly S. Barranger, chair of the Department of Dramatic Art at the University of North Carolina, Chapel Hill,

> The United States pioneered musical theater as the most popular form of commercial, nonprofit, and amateur entertainment. Broadway, the heart of New York City's theater district, became synonymous with the production of musicals—both revivals and new works—and with multimillion-dollar production costs. The American theater also became ethnically and ideologically diverse, beginning in the 1960s with the rise of African American, Latino, Asian American, feminist, and homosexual theater groups, to name a few.[6]

U.S. Theater Today

Broadway

In the twenty-first century, New York City's Broadway is regarded as the Theater Capital of the World because of the sheer numbers of plays and musicals performed there on a nightly basis. According to the Broadway League, an association representing New York theaters and producers, there were 36 productions on Broadway during the 2007–2008 year, with ticket sales of 12.27 million, grossing $938 million.[7] These numbers would likely have been even higher had the industry not come to a virtual standstill during a 19-day stagehands strike during November 2007.

Broadway productions employ approximately 14,000 people both directly (as actors, directors, producers, designers, etc.) and indirectly (as vocal coaches, agents, lawyers, etc.), according to League statistics. In addition, the theater industry contributes approximately $5.1 billion to the City of New York as it not only generates ticket revenues but tourist income for local shops, restaurants, and hotels. (The majority of New York's theatergoers are tourists—about 65%.)

Touring productions of Broadway shows also generate dollars. If a show is a hit on Broadway, it might be sent on tour, sometimes with the original cast but more often with an ensemble specifically cast for the road show. According to the Broadway League, touring productions of Broadway shows appear in approximately 240 North American theaters each year. During the 2006–2007 season, 17 million tickets were sold, grossing $950 million.[8]

Regional Theater

Beyond Broadway, a number of nonprofit regional theater companies provide entertainment to audiences in cities throughout the United States. These organizations are dedicated to bringing an affordable theater experience to the public through the production of plays that might, in some cases, be considered too controversial or not profitable enough by Broadway standards.

Among the better-known regional theater companies in the United States are the Guthrie Theater in Minneapolis; Arena Stage in Washington, DC; American Conservatory Theater in San Francisco; Alley Theatre in Houston; and La Jolla Playhouse near San Diego. Many of these were established in the 1960s, as the regional theater movement began to blossom in the United States as an alternative to the Broadway stage. Some regional theaters specialize in producing offbeat works or plays by new or relatively unknown playwrights. Some can also serve as launching pads for shows that may ultimately end up on Broadway— shows like *August: Osage County.*

Because of their nonprofit status, regional theaters depend heavily on government grants, private donations, and the support of local community members for their survival. According to Jim Volz, theater professor at California State University, Fullerton,

> Nonprofit theaters in America continue to emerge, struggle, flourish, and, hopefully, dig deep roots in their home communities.... Bonding with the home communities has emerged as a central theme for regional theaters eager to develop artistically and survive in a highly competitive American arts, entertainment, and tourist market.[9]

Children's Theater

Over the last few decades, a movement toward introducing youngsters to the theater at an early age—and maintaining their interest in it—has resulted in the growth of children's theater companies throughout the United States. Some of these are offshoots of regional theater companies, while others are stand-alone programs, such as the Children's Theater Company of Minneapolis and Seattle Children's Theater, the two largest children's theater programs in the United States.

In 2005, The John F. Kennedy Center for the Performing Arts in Washington, DC, completed a $9 million theater specifically designed for performances for children. An article in the *Washington Post* reported,

FRANK BUTLER

Production Director, Guthrie Theater
www.guthrietheater.org

The show must go on—and it must be on time and on budget. That's Frank Butler's motto when leading his team of 85 full-time employees at the Guthrie Theater in Minneapolis, MN. Butler is the production director, and he explains his position as the "boss of the boss of the people who run the shows."

But, Butler didn't always know that theater would be his life's calling. In high school, he was in a rock band. "I thought I was going to be the next Peter Frampton," Butler laughed, but performing on stage in front of people wasn't the best place for an introvert. So, he found himself gravitating toward sound equipment and lighting.

After graduating from Purdue University with a degree in Technical Theater, Butler set his sights on graduate school. It wasn't until his last semester at the University of Washington while finishing his M.F.A. in Lighting Design that he did an internship with a theater company and found his niche. His first job in the field was with the American Repertory Theatre in Cambridge, MA.

As production director at the Guthrie Theater, Butler is in charge of all elements of production including: personnel, budgets, union issues, and watching daily sales reports and performance reports. One of the things he loves about his job is "the mixture of technical, artistic, financial, and managerial" skills.

Another great thing about his job, he said, is he can go to the theater and watch a performance any night he would like, but he isn't required to be there every night to make sure the show goes off without a hitch. Instead, he spends most evenings at home with his family.

Butler said the best piece of advice he could give to someone wanting to get started in the field of entertainment is to find an institution or company that produces work you are passionate about, and align yourself with that institution. Don't worry so much about the job title or the pay. The proper title and pay will follow you—if you follow your heart.

» » »

It makes a statement about the escalating ambition of children's theater in the nation's capital and across the country, an increasingly diversified and grade-level specific genre that is exploring ways to usher 6- and 16-year-olds alike into the world of live drama.[10]

To attract children of all ages, over the years, children's theater productions have gotten more sophisticated, according to an article in *Time* Magazine.

> Children's theater—or theater for young audiences—is growing up. Once a place where community actors donned bright plaid costumes to act out fairy tales for little tykes, it has become a haven for some of the most committed and creative theater people in the country. These venues still draw the biggest crowds with the familiar kiddie favorites, from *Charlotte's Web* to *Go, Dog, Go!* But increasingly, they are commissioning new works, reaching out to older kids who typically stop going to theater when their parents stop dragging them, and pushing the boundaries in both style and subject matter.[11]

It is estimated that there are approximately 130 theater companies in the United States offering programs aimed at children and young adults.[12]

Challenges and Trends

Planning the Production

In any industry, one of the challenges of running a successful business is to offer a product or service that appeals to the audience for which it is intended. In theater, this product comes in the form of a show designed to engage the audience through the use of an interesting plot, colorful characters, attractive sets and costumes, and dazzling special effects.

For those working in theater management, coming up with the right show—one that will be both entertaining and profitable—is a significant part of the job. This task may vary depending on the nature of the theatrical enterprise. For those producing shows for Broadway or London's West End, for example, the focus may be on developing a single blockbuster that has the potential to entertain audiences for years to come, both in New York and London as well as on tour.

For those working in regional theater, the nature of the business may encompass coming up with a "season" of shows that can be used not only to generate one-time ticket sales but to maintain sufficient interest in the theater's offerings to encourage repeat business.

Managers of regional theaters are often guided by the organization's mission when deciding what to produce onstage. If a theater's mission is to showcase the talents of new playwrights or address topics considered thought-provoking or controversial, for example, this may be reflected in the line-up of shows offered. Often, theatergoers choose to see plays produced by a particular regional theater company because the organization's mission—and ultimately its show selections—is in accordance with their own personal values.

Appealing to the Audience

On Broadway, however, where productions must appeal to a mass audience, the task of choosing the subject of a show can be more complicated. This has become especially challenging in recent years, as the traditional theater-going audience is aging and being supplanted by a younger demographic of audience members with different tastes and values. This trend is having a significant impact on the state of the Broadway musical.

Back in the 1930s, '40s, and '50s—the heyday of the Broadway musical—a handful of writers and composers made their mark on the development of American musical theater. Individuals such as George and Ira Gershwin, Cole Porter, Irving Berlin, and Richard Rodgers and Oscar Hammerstein produced some of the classic musicals that are still performed today. They were followed by others such as Stephen Sondheim and Andrew Lloyd Webber who continued the musical tradition.

Today, however, the trend of having a few big-name composers churning out hit after hit has died out. Over the last two decades, they have been replaced by a wide variety of writers and composers with differing styles and varying rates of success with their productions. Consequently, theater producers have looked for other options as a means of choosing shows that will guarantee them a surefire hit.

Taking a Cue from Hollywood

One approach that has become extremely popular has been to develop musicals from tried-and-true Hollywood films. This trend began with the Disney Company's entry onto Broadway with its production of *Beauty and the Beast* in the mid-1990s. Disney's success in turning its animated cartoon into a stage musical was followed by other similar efforts—*The Lion King, Tarzan, Mary Poppins,* and *The Little Mermaid*. As Jeff Korbelik observed,

> There's money to be made from musicals based on movies. Lots of it. Disney's *The Lion King,* for instance, has grossed more than $563 million in its 10 years on Broadway.... *Mary Poppins* has grossed more than $81 million since opening in November 2006.[13]

Since 2000, a variety of "movicals"—musicals based on movies—have appeared on the Broadway stage. These include *The Producers, Hairspray, Chitty Chitty Bang Bang, Legally Blonde, Spamalot, The Wedding Singer, Xanadu,* and *Young Frankenstein*. As an article in the *San Francisco Chronicle* explained,

> Broadway's increasing fascination with the movies is a direct reflection of live-theater economics. With the decline of stars who could fill houses (and commit themselves to the long runs required to pay back the investment in them) and the spiraling costs of mounting a musical, producers needed something else that could generate interest and sell tickets. That's exactly what the name recognition of popular films offered.[14]

It appears that this trend will continue since, as of this writing, plans for future seasons include a slate of Hollywood movies intended for the Broadway stage.

Financing and Fundraising

One of the reasons for such concern about the potential success of a theatrical production is the prohibitive cost of launching a play or musical, particularly on the Broadway stage. The average Broadway musical costs more than $10 million to produce.[15] Couple this with the fact that 80% of Broadway productions lose rather than make money, and it's not that difficult to understand why producers want to hedge their bets when staging new shows.[16]

According to the *Wall Street Journal,*

> Typically, Broadway plays are financed by a group of investors, who can number as many as 50 or more. When a show does make a profit, which is rare, investors are paid back after initial costs like costumes and set design are recouped by producers.[17]

Therefore, a producer launching a show has to work diligently to seek out investors willing to take a gamble on a new production. For those who have already had a hit or two, the task is somewhat less daunting than for those looking to produce their first show.

Regional theaters generally function as nonprofit organizations, which means that profits are incorporated back into the operation of the organization. As a result, a regional theater can't afford to rely solely on ticket sales for its survival. Generally, regional theaters depend on a combination of government and foundation grants, private donations, patron subscriptions, and corporate sponsorships to supplement the income from individual ticket sales.

Some theaters also incorporate regular fundraising activities into their roster, such as annual campaigns or special events. The Savannah Children's Theatre, for instance, has raised money by partnering with a New York City art gallery to host an art auction and by sponsoring a masquerade gala for members of the local community.[18]

Some regional theaters have used building campaigns as a means of raising funds for new facilities. The Arena Stage in Washington, DC, raised more than $100 million in 2006 to construct a new theater complex.[19] Large-scale efforts like this, however, require years of advance planning and necessitate a strong donor support base prior to the start of the project.

Developing Innovative Marketing Strategies

One of the biggest trends the theater industry has witnessed in recent years is a shift in the way shows are marketed to the public. For many years, Broadway producers relied on traditional media to promote their shows—full-page advertisements in the *New York Times;* billboards; direct mail fliers; radio advertisements; and word of mouth. With the rising costs of theater tickets and a need to recruit a younger demographic of theatergoers, producers have begun to re-think the ways they attract their audiences.

One such producer is Jeffrey B. Seller, who has been partly responsible for the change in approach to theater marketing. As the producer of two hit shows, *Rent* and *Avenue Q,*

Seller has instituted some previously unheard of promotional tactics into his shows. According to an article in the *Wall Street Journal,*

> When Mr. Seller started producing *Rent,* he convinced his partners to institute a policy, now ubiquitous in the business, of offering a limited number of $20 front-row tickets to attract a younger crowd. For his short-lived 2002 effort, *La Boheme,* he incorporated ads into the set—a heresy for a "serious" theatrical production. He and his producing partner Kevin McCollum marketed *Avenue Q* with e-mails and ads that said, "Warning: Full Puppet Nudity."[20]

The latter show, *Avenue Q,* is a tongue-in-cheek, slightly risqué parody of *Sesame Street,* featuring a cast of live actors and puppets and addressing issues such as unemployment, homosexuality, racism, and homelessness. To build additional awareness of the show, Seller had the cast of actors and puppets stage a political rally in New York's Times Square shortly before the 2004 presidential election. Not only did this strategy draw the attention of the public, it was covered by "14 television networks, including two in Japan."[21] As an indirect result of all this publicity, when it came time for the coveted Tony Awards, *Avenue Q* beat out the favorite, *Wicked,* for the Best Musical award.

Another trend in marketing has been to capitalize on the popularity of celebrities to fill theater seats. More and more producers are importing movie and television stars into their shows. Julia Roberts, Brooke Shields, Morgan Freeman, Jennifer Garner, and Denzel Washington are only a few of the Hollywood stars who have displayed their talents on the Broadway stage in recent years.[22]

Marketers are also capitalizing on the success of popular television shows like *American Idol.* According to author Stuart Miller,

> A steady stream of *Idol* alums—Frenchie Davis in *Rent,* Constantine Maroulis in *The Wedding Singer,* Diana DeGarmo in *Hairspray,* Josh Strickland in *Tarzan*—have taken the New York stage, accompanied by a frenzy of press attention and a burst of ticket sales from their fans, often people who don't usually attend the theater.[23]

As an example, when it was announced that *Idol* alum Fantasia Barrio would be joining the cast of *The Color Purple,* "hits on the musical's website soared from 2,000 hits per day to 20,000, and advance sales, which had grown anemic, skyrocketed by $6.5 million."[24]

Although this trend has become popular with the public and its results embraced by those making money on these productions, it has angered some veteran theater actors. This was reflected in a 2008 Tony Awards acceptance speech given by author Tracy Letts who thanked the producers of his award-winning show, *August: Osage County,* and commented, "They did an amazing thing. They decided to produce an American play on Broadway with theater actors.[25]

In London's West End, the tremendous popularity of reality television programming has had a direct influence on the promotion of musicals through an unusual method of casting stars. A practice initiated by writer/composer/producer Andrew Lloyd Webber relies on reality television programs to search for musical leads. Webber's TV reality show, *How Do You Solve a Problem Like Maria?* resulted in the casting of unknown Connie Fisher to star in *The Sound of Music,* while TV reality programs called, *Any Dream Will*

Do and *I'd Do Anything* were used to cast the leads of *Joseph and the Amazing Technicolor Dream Coat* and *Oliver!,* respectively.

According to an article in The *Wall Street Journal,* "It's a strategy that has boosted West End ticket sales to new levels. London box-office revenue hit a record high of nearly $1 billion in 2007, up from about $786 million the previous year. Attendance at musicals shot up 19%."[26]

Some of these new marketing techniques may appear radical to those within the industry, but the financial results are proving that they are certainly appealing to a new generation of theatergoers.

Impact of Technology

Of the many topics covered in this book, live theater is one subject that has not been changed as dramatically by technology as some of the others such as television and film. However, even this segment of the entertainment industry has not been immune to the effects of new technologies.

The Internet, for example, has changed the way theatergoers purchase show tickets. Whereas tickets were once sold primarily at the box office and through telephone and subscription sales, it is now estimated that 40% of Broadway theater tickets are purchased online.[27] In London's West End, this number is reported to be as high as 75%.[28]

According to Pat Craig in the *Oakland Tribune,*

> Theater people are arriving a bit late to the game, but diving into cyberland with both feet, scrambling to build a memorable Internet presence with sophisticated multi-media Web sites, blogs and videos posted on MySpace, YouTube and other outposts in the wired wilderness.[29]

Theater companies now routinely use websites to promote their shows, often featuring bios of cast members, song clips, background information, and an opportunity to purchase show-related merchandise on their sites. "The biggest advantage of a Web site is the unique way it can help visitors understand and enjoy a play better," Craig observed.[30]

Social networking sites such as BroadwaySpace.com, MyBroadway.com, talkinbroadway.com, and BroadwayWorld.com are specifically geared toward the theater industry. The goal of many of these sites, explains *New York Times* reporter Caryn James, is to reach out to younger theatergoers and to show that "Broadway can be part of a big, wide world, and a means for people way outside New York to feel connected."[31]

Technology has also influenced an aspect of the theater business that some in the industry fear will have a long-term negative impact. The development of the "virtual orchestra"—music created digitally—has the potential to dramatically reduce the need for live musicians to accompany Broadway musicals.[32] The argument against the use of digital music on Broadway was the partial focus of a four-day musicians' strike in 2003. While a virtual orchestra can save on costs, hard-core theater lovers argue that it takes away from the live theater experience and takes jobs away from professional musicians. Although this issue is still being debated, its resolution could have a significant effect on the Broadway musical of the future.

JAN FRIEDLANDER SVENDSEN

Director of Marketing, The Broadway League
Chief Marketing Officer, The Tony Awards
www.broadwayleague.com

The person to ask if you are wondering which Broadway play or musical to see is Jan Friedlander Svendsen. In her position as Director of Marketing for the Broadway League, she sees everything that plays on Broadway—it's her job. The Broadway League is the national trade association representing 600 members who work on Broadway.

"I'm in charge of making sure people are aware of Broadway and excited to go to Broadway," Svendsen said. "I love the theater, and being able to promote and market it is really a great job."

Svendsen's job is diverse and hectic. A typical day might include working on traditional advertising such as print ads or putting together a television show all about Broadway. One of the things Svendsen enjoys about her position is that no two days are ever the same—it's always changing and always challenging.

One of her most memorable projects was when the mayor of New York City called her after the terrorist attacks on September 11, 2001, and wanted to put together a campaign to promote people coming back to the theater. Svendsen said, "It helped morale and lifted the spirits of people who worked and lived in the area."

The Broadway League is the organization that puts together the Tony Awards. Svendsen is the Chief Marketing Officer for the Tony Awards and has worked on several televised specials, including serving as Executive Producer for the Tony Awards Preview Show. Prior to joining the Broadway League, Svendsen worked in advertising as Vice President of Ogilvy & Mather and ran her own marketing consulting firm.

Svendsen believes finding work you are passionate about will sustain you over the course of a career. "Don't forget—you can reinvent yourself," she said. Svendsen never dreamed she would be working in New York City with the Broadway community when she graduated from the University of California, San Diego with a degree in sociology.

For young people hoping to follow in Svendsen's footsteps, she recommends internships. "They are one of the best things you can do." Through internships you can find out what you like—or maybe even more important—find out what you don't like.

» » »

Employment Opportunities

Finding a job in theater can be a challenge because of the highly competitive nature of the business, particularly on the performance side. However, a theatrical production requires people with many different types of skills, which provide options for those wanting to work in the industry. Jobs in theater can be roughly classified into three categories—performance, production, and administration.

Performance Jobs

The performance side of the field is where you find the people who are directly involved with the creative aspect of a show—the actors, writers, composers, singers, dancers, choreographers, musicians, etc. Those working in this segment of the industry generally bring a mixture of innate talent and specialized training to the table, such as a background in acting, writing, music composition, or dance.

If you are interested in this area of theater, it is important to understand that the competition can be fierce because the number of theatrical productions is limited, both on Broadway and in smaller regional theaters. One way to get involved while still in college is by trying out for school productions or working with local community theater groups to hone your skills. If you live in an area where there is a local theme park, you might also investigate the possibility of working in a theatrical production there for a summer. Any amateur theatrical skills that you can develop will help build your résumé and provide you with training and experience that may serve you well professionally in the long run.

Production Jobs

In addition to performance, there is a need for people to work on the production side of the business. Job titles in this area include producer, director, set and costume designer, lighting specialist, casting director, stage manager, etc. These are the people who shape a theatrical production by working with those on the performance side to get the right blend of talent and effects in order to create the perfect production.

The backgrounds of those working in this area of theater can vary. Producers, for example, need to be very entrepreneurial, as they are responsible for securing investors for a production and selling it to the public. A background in business is very useful for those interested in producing.

Directors work with the writers and actors to bring a play or musical to life. They provide guidance and instruction to those putting on the performance and need to have a vision of what they want the end results to be. For those interested in directing, it is helpful to have some previous experience working in theater in order to understand how a production takes shape.

Some of the other positions in this category, such as set and costume designers, require highly specialized skills and, in many cases, a background in art or design. Designers work with the director to help ensure that the scenery and costumes are in tune with the director's vision for the show. Many who work in this area have at least some professional training.

Administrative Jobs

Those working on the administrative side of the theater business are the ones responsible for the financial success of a production. These may include the managing director, finance manager, development director, publicity manager, etc. As with similar positions pertaining to other topics covered in this book, those working in these areas are crucial to the day-to-day operations of a theater venture. If you are interested in this aspect of the field, a background in management, communications, marketing, public relations, or finance is extremely helpful.

Education and Training

Although an advanced degree is not required for a successful career in the theater, for some of the jobs mentioned above it can be extremely helpful. A graduate program in theater provides you with an opportunity to learn additional skills beyond those acquired in college. According to Jim Volz, it also offers an opportunity to network with others in the industry and develop your résumé while gaining experience working on theatrical productions at the university level.[33]

The University/Resident Theatre Association offers information on graduate training programs for those interested in advancing their theater-related knowledge and abilities (http://urta.com). A number of regional theater companies also provide internship programs that are designed to help those interested in theater careers further develop their skills.

Figure 9: Theaters in the United States and Europe Offering Internship Programs

- » Alley Theatre, Houston: www.alleytheatre.org
- » American Conservatory Theater, San Francisco: www.act-sf.org
- » American Theatre Wing, New York: www.americantheatrewing.org
- » Arcola Theatre, London: www.arcolatheatre.com
- » Berkeley Repertory Theatre, Berkeley, CA: www.berkeleyrep.org
- » Berkshire Theatre Festival, Stockbridge, MA: www.berkshiretheatre.org
- » Guthrie Theatre, Minneapolis: www.guthrietheatre.org
- » John F. Kennedy Center for the Performing Arts, Washington, DC:
- » www.kennedy-center.org
- » Juilliard School, New York: www.juilliard.edu
- » La Jolla Playhouse, La Jolla, CA: www.lajollaplayhouse.org
- » Lincoln Center for the Performing Arts, New York: www.lincolncenter.org
- » National Theatre, London: www.nationaltheatre.org.uk
- » Steppenwolf Theatre Company, Chicago: www.steppenwolf.org
- » Wilma Theater, Philadelphia: www.wilmatheater.org
- » Wolftrap Foundation for the Performing Arts, Vienna, VA: www.wolftrap.org

Future Outlook

A variety of societal changes are likely to have an impact on the theater industry of the future. As Frank Rizzo observed in the *Hartford Courant*, "Demographics are shifting, deficits are growing, the whys and ways people buy tickets are changing, the Broadway product is not what it used to be."[34] Some of this is reflected in the trends discussed earlier in the chapter such as the reliance on Hollywood box-office stars and reality television programs to attract audiences. Other trends pertain to the composition of the future theater audience and how this will likely be reflected in the content of Broadway plays and musicals.

Appealing to the Boomer Generation

As the Baby Boomers gradually make the transition from mid-life to their twilight years, it is likely that this change will impact production offerings, both on the Broadway stage and in regional theaters. The last few years have witnessed the development of what has become known as the "jukebox musical," one that "uses existing pop songs for its score, usually the catalog of a particular artist rather than an original score,"[35] according to theater critic Everett Evans.

Mamma Mia!, which featured the music of ABBA, and the Tony award-winning *Jersey Boys*, which highlighted the songs of Frankie Valli and the Four Seasons, are two examples of shows that fall into this category. Likewise, two recent hits based on the 1980s films of cult director John Waters—*Hairspray* and *Cry-Baby*—were also intended to appeal to the Boomer generation.[36]

The surprise hit *Menopause The Musical* "takes classic baby boomer rock and pop hits and changes the lyrics to comment on all aspects of menopause, from memory loss to mood swings, night sweats to food cravings," according to Jim Kershner in the *Spokesman Review*.[37] While not likely to appeal to the under-40 crowd, the show has been a tremendous hit with Boomers, playing off-Broadway for three years and touring to more than 200 U.S. cities. As Baby Boomers continue to age, signs indicate that theater producers will cater to their needs and interests with future productions that continue to rely on what appears to be a highly successful formula.

Attracting a Diverse Audience

The changing racial and ethnic diversity of the theater-going public has resulted in a movement toward what Howard Shapiro calls, "color-blind casting—putting actors in roles irrespective of race" as a means of appealing to this diverse audience.[38] The 2007–2008 theater season, for example, included *The Country Girl*, featuring Morgan Freeman and Frances McDormand in a mixed-race marriage as well as an entirely African American cast of the Tennessee Williams play, *Cat on a Hot Tin Roof*.

The same season saw the popularity of musicals with ethnic themes such as the Tony award-winning *In the Heights*, which takes place in a Latino neighborhood in Manhattan's

Washington Heights.[39] Other shows, such as *Hairspray* and *Avenue Q* have confronted the issues of race and ethnicity in their story lines in previous seasons. While addressing racial and ethnic issues onstage is not a new concept, the proliferation of recent shows that address these issues suggests that future plays and musicals will continue to blur racial and ethnic lines in an attempt to reach out to an increasingly diverse theater-going public.

Reaching Out to Young Audiences

Finally, one trend that is expected to continue is the growing interest in children's theater. As theater companies try to attract younger audiences, the need to get people hooked on theater at an earlier age has become more important. One program designed to do just that is called "Kid's Night on Broadway." Sponsored by the Broadway League, it offers audience members between the ages of 6–18 the opportunity to attend a Broadway musical for free when accompanied by a paying adult.

Another endeavor launched in 2008 by U.S. Airways reflects a trend of theaters partnering with corporations eager to tap into the youth arts market. Called, "Imagination Begins with US," the airline-sponsored program featured theater performances for young audiences put on by local regional theater companies in three of the airline's hub cities—Philadelphia, Phoenix, and Charlotte.[40] Given the growing interest on the part of those in the theater industry to expand their audiences, it is likely that the future will bring more events like these, specifically aimed at engaging young people.

Summary

In an era when so much entertainment is delivered in an electronic form, live theater continues to stimulate, captivate, and engage audiences. Since the days of the classical Greeks and Romans, theatergoers have been enchanted by the experience of seeing performers acting out stories onstage. Watching a live theatrical performance enables audience members to lose themselves for a few hours in dramas, comedies, and musicals that are routinely performed in a variety of venues—the Broadway stage, the West End, the neighborhood regional theater, and even the local high school.

Among the challenges faced by those working in the theater industry is the need to develop new productions that are likely to appeal to a changing demographic of theatergoers. Producing a show with sufficient audience appeal has become crucial to the financial success of a performance or, in the case of regional theaters, a series of performances. Innovative marketing strategies and new technologies reach out to potential audiences and offer promising possibilities to help meet these challenges.

Employment in theater can be highly competitive because of the structure of the industry and the limited number of professional performance venues. However, because jobs within the field are highly diverse, opportunities exist for individuals with a variety of backgrounds, skills, and training.

It is expected that in the future, demographics will continue to influence the industry, as Baby Boomers age, audiences diversify, and theater companies develop new strategies for reaching out to younger audiences. In general, live theater is expected to continue to remain a unique segment of the entertainment industry.

ADDITIONAL RESOURCES

Associations and Organizations

American Theatre Wing: www.americantheatrewing.org
The Broadway League: www.broadwayleague.org
League of Resident Theaters: www.lort.org
National Alliance for Musical Theater: www.namt.org
Theater for Young Audiences/USA: www.assitej-usa.org
University/Resident Theatre Association: www.urta.com

Job-Hunting Resources

American Theatre Resources: www.theatre-resources.net
Artsearch: www.tcg.org
Backstage Jobs: www.backstagejobs.com

Books

Bekken, Bonnie Bjorguine. *Opportunities in Performing Arts Careers.* Lincolnwood, IL: VGM Career Books, 2001.

Field, Shelly. *Career Opportunities in Theater and the Performing Arts,* 3rd ed. New York: Ferguson, 2006.

Fraser, Neil. *Theatre History Explained.* Wiltshire, England: The Crowood Press, 2004.

Lee, Robert L. *Everything About Theatre!* Colorado Springs, CO: Meriwether Publishing Ltd., 1996.

Volz, Jim. *How to Run a Theater.* New York: Backstage Books, 2004.

Volz, Jim. *The Backstage Guide to Working in Regional Theater.* New York: Backstage Books, 2007.

Webb, Duncan M. *Running Theaters: Best Practices for Leaders and Managers.* New York: Allsworth Press, 2004.

Magazines and Trade Publications

American Theatre: www.tcg.org
Dramatics: www.edta.org
Stage Directions: www.stage-directions.com
Theater Magazine: www.dukeupress.edu/theater

Blogs

AmericanTheater Web: http://atw-blog.blogspot.com

ENDNOTES

1. Deanna Dunagan, 2008 Tony Awards television broadcast, June 15, 2008.
2. See Robert L. Lee, *Everything About Theatre!* Colorado Springs, CO: Meriwether Publishing Ltd., 1996: 15.
3. Lee, 70.
4. See Neil Fraser, *Theatre History Explained*, Wiltshire, England: The Crowood Press, 2004: 35.
5. Lee, 109.
6. Milly S. Barranger, *Theater*, http://encarta.msn.com.
7. The Broadway League, www.broadwayleague.com.
8. Ibid.
9. Jim Volz, *The Backstage Guide to Working in Regional Theater*, New York: Backstage Books, 2007: 72 and 75.
10. Peter Marks, "Children's Theater Comes of Age at Kennedy Center," *Washington Post*, 9 December 2005, A1.
11. Richard Zoglin, "Setting a New Stage for Kids," *Time* 164:20 (November 15, 2004): 104.
12. See Volz, 311.
13. Jeff Korbelik, "The Mighty Movical," *Lincoln Journal Star*, 27 April 2008, 1.
14. Steven Winn, "Broadway-Hollywood Connection," *San Francisco Chronicle*, 13 April 2008, N19.
15. See "Broadway: The American Musical," www.pbs.org/wnet/broadway.
16. See Brooks Barnes, "Song and Dance: To Push Musicals, Producer Shakes Up Broadway Tactics," *Wall Street Journal*, 10 March 2005, A1.
17. Robert J. Hughes, "Hollywood Report: Broadway's New Deal," *Wall Street Journal*, 11 March 2005, W1.
18. See John Stoehr, "Theater Tries Innovative Fundraising Strategy," *Savannah Morning News*, 5 December 2006, 1C; and "Gala Benefits Savannah Children's Theatre," *Savannah Morning News*, 4 October 2007, 7E.
19. See Jacqueline Trescott, "Gift Opens Act 2 for New Arena Stage," *Washington Post*, 7 December 2006, C1.
20. Barnes, A1.
21. Ibid.
22. See David Ward, "Theater Coverage Broadens Off the Beat," *PR Week* 10:39 (October 8, 2007): 11.
23. Stuart Miller, "Former 'Idols' Bringing Business to Broadway," *Times-Picayune*, 8 April 2007, 10.
24. Patrick Pacheco, "Crowd Control: The Great Pop-Culture Marketing Machine Discovers Just What Fans Will Do for Love," *Los Angeles Times*, 8 April 2007, F1.
25. Tracy Letts, 2008 Tony Awards television broadcast, June 15, 2008.
26. Lauren A.E. Schuker, "Let's Go On with the (TV) Show; How Television Is Transforming London Theater, and Vice Versa," *Wall Street Journal*, 16 February 2008, W1.

27. See, for example, Paul Lieberman, "Attendance Revival on Broadway," *Los Angeles Times,* 10 June 2007, A1.

28. See Robin Eggar, "Youth Enters, Stage Right," *London Times,* 8 April 2007, 26.

29. Pat Craig, "For Theater, the Web's the Thing," *Oakland Tribune,* 29 January 2008, 1.

30. Ibid.

31. Caryn James, "Broadway Web Sites: Now for Fans as Well as Fanatics," *New York Times,* 16 January 2008, E4.

32. See Michael Phillips, "Broadway Shrinks the Pit Orchestra, Boosts Impact of 'Virtual' Musicians," *Knight Ridder Tribune Business News,* 16 March 2003, 1; and Gregory M. Lamb, "Robo-music Gives Musicians the Jitters," *Christian Science Monitor,* 14 December 2006, 13.

33. See Volz, 347.

34. Frank Rizzo, Theaters Need to Change Their Wicked Ways," *Hartford Courant,* 11 January 2004, G5.

35. Everett Evans, "Pop Goes the Musical?" *Houston Chronicle,* 3 February 2008, 24.

36. See Sid Smith, "Invasion of the Boomers," *Chicago Tribune,* 20 April 2008, 1.

37. Jim Kershner, "In a Flash, a Legend is Born," *Spokesman Review,* 30 March 2008, D3.

38. Howard Shapiro, "Color-blind Casting; Racial Diversity Onstage Brings New Dimensions to Old Plays, Both Regionally and on Broadway," *Philadelphia Inquirer,* 1 May 2008, E1.

39. See Ed Morales, "Latinos Conquer Broadway with *In the Heights,*" *McClatchy-Tribune News Service,* 11 June 2008.

40. "US Airways Gives Wings to Theatre for Young Audiences," *PR Newswire,* 11 March 2008.

6

Music BETH BINGHAM EVANS

Deep inside the Washington, DC, headquarters of the Recording Industry Association of America (RIAA), there is a room staffed with young men and women who are part of the team doing investigative work for the music trade association. The workers' identities are carefully protected, and tinted windows keep visitors from being able to see their faces. These young people are hard at work trying to save the music industry.

It might sound like a plot for the latest action film, but this is reality. These young people are part of the team trying to find people who share music illegally over peer-to-peer networks. The RIAA believes prosecuting people who break the law is one way to stop Internet piracy.

Emotions run so high when it comes to music sharing and the law that some of the attorneys and music executives involved in these lawsuits have received death threats. The RIAA is the trade organization that represents the recorded music industry. The RIAA started its litigation campaign against people who illegally download music in 2003. Since then, thousands of people have been slapped with lawsuits for downloading music illegally and sharing those illegal files. Almost all of the lawsuits have been settled out of court.

In May 2008, a jury in Alexandria, VA, handed down a guilty verdict in the first-ever criminal outlaw music piracy trial. Twenty-five-year-old Barry Gitarts of Brooklyn, NY, was convicted of being part of a group that uploaded and downloaded hundreds of thousands of copies of pirated music, movies, software, and video games. The jury reached a guilty verdict after two days of deliberations. Gitarts now faces up to five years in prison and a $250,000 fine.[1]

The RIAA believes illegal piracy is the biggest threat to the music industry. If something isn't done to curb illegal piracy, the RIAA believes the music industry may be damaged forever. This chapter will discuss music piracy and other issues affecting the recorded music industry and explore industry trends and employment opportunities in the field.

History and Background

Music is a universal language appealing to all demographics. While music has been around since the beginning of time, recorded music as an entertainment medium has been around just over 100 years. The term *music industry* refers to the business of recording, publishing, distributing, and marketing recorded music.

Early Years

Thomas Edison invented the first phonograph that recorded and replayed sound in 1877. Edison's device recorded the music onto a tinfoil sheet wrapped around a cylinder. The stylus used an up-and-down motion, similar to the way player pianos of the late nineteenth century worked. Music started to be mass-produced on these cylinders in the 1890s.

In the early part of the twentieth century, Columbia Records started making disc records. These records had recordings pressed on both sides and soon became more popular than the cylinder recordings, especially since the discs were easier and cheaper to store in bulk. Vinyl records became the most popular recording medium for most of the twentieth century, only to be replaced by digital media in the 1980s.

Radio and Rock 'n' Roll

As radio reinvented itself in the 1950s in the wake of television, recorded music became the dominant programming format. Most of the earlier radio programming, vaudeville shows, sitcoms, and dramas, all migrated to television. Recorded music was now the format for most radio stations, and during the 1950s, rock 'n' roll music became very popular. As more and more young people listened to the new rock 'n' roll music on the radio, more of them also bought records. The recorded music companies saw an increase in sales during this time.

Digital Music

The compact disc or CD was introduced in the 1980s. This was the first digital recording of music for mass audiences. The recorded music companies saw a surge in sales with the introduction of CDs because many people replaced their analog vinyl collections with CDs.

The MP3 format, a compressed digital file with little or no loss of sound quality, was introduced in the 1990s. This digital compressed version was so small it could easily be sent via the Internet. The MP3 format allowed music to be uploaded or downloaded through a personal computer at a high speed that eventually led to massive piracy issues in the music industry.

Oligopoly

For just about its entire history, the recorded music industry has been in a state of tight oligopoly.[2] Oligopoly is defined by the Merriam-Webster online dictionary as "a market situation in which each of the few producers affects but does not control the market."[3] What all of this means is the music industry was and continues to be controlled by just a few major companies. In the early twentieth century, the recorded music industry was controlled by Edison, Columbia, and Victor. All three of these companies had patents for the recording technology. Their dominance would last until the 1950s.

Rock 'n' roll music ushered in a new sound and independent music labels.[4] For the first time since the recorded music industry began, the tight oligopoly was broken. Many independent labels gained a significant market share when they started signing rock 'n' roll and R&B artists. "The public's demand for the new music drove sales of recordings up with a 44 percent increase in sales volume from 1955 to 1956," explained Albert N. Greco.[5]

By the 1970s, the music industry was back to a tight oligopoly with just a few companies controlling the majority of albums sold. During the 1990s, several companies merged, and by 2008, just four record companies controlled the majority of sales. Those four companies were Sony/BMG, Warner Music Group, EMI, and Universal Music Group.

Digital Downloads

The introduction of the MP3 format in the 1990s, combined with that fact that more people were using high-speed Internet connections, led to the problem of music files being downloaded and shared illegally through the World Wide Web. In 2001, the Recording Industry Association of America (RIAA) reported that 10% fewer albums were sold than in 2000. The RIAA also reported that seizures of counterfeit, pirated, or bootlegged music soared nearly 500% in 2001.[6] The problem of music piracy was underway.

In 2003, the RIAA filed the first 261 lawsuits against people who had illegally downloaded music and shared the files. Eventually, thousands of lawsuits would be filed in an effort to crack down on piracy, but it appeared the lawsuits were having little effect.

In August 2008, the RIAA reported that global music piracy (both street piracy and online piracy) caused "$12.5 billion of economic losses over a year period, and 71,060 U.S. jobs had been lost."[7]

The music industry was slow to respond to the fact that music lovers, especially young people who were technologically savvy, wanted to get the latest music digitally. In the early part of the twenty-first century, there were few ways to buy music online, but by 2008, dozens of online stores had been set up to give music lovers the choice to buy music online legally.

DAVID HELFANT

Entertainment Attorney/A&R
Immergent Records
www.immergent.com

David Helfant has worked with some of the biggest names in entertainment, including Van Halen, Johnny Carson, Savage Garden, Jennifer Love Hewitt, and Rita Coolidge to name just a few. Helfant is an entertainment attorney who specializes in music. He is also in charge of the Artist and Repertoire (A&R) division at Immergent Records.

Helfant graduated from State University of New York at Binghamton and then went on to study law at Southwestern University School of Law in Los Angeles. He has always loved music—he plays the guitar, drums, and keyboard, and he sings. There was never a question of what area of entertainment he would work in—the question was, could he make it as a musician?

"If I'm a musician, I'm going to starve," he thought. Once he realized that playing music wasn't going to pay the bills, Helfant decided practicing law and specializing in music was his calling.

Helfant has moved seamlessly from private practice to working for some of the biggest companies in entertainment. At Paramount Pictures, he supervised production of several soundtrack albums including *How to Lose a Guy in 10 Days, School of Rock,* and *Team America.* As head of his own law firm, Helfant served as executive producer on Lowell George's tribute album, *Rock and Roll Doctor,* and the Buddaheads' debut album, *Blues Had a Baby.*

"I love to be able to straddle the fence between creative and being able to strengthen the deals at the same time," he said.

Helfant admitted the hardest part of his job is the long hours. He typically works 14 hours a day and rarely takes the weekend off.

"I probably go to sleep at 2 A.M. every night. I'm on my computer doing business with international clients," he explained.

Helfant said life is too short to not love what you do for a living. He offered this piece of advice to others wanting to start a career in the entertainment business: "Don't ever let anyone tell you you can't follow your dreams. If you love the business, you'll figure a way to get a foot in the front door or the back door."

» » »

Figure 10: Legal Music Sites: Some of the More Popular

Legal Online Music Sources		
amazonMP3	AOL Music	Apple's iTunes Music Store
Artist Direct	AudioCandy	BestBuy
BET	BuyMusic.com	Catsmusic
CD Baby	Circuit City	Dimples Music
Electric Fetus	Emusic	FYE
Gallery of Sound	imeem	iMesh
Independent Record	Latin Noise	Lifeway
LiquidAudio	MP3.com	Music Millennium
Music Rebellion	Napster	Passalong
Pro-Music	RasputinMusic	RealNetworks' Rhapsody
Record and Tape Trader	Rolling Stone	Ruckus
Sam Goody	Spinner	SpiralFrog
Tower Records	Wal-Mart	Windows Media
Yahoo! Music	Zune	

Source: Recording Industry Association of America, August 2008

ASCAP and BMI

The concept of protecting copyrighted music is nothing new. The music industry was one of the first to organize to protect copyrighted work. The organizations of ASCAP and BMI were created to protect the rights of musical artists. ASCAP, or The American Society of Composers, Authors and Publishers, was created in 1914 and is made up of more than 300,000 composers, songwriters, lyricists, and music publishers of every genre.[8] ASCAP protects the copyrighted material of its members by licensing and distributing royalties for their works.

BMI or The Broadcast Music, Inc. is the other organization that protects the rights of its members by issuing licenses to various users of music including television, radio stations, and some new media. BMI was started in 1939 when radio broadcasters were unhappy with ASCAP's monopoly.[9]

Challenges and Trends

Piracy

Music piracy continues to be one of the biggest challenges in the recorded music industry. The biggest concern in music and throughout the entire entertainment industry is maintaining control of content. The RIAA has devoted much of its resources to protecting intellectual property rights and fighting piracy. Piracy hurts the artists and the record label companies, but it also hurts employees who make their living in the music business, people like songwriters, administrative assistants, and new artists who have had a harder time getting signed and breaking into the business.

Many young people are convinced that CDs are overpriced and feel no guilt about downloading music illegally. Some young people go as far as to say the artists make so much money they don't need more. Successful artists say it isn't a matter of how much money they have but rather that the majority of artists want to be compensated for their work.

In 2003, during a session on the problem of music piracy before the Senate Permanent Subcommittee on Investigations, rap artist LL Cool J said,

> Do people in the entertainment industry have the same rights as other Americans to get fair pay for fair work? If a contractor builds a building, should people be able to move into it for free, just because he's successful? That's how I feel when I make an album, and it zips around the world on the Internet.[10]

The RIAA compares illegal downloading to shoplifting. The RIAA states that both are stealing, and both are illegal; the difference is that downloading music illegally is usually done anonymously from a home computer. The RIAA has been successful in tracking down heavy downloaders through peer-to-peer (P2P) networks. "The P2P software has a default setting that automatically informs the network of your user name and the names and sizes of the files on your hard drive that are available for copying," according to the RIAA.[11] All of the information is public, so it's relatively easy to see who is sharing copyrighted music files.

Remember those young people sitting in the room deep inside the RIAA headquarters? Those folks are looking for copyrighted materials on hard drives through P2P network software. When the RIAA files a lawsuit, it's against "John Doe" at a specific ISP address. When the lawsuit is filed, the RIAA does not know any personal information about the individual allegedly engaged in illegal file sharing except the unique number assigned to that person's computer from an Internet service provider.

With the exception of the original Napster online music file-sharing service, the RIAA can't do much about technology or software that is used to share music online. The RIAA agrees that devices and technology are not the problem: It believes the problem is that people use the technology for illegal purposes.

The original Napster's P2P file-sharing service is different from many of the other P2P software. Napster used a centralized computer to distribute music. Because Napster supplied the server, the recording industry went after the company. Other P2P software allows users to connect directly to another user's computer instead of to a central computer. RIAA sued Napster in December 1999, alleging copyright infringement. Napster lost its case and eventually declared bankruptcy in 2002. Its brand and logo were purchased after the company closed its doors and reopened as a pay-online music site using the same name.

Figure 11: Top Selling Albums of All Time

1.	Eagles: Greatest Hits 1971–1975	Eagles
2.	Thriller	Michael Jackson
3.	Led Zeppelin IV	Led Zeppelin

4.	The Wall	Pink Floyd
5.	Back in Black	AC/DC
6.	Double Live	Garth Brooks
7.	Greatest Hits Volume I & II	Billy Joel
8.	Come on Over	Shania Twain
9.	The Beatles	The Beatles
10.	Rumours	Fleetwood Mac
11.	Boston	Boston
12.	The Bodyguard (Soundtrack)	Whitney Houston
13.	No Fences	Garth Brooks
14.	Cracked Rear View	Hootie & The Blowfish
15.	Greatest Hits	Elton John
16.	Jagged Little Pill	Alanis Morissette
17.	Hotel California	Eagles
18.	The Beatles 1967-1970	The Beatles
19.	Physical Graffiti	Led Zeppelin
20.	The Beatles 1962–1966	The Beatles
21.	Born in the U.S.A.	Bruce Springsteen
22.	Appetite For Destruction	Guns 'N Roses
23.	Dark Side of the Moon	Pink Floyd
24.	Saturday Night Fever (Soundtrack)	Bee Gees
25.	Greatest Hits	Journey

Source: Recording Industry Association of America, August, 2008

Slumping Album Sales

Another challenge for the music industry is the slump in album sales. CD sales have declined steadily for the eight-year period from 2000 to 2008.[12] The drop from 2007 to 2008 alone was 20%.[13] Meanwhile, the number of legal downloads has been increasing from 2004 (the first year that the record labels saw profits from legal downloads) to 2008. In 2007, the number of songs legally downloaded reached an all-time high of 809 million.[14] The increase in single downloads, however, wasn't enough to make up for the declining CD sales.

The drop in album sales appears to be an indication of listener preferences. Music buyers were more likely to buy a single than an entire album, partly because of advances in technology. Devices such as the iPod allow listeners more freedom to build individual play lists of songs from multiple artists.

Another reason album sales might have slumped is because many music buyers today prefer to buy just a song or two from an album instead of being forced to pay for the entire album, including the songs that they don't like.

iPod and Digital Sales

A big step forward for the recorded music industry came in the form of the iPod. Actually, it wasn't exactly the iPod that helped the industry; it was the iTunes Music Store. But, the iPod and iTunes go hand and hand. And if that wasn't enough, Apple introduced the iPhone, which further expanded the iTunes reach. When the iPhone was first available for purchase, it was all the rage. However, many people didn't realize it required users to sign up for iTunes downloadable service even if the iPhone's user didn't want to download music. In late 2007, the iTunes store was realizing tremendous success. Sales exceeded three billion songs, in addition to 100 million TV shows and two million feature films since 2003.[15]

iPod sales really took off in 2002 when Apple introduced its larger capacity 10-GB unit. The iTunes Music Store was offered initially as a way to boost iPod sales. It seemed to work. By April 2007, more than 100 million iPods had been sold worldwide. At that time iPod held approximately 66% of the digital music player market.[16] The iTunes Music Store is very simple to use and offers a broad selection of songs and types of music for $0.99 a song. The success of iTunes was evidence that music lovers were happy with downloading music and paying for it. Music companies were also happy with iTunes as they received $0.65 in gross revenue per song.[17]

Consumers seem to have embraced the pay download sites. Not only is iTunes a success, but many other legal download sites are up and running. All indications point to the fact that the music industry was too slow in embracing a new way to deliver the product to the consumer, so the only choice initially was downloading illegally.

Stores Closing

As the number of songs being downloaded legally has continued to rise, the number of CD albums sold has continued to decline. Fewer CDs sold continues to be a challenge for the brick and mortar music stores. The Baby Boom generation remembers going to the local record store to spend the afternoon listening to new albums, checking out album covers, and deciding which album to buy and take home to listen to. The long afternoons spent at the record store are a thing of the past because very few of these stores are still in business. The most common place for people to buy albums these days (if they aren't buying online) is the big-box chain store. One advantage the big-box stores have over the mom and pop record stores is more competitive pricing. The big stores can buy in bulk and get a better price, which usually translates into a lower price for consumers.

Many of the small, independent music stores across the United States have gone out of business, and many of the chain stores like Tower Records, which went out of business in 2006, are closing individual stores. As more consumers turn to downloading music, it's likely that music stores will continue to close. Or maybe they will reinvent their purpose. Alan Greenblatt suggests that

> Physical record stores may become filling stations for music featuring kiosks that allow easy downloading for people who haven't invested in MP3 systems that grant them access to thousands of songs at the touch of a button.[18]

Social Networking Sites

Social networking sites just might be the next big way to promote artists and music. Hundreds of social networking sites are up and running, and millions of people are flocking to them. The recording industry has taken notice and is increasingly embracing these sites as a way to promote music.

In April 2008, News Corp, which owned the Fox Television Network, 20th Century Fox, and MySpace, announced plans for the launch of MySpace Music. MySpace Music is intended to be a place to buy music from at least three of the four major music companies: Sony/BMG, Universal Music, and Warner Music Group. The idea behind MySpace Music was to provide visitors with an ad-supported, pay-for-download music site [19]

The fourth major music company, EMI, was expected to join the venture as well. The recorded music industry saw the potential in leveraging one of the fastest-growing platforms appealing to young people—a demographic that traditionally has bought a lot of music.

360-Degree Deals

After experiencing years of slipping CD sales and lost revenue because of piracy, the major music companies decided it was time to reinvent the contract between the artist and the label. The 360-deals, sometimes referred to as multiple rights, are the new contracts that artists and record companies are signing. The new deal gives the record label a percentage of the artists' income from record sales, but it also includes income from ancillary sources such as concerts, merchandise, and endorsement deals.

One of the first 360-deals was between Robbie Williams, the British pop singer, and EMI in 2002. One of the most publicized was Madonna's $120 million deal with the concert promoter Live Nation.[20] The recording companies say the deals make sense since the labels invest the most money in the risky business of developing new talent, so why shouldn't they get a larger share once the artist is a success?

The 360-deals have the potential to earn the labels tremendous money from concert tours. Traditionally, successful concert tours have been cash cows for musicians. It was not uncommon for an artist to make much more money while on tour as compared to the money made from album sales. Consider this: *Forbes* magazine listed the top money-making pop music superstars, and Madonna ranked at the top. She earned an estimated $194 million dollars worldwide from her 2006 *Confessions* concert tour alone.[21] And now, labels want a slice of the revenue they feel they've earned since they helped make the artists popular by promoting the albums and encouraging radio stations to play the artists' music.

The 360-degree deals could eventually impact the types of artists who are signed to a particular label. It is speculated that the 360-degree deals could lead to more artists being signed who have potential in the concert and merchandise arenas even though they are not necessarily the best artists. But the recording companies disagree. They say 360-degree contracts are better for all musicians since they provide less pressure for the artist to make back the label's money immediately.

Figure 12: Top Selling Artists

1. The Beatles
2. Garth Brooks
3. Elvis Presley
4. Led Zeppelin
5. Eagles
6. Billy Joel
7. Pink Floyd
8. Barbra Streisand
9. Elton John
10. AC/DC
11. George Strait
12. Aerosmith
13. The Rolling Stones
14. Bruce Springsteen
15. Madonna
16. Mariah Carey
17. Michael Jackson
18. Metallica
19. Van Halen
20. Whitney Houston
21. Kenny Rogers
22. U2
23. Celine Dion
24. Fleetwood Mac
25. Neil Diamond

Source: Recording Industry Association of America, August 2008

Ring Tones

Ring tones have become a big money maker for the music industry. In 2007, ring-tone revenue hit $550 million.[22] *Billboard* magazine keeps track of the top ring tones week to week. As of August 2008, Koji Kondo and the song "Super Mario Brothers Theme" had been at the top of the ring tone charts for almost four years. "Best Friend," by 50 Cent & Olivia, with their song had been at the top of the charts for two years.[23] The record companies and cell phone companies are taking notice.

Musical ring tones took off when cell phone companies started offering their customers phones that could download music. Motorola's RAZR V3i phone plays songs downloaded from iTunes with a capacity of 100 songs. But 100 songs aren't very much considering some people have thousands of songs on their iPods. According to Plunkett Research, "Nokia hoped to solve the storage problem with its Nseries phones, which feature 4-gigabyte hard, drives capable of storing 1,000 songs."[24]

Music companies see ring tones as a way to make money as well as a way to promote music. One of Madonna's most successful singles, "Hung Up" was offered first as a ring tone. Warner Music Group released the single as a ring tone a month before the song was available anywhere else.[25] The idea behind the early ring tone release was to increase awareness and demand for Madonna's new song before it was even played on the radio. And with a song called "Hung Up," it was a natural as a ring tone.

Employment Opportunities

The music industry is enormous. Even though many jobs have been lost because of music piracy, there still remain many opportunities to work in the industry. Of course, music label executives are always looking for the next great sound or a promising performer. Many musicians find plenty of ways to make a living even before signing with a label. But since this chapter is focused on the recorded music industry, the areas with the most potential for getting started in the recorded music industry are in distribution, marketing, and A&R.

A&R

An Artist and Repertoire (A&R) representative is essentially a talent scout looking for the next great recording artist. A&R reps listen to demo tapes, travel, and attend concerts in an effort to keep up on the latest trends in music. It's not uncommon for an A&R rep to spend every night out listening to artists in small nightclub venues.

Once a label signs a new artist, the A&R rep is responsible for working with the artist every step of the way to get the recording finished. The A&R administrative staff handle all clearances for music and make sure everyone gets proper credit on an album. They also coordinate delivery of the master recording, the artwork, and all other materials to coincide with the release date of the album.

Producer

Music producers are in charge of the recording process and the finished product. The producer works with the artist before and during the recording of the music. The producer helps the artist with the sound to make it commercially pleasing. The producer will also work with the marketing staff to decide on the packaging for the CD and come up with the artwork and publicity materials for the artist. Producers must keep up on trends in the music industry. Producers can be freelance or on staff with the music label. Many established artists work repeatedly with the same producer.

Marketing

The marketing team works to get the recording airplay on local radio stations. Marketing executives are also responsible for getting the CDs to consumers through retail sales and for promoting customer awareness of the album. Marketing executives usually have a close working relationship with the program directors at radio stations.

Public Relations

The public relations team's work includes getting the artist editorial exposure in newspapers, magazines, television, and radio. Public relations executives also work to get the artist publicity during a concert tour. Junkets are sometimes held for artists when they release a new album. Junkets allow the public relations team to bring together the musicians and the press for interviews in an effort to generate exposure in the media. Public relations work is sometimes handled by an outside company that specializes in that type of work.

Distribution / Sales

The distribution or sales department is responsible for getting the recordings to the places where consumers can buy the CD. The sales team may work closely with the marketing team to get the artist's music to websites, such as MySpace.com.

Advertising

The advertising team creates the ad campaign that will go with a particular album or single. The ad team will decide where to place ads in radio, print, and television. Sometimes the advertising is handled by an outside agency.

Future Outlook

Whether it's listening to our favorite artist on an iPod or singing at the top of our lungs from the safety of our automobile when our favorite song plays on the radio, we love music. We turn to music when we celebrate, and we turn to music when we are more introspective. Music is here to stay. But what isn't so clear is what is going to happen to the major recorded music companies.

In a 2003 article, Alan Greenblatt asked, "Will the Major Music Labels Survive the Digital Age?"[26] The recorded music companies have been badly hurt by copyright infringement and illegal downloads. According to the RIAA, computer users illegally download more than 2.6 billion copyrighted files every month.[27] Most of those files are music files. The only thing that we appear to love more than music is free music.

Even the lawsuits filed by the RIAA have done little to stop people from violating copyrights. Many in the music industry are wondering what can be done to stop the flood of illegal downloads. The music industry isn't sure what needs to be done. And it's not just the executives in charge of the labels who are worried. Executives across the entertainment spectrum are watching the music industry closely. Many entertainment chiefs know that file swapping and illegal downloading isn't a problem that is limited to the music industry. If it can happen with music, it can certainly also happen in the film or television industries.

DAN SAVANT

Music Producer, Savant Productions, Inc.
www.savantproductions.com

Dan Savant has always loved music. The Los Angeles-based music producer plays the trumpet, an instrument he picked up for the first time at the age of 6. Savant even quit college for a while to play with a band and tour the country.

So, when it came time to get back to his studies and finish his degree, there was little question what his major would be—accounting. Savant said the accounting degree was something he could fall back on if he didn't make it in the music business, but, he did make it—both as a performer and a producer.

Savant runs his own company, Savant Productions. He estimated he spends about 40% of his time as a trumpet player and 60% as a producer. As a producer, he has worked on the music for the films *Passion of the Christ* and *Freaky Friday.* As a trumpet player, he has been featured on the soundtrack for *Sideways* and *Sin City.*

"You need to have a picture in your head to imagine what you really want to do," Savant said about making it in the business. He added that if you aim high, your dreams just might come true.

Savant's degree in accounting from California State University, Northridge has come in handy in running his own company. He said he offers clients the best of both worlds. Savant knows the music business, and he understands the business behind the music.

"It's a business first and foremost," he said. While he doesn't always agree with his clients' choices for music and production, he believes that making sure the clients get what they want is one of the keys to making it in the music industry as a producer.

Savant encourages musicians to take a shot at making it big as a performer. "If they are playing an instrument, definitely try it. Anyone can do anything in the United States," he added, "but keep in mind that other jobs in the field might be just as fulfilling."

» » »

But everything in the music industry isn't gloom and doom. Several technological advances are creating new opportunities to sell music and make money. Ring tones continue to be an increasing area of money making. Also, legal download sites continue to see sales increase. All indications point to the fact that there is nothing that can stop the iPod. The portable listening device has become the gadget just about everyone carries when away from the house. iPod has become synonymous with music on the go.

It's too early to predict the demise of the major music labels, but it's too early to predict a turnaround in losses. What is safe to predict is that technology will be leading the way. It is safe to assume that we haven't seen the latest in music technology and that if the major music labels find a way to embrace the technology instead of changing it, music executives will find a way to turn around their companies and start showing profits. Don Van Cleave, a Birmingham, AL, record store owner who was forced to close his doors because of a slowdown in CD sales predicts, "The next 10 years are going to be the most interesting business shift any of us has ever seen."[28]

Summary

The recorded music industry started in the late nineteenth century with the introduction of the phonograph. Music was first recorded onto a cylinder and sold in tubes. The vinyl record took over as the industry standard in the 1920s and continued as such until the beginning of the digital age. Music companies saw a boost in sales during the 1980s when the first digital format, the CD, was introduced.

Everything changed for the major music labels with the introduction of the MP3 format. The MP3 format would rock the music industry to its core. Not directly because of the new format but because of the possibilities in sending the files through the Internet. The MP3 format was a compressed file and small in size, which allowed it to be sent very quickly via personal computers. The MP3 format was easily exchanged through peer-to-peer software. Napster was a file-sharing system that allowed music files to be easily transferred from computer to computer. Downloading music became extremely popular. It also was illegal. When Napster first started there were no other websites offering the opportunity to buy music legally.

The widespread availability of free music caused sales to plummet and resulted in huge numbers of layoffs at the recorded music companies. Almost 30 years later, the music industry is trying to find its footing.

Several growth areas are helping the music industry recover some of its losses. Ring tones are popular as well as pay sites such as the iTunes Music Store. The 360-degree contracts are also helping music labels make more money off successful artists.

Many industry analysts believe the future of music lies with the Internet. Eventually, all music will be bought and sold electronically, and the CD will become a relic or even an antique. CDs just might eventually go the way of the cylinder recording or the vinyl record. The CD might become something people might collect even if they don't have a way to listen to the music on it in the digital age.

ADDITIONAL RESOURCES

Associations and Organizations

American Federation of Musicians (AFM)
1501 Broadway, Suite 600
New York, NY 10036
(212) 869–1330
www.afm.org

American Society of Composers, Authors & Publishers (ASCAP)
ASCAP Building
One Lincoln Plaza
New York, NY 10023
www.ascap.com

Broadcast Music, Inc. (BMI)
320 West 57th Street
New York, NY 10019–3790
www.bmi.com

National Music Publisher's Association of the United States (NMPA)
101 Constitution Avenue NW
Suite 705 Easy
Washington, DC 20001
(202) 742–4375
www.nmpa.org

Recording Industry Association of America (RIAA)
1025 F Street NW
10th Floor
Washington, DC 20004
(202) 775–0101
www.riaa.com

Society of Professional Audio Recording Services (SPARS)
9 Music Square South, Suite 222
Nashville, TN 37203
(800) 771–7727
www.spars.com

Job-Hunting Resources

Mediawebsource.com: mediawebsource.com/musicjobs.htm
MyMusicJob.com: www.mymusicjob.com

Sony Music: www.sonybmg.com/careers.html

Magazines and Trade Publications

Billboard Magazine: www.billboard.com

Music Trades: www.musictrades.com

Q4Music: www.q4music.com

Radio and Records: www.radioandrecords.com

Books

Britten, Anna, and Alan McGee. *Working in the Music Industry: How to Find an Exciting and Varied Career in the World of Music.* Oxford, England: How to Books, 2005.

Crouch, Tanja L. *100 Careers in the Music Business.* Hauppauge, NY: Barrons Educational Series, 2008.

Hatschek, Keith. *How to Get a Job in the Music Industry,* 2nd ed. Boston, MA: Berklee College, 2007.

Hull, Geoffrey. *The Recording Industry,* 2nd ed. New York: Routledge, 2004.

Schulenberg, Richard. *Legal Aspects of the Music Industry.* New York: Billboard Books, 2005.

ENDNOTES

1. "Member of Music Piracy Group Convicted of Conspiracy," *PR Newswire,* 22 May 2008.
2. Albert N. Greco, *The Media and Entertainment Industries,* Needham Heights, MA: Allyn & Bacon, 2000: 76.
3. *Merriam-Webster Dictionary,* www.merriam-webster.com.
4. Greco, 78.
5. Ibid.
6. Recording Industry Association of America, www.riaa.com.
7. Ibid.
8. American Society of Composers, Authors and Publishers, www.ascap.com.
9. Broadcast Music Inc., www.bmi.com.
10. Alan Greenblatt, "Future of the Music Industry: Will the Major Music Labels Survive the Digital Age?" *CQ Researcher,* 21 November 2003, 3.
11. Recording Industry Association of America, www.riaa.com.
12. Ibid.
13. Ibid.
14. Ibid.
15. Ibid.
16. "Apple's iPod Revitalizes the Music Industry," Plunkett Research Ltd., 18 February 2008, www.plunkettresearchonline.com.
17. Ibid.
18. Greenblatt, 16.
19. Ibid.

20. Tuna N. Amobi, "Movies and Home Entertainment: Current Environment," *Standard & Poor's Industry Surveys,* 3 July 2008, 9.

21. Louis Hau, "Material Girl to Cash In?" *Forbes,* October 11, 2007, www.forbes.com.

22. "Music Plays a Major Role in New Cell Phones," Plunkett Research, Ltd., 17 July 2008, www.plunkettresearchonline.com.

23. *Billboard* magazine, www.billboard.com.

24. "Music Plays a Major Role in New Cell Phones," Plunkett Research, Ltd., 17 July 2008, www.plunkettresearchonline.com.

25. Ibid.

26. Greenblatt, 1.

27. Recording Industry Association of America, www.riaa.com.

28. Greenblatt, 21.

7

Museums ANDI STEIN

Who would imagine that an exhibit of hollowed-out cadavers would appeal to more than 25 million people? Yet "Body Worlds," which made its museum debut in Japan in 1995, has done just that. This unusual exhibit has been shown at 35 museums since it first opened. It offers audiences a chance to learn about the innerworkings of the human anatomy with a display of preserved bodies that essentially "let it all hang out"—muscles, tissue, organs—the works. Three different versions of the exhibit have brought in record-breaking crowds. For some museums, such as the Milwaukee Public Museum, interest in the exhibit has helped generate previously unheard of revenues for its hosts.[1]

Museums have been entertaining and educating audiences for literally thousands of years. The human desire to collect and display artifacts for others to gawk at is a strong one and has led to the establishment of some of the world's most famous museums—the British Museum in London, The Louvre in Paris, and the Smithsonian Institution complex in Washington, DC, to name just a few. These and other museums offer the public an opportunity to learn about art, history, science, popular culture, etc., by giving patrons a first-hand glimpse of objects that showcase the best of these fields.

Some of the earliest museums were essentially libraries or "cabinets" of curios that began with people's personal hobbies or interests in collecting specific items such as paintings or other decorative objects. As these collections were made available to the general public over the years, the museum evolved into a place where people could be both entertained and educated by these collections.

Today, with an increased focus on technology and hands-on interactivity, the museum has become a place where visitors can see, touch, and even actively engage with the various artifacts on display within it. Traditional museum exhibits featuring well-known paintings and scientific curiosities have been expanded to include a widespread array of items that encompass everything from costumes to computers to the cadavers featured in the Body Worlds exhibit.

Today's museums have even gone beyond the scope of place, as the Internet and World Wide Web have allowed for the creation of the virtual museum, where interested patrons can view museum collections online in the comfort of their own homes.

As with any entertainment venue, the operation of a museum comes with its own set of challenges. Funding, promotion, and security are all issues regularly discussed by museum directors, curators, and development directors. Keeping the public interested and encouraging repeat business are also crucial and have resulted in a shift toward traveling exhibits over permanent collections in the last few decades.

This chapter will explore the role that museums play in entertaining and educating the public. It will provide information on the evolution of the museum over time and discuss how today's museum professionals grapple with some of the issues and challenges of the industry.

History and Background

Early Museums

The word museum evolved from the Greek term, "mouseion" and translates to "seat of the Muses." While use of the word did not become popular until the early seventeenth century, it appropriately characterized some of the early incarnations of museums, which highlighted relics of art and culture.[2]

The earliest known museums, which date back thousands of years, were more like libraries than the museums in existence today. They were generally intended to house personal collections of books and artifacts, like that owned by Egyptian Pharaoh Akhenaton, who constructed a library-like museum to hold the collection of gifts given to him during his reign in the mid-1300s B.C.

One of the earliest museums on record, also in Egypt, was founded by King Ptolemy I in the third century B.C. It contained a collection of scientific instruments, statues, books, manuscripts, and even a small zoo of live animals. It is still in existence today as the Museum of Alexandria.

In ancient Greece, the fall of the empire of Alexander the Great in the third century B.C., led to the public display of paintings, sculptures, and other objects of art that were looted from abandoned towns. Religious houses of worship such as churches and cathedrals later contributed to the development of the museum with their vast collections of religious objects and illuminated manuscripts.

A number of the museums that are today considered to house some of the world's greatest treasures grew out of private collections that were eventually opened to the public. During the Renaissance, for example, as commerce flourished, individuals who acquired money used this wealth to purchase artworks, jewels, tapestries, etc. The Medici family in Italy, for example, established a large-scale "galleria" in their home in Florence where they displayed some of the artwork they had acquired. This term "galleria" evolved into "gallery," which now refers to a place where artwork is displayed. The Medici collection was ultimately given to the people of Italy in 1743 and is known today as the Uffizi Gallery, one of Florence's premier museums.

Some early collectors displayed their collections in large pieces of furniture called, "Kabinetts" (from the German) or "cabinets of curiosities" to preserve them.[3] One of these was Britain's John Tradescant the Elder, who, with his son John Tradescant the Younger, began allowing the public to view their collection of natural history specimens in the mid-1600s. After their deaths, the collection was donated to the University of Oxford, where it eventually became the Ashmolean Museum in 1683. This was the world's first natural history museum open to the general public, and it firmly established the official use of the word "museum."

From Private to Public

By the mid-eighteenth century, the trend of making private collections public had caught on in both Europe and Asia. In England in the mid-1700s, a naturalist named Sir Hans Sloane left his collection of gemstones, archeological objects, and coins to the city of London. These were combined with a collection of manuscripts left to the city by Sir Robert Cotton and Robert Harley and formed the basis for what today is the British Museum.

In France, the Louvre was opened to the public in 1793, showcasing artwork that had been collected over the years by French royals. A collection of the Batavia Society of the Arts in Jakarta, Indonesia, evolved into the Central Museum of Indonesian Culture in 1778, while in India, a private collection of the Asiatic Society of Bengal became the Indian Museum in Calcutta in 1784.

These were followed by the development of museums worldwide that featured prime examples of art, scientific objects, and natural history specimens: the Prado in Madrid in 1819; Argentine Museum of Natural Sciences in Buenos Aries in 1812; and the Australian Museum in Sydney in 1829, among others.

U.S. Museum Development

As the United States began to develop in the eighteenth century, the museum concept made its way across the Atlantic Ocean. The oldest U.S. museum is the Charleston Museum in South Carolina, which opened in 1773. One of the early pioneers of the U.S. museum was the artist Charles Wilson Peale, who began displaying his own artwork and natural history specimens in a gallery in his Philadelphia home in 1786. When his collection outgrew his residence, he opened Peale's American Museum, which remained in existence until 1854.[4]

Some of the most prominent American museums soon followed in the nineteenth century: the Smithsonian Institution in Washington, DC, in 1846; Metropolitan Museum of Art in New York in 1870; Philadelphia Museum of Art in 1871; and the Field Museum in Chicago in 1893.

The nineteenth century also saw the rise of the "dime museum," which brought culture to the masses by presenting collections of artifacts and curiosities to the working class for a low admission price. Perhaps the most famous of these was P.T. Barnum's American Museum, which opened in New York City in 1841. Barnum was a showman who specialized in finding human and non-human oddities and putting them on display for all to see, according to Andrea Stulman Dennett:

> Dime museums attempted to bridge the ever growing gap between elite and popular audiences.... For a low, onetime admission charge, the dime museum dazzled men, women, and children with its dioramas, panoramas, georamas, cosmoramas, paintings, relics, freaks, stuffed animals, menageries, waxworks, and theatrical performances. Nothing quite like it had existed before.[5]

A Change of Focus

The twentieth century led to a shift in the focus of the museum as a result of changes in government, war, and a growing interest in heritage preservation. The Russian Revolution in 1917, for instance, brought Russia's museums under state control and led to the development of museums designed to highlight the country's cultural heritage. Likewise, the end of World War I in Germany resulted in the creation of regional museums to promote German nationalism. This was followed in other countries by the creation of open-air museums, such as the Welsh Folk Museum in Cardiff, and Colonial Williamsburg in Virginia, where visitors could see people in period costume reenacting the past as a way to learn about the heritage and history of their countries and communities.

After World War I, the mission of the museum in the United States and Europe began to change from one purely focused on entertaining members of the public to educating them as well. Regional and specialty museums proliferated, focusing on informing patrons about political and social issues and trends and complementing the established tradition of simply displaying collections of art and artifacts.

Museums began partnering with schools and community groups as a means of extending beyond traditional walls and educating people about the stories behind their collections. In addition, a greater focus on interactivity at places like the Exploratorium in San Francisco and the Please Touch Museum in Philadelphia has allowed museums to shift from primarily being "static storehouses for artifacts into active learning environments for people."[6]

In the past few decades, a rise in the number of traveling museum exhibits has enabled people to see collections from museums around the world they might otherwise not be able to access. In addition, the Internet and the World Wide Web in the twenty-first century have expanded the reach of the museum even further with the development of the virtual museum, which enables people to view museum collections online.

Museums Today

The public's fascination with collecting interesting objects and sharing these objects with others has led to the continued growth and development of the museum over time. Today there are approximately 17,500 museums in the United States alone, according to the American Association of Museums, with thousands more estimated throughout the world.[7] These include traditional museums that showcase art, history, science, and natural history, as well as regional and specialty museums that highlight everything from baseball to rock and roll. Some museum collections are housed in large complexes like the Smithsonian Institution in Washington, DC, which showcases a little bit of everything. Others may be displayed in one or two rooms that focus on presenting items pertaining to a single topic, such as the Route 66 Museum in Clinton, OK.

Several government and nonprofit organizations and trade associations serve the museum industry by providing information, establishing standards for best practice and helping to link museum professionals. In addition, an online resource called MuseumSpot. com offers information about the industry (www.museumspot.com).

Figure 13: A Sampling of Museums Around the World

Art
Art Institute of Chicago: www.artic.edu
Asian Art Museum of San Francisco: www.asianart.org
Getty Museum, Los Angeles: www.getty.edu
The Louvre, Paris: www.louvre.fr
Metropolitan Museum of Art, New York: www.metmuseum.org
Philadelphia Museum of Art: www.philamuseum.org
Shanghai Museum, China: www.shanghaimuseum.net
Hermitage, St. Petersburg, Russia: www.hermitagemuseum.org

History
British Museum, London: www.britishmuseum.org
Colonial Williamsburg (open-air): www.colonialwilliamsburg.com
National Gallery of Canada, Ottawa: www.gallery.ca
National Museum of American History, Washington, DC: americanhistory.si.edu

Natural History
Academy of Natural Sciences, Philadelphia: www.ansp.org
American Museum of Natural History, New York: www.amnh.org
Carnegie Museum of Natural History, Pittsburgh: www.carnegiemnh.org
Field Museum, Chicago: www.fieldmuseum.org

Science
Exploratorium, San Francisco: www.exploratorium.edu
Franklin Institute, Philadelphia: www.fi.edu
Museum of Science, Boston: www.mos.org
Museum of Science and Industry, Chicago: www.msichicago.org

Specialty
American Jazz Museum, Kansas City, MO: www.americanjazzmuseum.com
Heard Museum, Phoenix: www.heard.org
International Spy Museum, Washington, DC: www.spymuseum.org

National Baseball Hall of Fame, Cooperstown, NY: www.baseballhalloffame.org
National Air and Space Museum, Washington, DC: www.nasm.si.edu
United States Holocaust Memorial Museum, Washington, DC: www.ushmm.org

Challenges and Trends

Funding and Fundraising

Museums rely heavily on a variety of funding sources to keep themselves going and need a steady source of revenue to keep their collections up-to-date, pay their staffs, and develop promotional activities that will help generate business. Funding for museums can come from a variety of sources, and these sources depend on the nature of the museum and the circumstances under which it operates.

Primary Sources of Revenue

Many museums operate as nonprofit organizations and rely on government grants and revenues to sustain themselves. This can be problematic during hard economic times when museums are sometimes forced to compete with other types of nonprofits for a share of what may be a limited pool of resources.

This often requires creativity and advocacy on the part of a museum's administrators. When the city manager of Alameda, CA,, proposed a 10% cut in funds to the Alameda Museum, for example, curator George Gunn appealed to the Alameda City Council for help according to an article in the *Oakland Tribune*. Arguing that a funding cut could hurt the museum's existence, Gunn brought relics of the museum's collection to the Council meeting to show members how the loss of the museum could result in the loss of artifacts crucial to the town's history. His plea worked, and the Council voted against the funding cuts.[8]

To avoid scenarios like this, many museums turn to private funding sources as a means of supplementing government monies. According to the American Association of Museums' 2006 Museum Financial Information Survey, private donations typically make up approximately 35% of a museum's funding.[9] Sponsorships from corporations, trade associations, or organized professional groups can often serve as sources of funding to help maintain a museum's collection or provide seed money for the creation of a new museum. In 2007, for example, a $100,000 pledge from the National Organization of Black Law Enforcement Executives (NOBLE) helped fund the groundbreaking for the National Law Enforcement Museum in Washington, DC, slated to open in 2011.

Some donations come in the form of objects rather than dollars. A couple in Maine was touted by the press for their philanthropy when they donated $100 million worth of artwork to the Colby College Museum of Art in Waterville.[10]

Alternate Sources of Revenue

Given the constant need for money, museums have found other ways to sustain themselves as well. Entrance fees, which can range from a few dollars to double digits, help defray operational costs. Museum shops selling exhibit-related souvenirs or on-site cafes or snack shops often can bring in additional revenues.

Organized fundraising activities such as capital campaigns have become a routine way for museums to generate income, especially when trying to expand their facilities or collections. Museums can also raise funds by renting space to corporations for special events or parties. According to an article in the *Rochester Business Journal*, one example of a museum that uses this technique is the George Eastman House International Museum of Photography and Film, which "brings in close to $100,000 a year on event revenues and has up to 150 functions a year, including corporate meetings, lectures, weddings and garden parties."[11]

Like those in charge of many nonprofit organizations, museum personnel are finding that adopting a business model when it comes to funding and fundraising can be beneficial. A program founded by the Center for Curatorial Leadership, for instance, was designed to help those working as museum curators learn more about business. The program's aim was to provide curators with information on topics such as endowment management, branding, budgeting, etc., "to help the next generation of museum directors cope with the growing financial pressures on arts institutions as they compete for visitors with one another and with the pop-culture industry."[12]

Marketing and Promotion

Getting people through the doors is one of the constant challenges faced by museum personnel. Museums routinely seek new and innovative ways to generate interest in what they have to offer and rely on a variety of marketing and promotional techniques to sustain this interest.

Traveling Exhibitions

One approach that has become extremely popular and profitable for museums in recent years is the hosting of traveling exhibitions. In the past, many museums relied on their permanent collections to draw in audiences; today these organizations have found that adding traveling exhibits into the mix can bring in visitors who might never have stepped inside the museum in the past. This, in turn, helps bring the museum's permanent collection to the attention of these first-time visitors and can result in repeat business.

The Body Worlds exhibit is a prime example of a successful traveling exhibition, as the unusual nature of its content has aroused the curiosity of millions of people. Not only does an exhibit like this enable visitors to see something they might not otherwise be able to, it also serves as a means of generating tremendous revenues for its host organization.

Today's traveling exhibits can be especially appealing to the public because they frequently are designed to focus on subjects that have great intrigue or mystique. An example

STEPHANIE MELCHERT-SMITH

Director of Development, National Cowgirl Museum and Hall of Fame
www.cowgirl.net

"This week is crazy," Stephanie Melchert-Smith admitted during a phone call prior to a big event she was working on. But then, just about every week is crazy for Melchert-Smith, who is the Director of Development at the National Cowgirl Museum and Hall of Fame in Fort Worth, TX. Melchert-Smith was in the midst of preparing for the museum's annual induction luncheon and ceremony, held every year to recognize and honor women of the American West. She was in charge of the lunch for 1,000 guests, invitations, catalogues, an art exhibit, and all festivities tied to the ceremony. "Multi-tasking is part of my job. I'm a stacker," she said, referring to the paper stacks on her desk. "I'm in the middle of six projects."

The National Cowgirl Museum is the only one of its kind and features exhibits, education programs, and research all about cowgirls and the Wild West. Melchert-Smith always had a love of horses but never imagined she'd spend her workdays talking about horses and cowgirls when she was in college at Iowa State University. As a double major in marketing and fashion merchandising, she planned to be an international buyer for a clothing store. But after three months studying that line of work in Paris right after graduation, she was convinced otherwise.

"I didn't like anything about the work," she explained. After a few stints in corporate marketing, she eventually landed with the non-profit organization, The United Way. She moved to the National Cowgirl Museum in 2008. "I love the non-profits. Sure, I could be making three times as much money at a for-profit company, but sometimes it's not all about the money," she said.

Her job as Director of Development requires her to do everything associated with raising money for the museum through private donations, corporate sponsors, and grants. While most days are hectic, she said, she loves what she does.

Melchert-Smith offered advice to others wanting to follow in her footsteps. "It's all about relation-ships, networking, and follow-up. If you say you're going to do something, you need to get it done, preferably within 24 hours."

Working at the National Cowgirl Museum is also fulfilling her life-long love of horses. Since the age of three, Melchert-Smith always wanted to own a horse. Although she still doesn't own one, she spends her days talking to and working around cowgirls and horses. And now she knows dozens of people who invite her horseback riding anytime she likes.

» » »

was an exhibit about King Tut called, "Tutankhamun and the Golden Age of the Pharaohs." When it appeared at the Franklin Institute in Philadelphia in 2007, the appeal was so great that the museum kept its doors open for 24 hours a day during the exhibit's final weekend.[13]

Other traveling exhibits of note have been "Pompeii: Tales From an Eruption," which included 500 artifacts from the eruption of Mount Vesuvius; "In the Dark," a look at creatures that flourish in darkness such as owls, bats, and bobcats; and "The Quilts of Gees Bend," featuring a collection of hand-made quilts produced by four generations of African American women from a community in rural Alabama.

Special Events

Organized special events can also provide museums with an opportunity to reach out to prospective visitors. These can come in many different forms, ranging from the showing of films to invited lectures affiliated with specific exhibits to on-site fairs that are open to the general public like the Bellevue Art Museum's "ArtsFair." This event, which has been an annual activity at the Bellevue, WA, museum for more than 60 years, features artists' booths, music, food, and an art auction. It serves as a major fundraising event for the museum as well as a promotional tool.[14]

Some museums have found it beneficial to partner with others in their communities to promote the museum-going concept on a broader scale. In Washington, DC, a promotion called, "Warm Up to a Museum" advertised 35 different programs offered by the city's museums during the cold winter months.[15] Likewise, galleries and museums in the United Kingdom band together every spring for "Museums and Galleries Month," which encompasses 1,200 galleries and museums and is designed to promote the arts throughout the UK.[16]

Educational Outreach

Educational outreach is now a key element of museum management and often falls under the broader umbrella of marketing and promotion. Teaching people about a museum's collection is a way of making them aware of the museum and what it has to offer. School programs, in particular, are excellent outreach vehicles for showing children what museums can offer in the hope that they will grow up to become regular museum-goers.

Some museums offer discounted fees to school groups or tailor specialized programs to suit their needs. Some will even send museum representatives into the schools to show off items from their collections, hoping students will be encouraged to visit the museum with their families at a later date to see more.

Other museums build partnerships with schools around exhibits. The Anniston Museum of Natural History in Alabama developed an education program centered on a visiting skeleton of a *Tyrannosaurus Rex* named "Sue." The museum worked with local schools to develop activities at the museum that could be tied into the schools' curricula. During the exhibit's 15-week stay at the museum, more than 10,000 students came to see Sue.[17]

Educational outreach programs can be targeted to appeal to students of all ages. The Amon Carter Museum in Fort Worth, TX, offers a tour designed for medical students at the University of North Texas Health Science Center. The museum has also started experimenting with distance education versions of its school tours by "filming the tours and inviting artists to the galleries to be videotaped. The interviews, demonstrations and tours are subsequently broadcast to schoolrooms hundreds of miles away."[18]

Theft Prevention

Protecting a museum's collection from theft can present a challenge to security personnel. Some art theft cases make international headlines, such as in 2004 when two Edvard Munch paintings were stolen from the Munch Museum in Oslo, including his famous work, "The Scream." Although the paintings were eventually recovered in 2006, the theft caused many other museums to question the vulnerability of their own collections.

Museums try to devise ways to protect their collections from thieves and vandals. Leonardo Da Vinci's famous "Mona Lisa" is protected by glass at the Louvre in Paris, for example. According to an article in the *Wall Street Journal,* "Some museums resort to rudimentary steps like displaying their high-value works away from exits, and such steps can help."[19]

An increase in art theft in recent years has also resulted in the creation of a new field— art recovery. In 1991, Julian Radcliffe founded the Art Loss Register, a database of stolen artwork that holds records of "more than 175,000 stolen objects, from paintings and sculpture to jewelry and rare antiques."[20] The existence of the database has helped art detectives track down those who may have information about the stolen works, which can lead to their recovery. Other organizations established to help with the recovery of stolen art and antiquities include the International Council of Museums (ICOM) and MuseumSecurity.Org. (www.museumsecurity.org).

Ownership Issues

In recent years, questions have arisen about ownership claims related to some of the art treasures displayed in museums throughout the world. A number of these pertain to the rights of one country to display artwork that originally came from another, often through unlawful means. These situations can have unfortunate consequences for the museums involved.

In 2008, for instance, artifacts from the Bowers Museum in Santa Ana, CA, were seized by the police for being obtained illegally. It appeared that the museum's former curator had purchased them from a dealer who had allegedly smuggled them out of Thailand. For the small Southern California museum, which had worked hard over the years to hold its own against its Los Angeles competitors, the negative publicity that resulted from the incident was quite a blow.[21]

In past years, a great deal of attention has been given to artwork that was looted from Jewish families by the Nazis during World War II. Some of these works eventually ended up on display in museums whose administrators were unaware of their origins. As the sources of many of these works have been uncovered, some museums have had to return them to the families of their original owners or compensate these families in order to keep them in their collections.

Employment Opportunities

If you are interested in pursuing a career in museum work, the field offers a variety of job choices. Museum staffs can generally be divided into two groups—administration and collections.

Museum Administration

The first group encompasses those responsible for the museum's administration and operations. These can include the director and assistant director, who are in charge of the overall management of the museum and its day-to-day operations. This group also encompasses those staff members who are responsible for activities such as public relations and marketing, development (fundraising), community outreach, education, and information management. Depending on the size and financial status of the museum, some of these jobs can be combined into a single job title. For example, in a small museum, the public relations director may also be in charge of fundraising and/or community outreach.

Collections Management

The second group is comprised of those responsible for the care and management of the museum's collection. This group includes curators who are responsible for overseeing the collections, deciding on exhibits, arranging for traveling exhibitions, etc. It also includes exhibit designers who work with the curators to design and arrange the exhibits to show them off in an aesthetically pleasing manner.

Museum registrars are part of this group as well, as they catalogue the museum's collection and maintain records of information related to each item. In addition, museum conservators are responsible for the physical care of the collection and make sure conditions are right for preserving and displaying the artifacts.

Museum Volunteers

Some smaller museums rely heavily on volunteers if they don't have the funds to hire sufficient full- or part-time staff. Many museums, for instance, rely on trained volunteers called "docents" to act as tour guides or work with school groups. Volunteering at a museum is an excellent way to learn about the business if you want to find out if it would be a good field for a long-term career.

Figure 14: U.S. Colleges and Universities Offering Advanced Degrees in Museum Studies

» Baylor University: www.baylor.edu/museum_studies
» Georgetown University: www8.georgetown.edu/departments/amt/mastudies_top.html
» New York University: www.nyu.edu/fas/program/museumstudies
» San Francisco State University: www.sfsu.edu/~museumst
» University of the Arts: www.uarts.edu/academics/cad/musstudies.html
» University of Florida: www.arts.ufl.edu/mstudies
» University of Kansas: www2.ku.edu/~museumst
» University of Michigan: www.umich.edu/~ummsp/home.htm
» University of Washington: www.museum.washington.edu/museum

Figure 15: Museums in the United States and Europe Offering Internship Programs

» Art Institute of Chicago: www.artic.edu/aic/jobs/interninfo.html
» Cincinnati Art Museum: www.cincinnatiartmuseum.org
» Field Museum, Chicago: www.fieldmuseum.org/dbAdminTool/Internships_Print.asp
» Georgia O'Keeffe Museum, Santa Fe, NM: www.okeeffemuseum.org/opportunities/internships.html
» Getty Museum, Los Angeles: www.getty.edu/grants/education/grad_interns.html
» Guggenheim Museum, New York: www.guggenheim.org/education/get_involved.shtml#internships
» Museum of Modern Art, New York: www.moma.org/education/internships.html
» Museum of Science, Boston: www.mos.org/visitor_info/about_the_museum/internships
» National Baseball Hall of Fame, Cooperstown, NY: www.baseballhalloffame.org
» Philadelphia Museum of Art: www.philamuseum.org/information
» Seattle Art Museum: www.seattleartmuseum.org/Jobs/internship.asp
» Smithsonian Institution, Washington, DC: www.si.edu/ofg/internopp.htm
» Victoria and Albert Museum, London: www.vam.ac.uk/res_cons/conservation/training/internships/index.html

Education and Training

While an undergraduate degree is a necessity for many of these positions, a number of them also require advanced degrees or specialized training. A museum director or assistant director might require an advanced degree in museum studies or a master's in business administration. A museum curator is likely to need an M.A. or Ph.D. in a specialized field related to the type of museum that he or she wants to work in—art, history, natural sciences, etc.

A number of U.S. universities offer master's degree programs in museum studies. These programs may combine specialized training in a specific field with courses in museum education. Internships are often integrated into museum studies programs, and, as a result, a number of museums offer formalized internship programs to encourage students to learn about the industry from the inside out. Some of these programs are open to undergraduate as well as graduate students.

The American Association of Museums (AAM) offers a variety of publications on museum careers, which can be ordered through the organization's online bookstore (www.

JENNIFER RING

Director of Registration and Collections Bowers Museum

www.bowers.org

Jennifer Ring traveled to China three times in 2008. She also traveled for business to Denver and Houston the same year. Her schedule for 2009 looked even busier with trips planned to Poland, Japan, and China again.

Travel goes with the job as the Director of Registration and Collections at the Bowers Museum in Santa Ana, CA. Ring is in charge of all the priceless art that belongs to the museum.

"I go everywhere our artwork goes," she said. If a collection owned by the Bowers Museum is on loan to another museum, Ring travels with the collection and makes sure everything arrives safe and sound. She is also responsible for any artwork loaned to the Bowers Museum.

One of the first collections Ring oversaw when she started at the museum was a Roman glass collection. She said she was horrified and nervous at first about handling the priceless works of art. "The only thing between the Roman glass and the cement floor was my hands," she said. But Ring quickly got over the fear of touching ancient artifacts and now thinks that's one of the best parts of the job. "How many people can say they have touched the Dead Sea Scrolls or Egyptian mummies?"

Ring didn't figure out her career path until her last year of college. As a history major at California State University, Fullerton, she wasn't sure what she would do for work. All that changed after she did an unpaid internship with the Bowers Museum.

Ring said the best part of the job is being surrounded by the world's finest art every day. The worst part is the mounds of paperwork that accompany every artifact. "Data entry can be mind-numbingly boring, and there can be a lot of it," she explained.

It can be very competitive to find positions as collections managers at museums, and Jennifer admitted the job isn't for everyone. "It's not like *Indiana Jones.* Investigate the job. You must be an intern or a volunteer in order to get hired." Unpaid work is expected prior to landing a job as a collections manager, she said, because there is no other way to get the training and experience for the job.

» » »

aam-us.org). The Smithsonian Institution has extensive information on its website related to careers in museums and educational opportunities (http://museumstudies.si.edu).

Future Outlook

Virtual Museums

As noted earlier, technology has had a profound impact on the way museums are able to share their collections with the public, and it will continue to influence this practice in the future. This has been evidenced by the growing popularity of virtual museums, which allow people to view museum collections via their computers. As Joel Garreau observed in the *Washington Post*, "It is only a matter of time before our computers display the entire content of every museum on Earth—plus everything in their warehouses...."[22]

The virtual museum is not likely to replace the experience of visiting a museum in person, but it has presented new challenges for those museums trying to keep up with the times and with their competitors online. Some have responded by developing sophisticated features that give users tremendous flexibility and options online. The website of the Hermitage in Russia, for instance, allows users to search for artwork by certain attributes like painting styles or genres (www.hermitagemuseum.org), and the website of the Getty Museum in Los Angeles enables virtual visitors to watch videos about the collection as well as view artwork online (www.getty.edu).

Increased Interactivity

Another trend that is likely to become more developed in the future is the incorporation of interactivity into museum exhibits. Although viewing a museum's collection has traditionally been a passive activity involving looking rather than touching, some museums have incorporated interactive exhibits into their mix. At the Franklin Institute in Philadelphia, for example, visitors can walk through a large-scale replica of the human heart, a feature that has been part of the museum since 1954. San Francisco's Exploratorium, founded by Frank Oppenheimer in 1969, was one of the first science museums to allow visitors to learn about science through hands-on interaction with its exhibits.

For the most part, though, until recently these museums have been the exceptions rather than the rule. However, as innovations in technology have made interactivity a staple of the entertainment industry, museums are realizing that they, too, need to continue to build visitor interaction into the museum experience. One example of a museum that has addressed this issue is the Newseum in Washington, DC, a museum about the journalism profession. Operated by the Freedom Forum, it bills itself as "The Interactive Museum of News." Along with displays on the history of journalism and noted journalists, the museum offers visitors a chance to "pick up a microphone, step before a camera and experience what it's like to be a TV reporter."[23]

The popularity of virtual reality games such as Second Life may also have an impact on the museum of the future. As the Newseum readied its physical building for the public, for example, it simultaneously developed a 3-D version of the museum that users could experience by using their avatars to "walk through" the museum online.[24] It is only a matter of time before other museums follow suit.

Summary

Museums once were designed to be places where people could passively view collections of art, artifacts, and natural specimens as a means of entertainment. Today, museums not only give patrons things to look at but also offer them a way to learn, often allowing them to be an active part of this learning experience.

An increase in the number of traveling exhibits has made it possible for museums to transport their collections beyond the confines of their own walls, so that people all over the world can see and enjoy them. The Internet and World Wide Web have also allowed for the expansion of the modern-day museum through the development of the virtual museum, which brings collections to the public via computer. This has enabled more people to become electronically exposed to art, history, science, and popular culture without ever leaving their living rooms.

Some of the challenges for those working in the museum business include fundraising, promotion, and security. Museums offer employment opportunities for those with backgrounds in art, science, history, business, and communications, among other fields, as their jobs are distributed between administration and collections management.

In the future, it is expected that museums will implement more interactive exhibits and further develop the concept of the virtual museum, enabling even more people to be entertained and educated by the museum experience.

ADDITIONAL RESOURCES

Associations and Organizations

American Association of Museums: www.aam-us.org
International Council of Museums: www.icom.org
Institute of Museum and Library Sciences: www.imls.gov

Job-Hunting Resources

Global Museum: www.globalmuseum.org

Museum Careers: www.aam-us.org/aviso

Museum Employment Resource Center (MERC): www.museum-employment.com

Museum Jobs: www.museumjobs.com

Books

Burdick, Jan E. *Creative Careers in Museums*. New York: Allworth Press, 2008.

Camenson, Blythe. *Opportunities in Museum Careers*. New York: McGraw-Hill, 2006.

Dennett, Andrea Stulman. *Weird and Wonderful: The Dime Museum in America*. New York: New York University Press, 1997.

Rubin, Saul. *Offbeat Museums: The Collections and Curators of America's Most Unusual Museums*. Santa Monica, CA: Santa Monica Press, 1997.

Schlatter, N. Elizabeth. *Museum Careers: A Practical Guide for Novices and Students*. Walnut Creek, CA: Left Coast Press, 2008.

Magazines and Trade Publications

Museum: www.aam-us.org.

Museums Journal: www.museumsassociation.org

Smithsonian Magazine: www.smithsonianmag.com.

Websites

Museum Marketing: www.museummarketingtips.com

Museum Spot: www.museumspot.com

ENDNOTES

1. See Steve Schultze, "Corpses May Revive Museum," *Milwaukee Journal Sentinel*, 15 January 2008, A1.

2. See Geoffrey D. Lewis, "History of Museums," *Encyclopedia Britannica Online*, www.britannica.com.

3. See Ellen Hirzy, "History of Museums," *Encarta*, encarta.msn.com.

4. See Charles Coleman Sellers, *Mr. Peale's Museum: Charles Wilson Peale and the First Popular Museum of Science and Art*, New York: Norton, 1980.

5. Andrea Stulman Dennett, *Weird and Wonderful: The Dime Museum in America*, New York: New York University Press: 1997, p. 5.

6. Eileen Hooper-Greenhill, *Museums and the Shaping of Knowledge*, London: Routledge, 1992: 1.

7. See American Association of Museums, www.aam-us.org.

8. See Kelly Rayburn, "Alameda Council Agrees to Keep Funding Museum," *Oakland Tribune*, 23 June 2007, 1.

9. American Association of Museums, www.aam-us.org.

10. See Bob Keyes, "Art Community Thrilled with Donation to Colby: The Major Gift Will Make a Big Impact on Waterville and the State as a Whole," *Portland Press Herald*, 19 May 2007, A1.

11. Lynette Haaland, "Cultural Sites Eye Revenues, Place Importance on Events," *Rochester Business Journal,* 27 July 2007, 20.

12. Randy Kennedy, "Learning to Mix Business with Art," *New York Times,* 30 January 2008, E1.

13. Peter Dobrin, "Tut Exhibit Eyes Record for Visitors," *Philadelphia Inquirer,* 5 September 2007, A1.

14. See Ashley Bach, "Museum Budget Relies on ArtsFair," *Seattle Times,* 27 July 2007, B3.

15. See Kathy Orton, "Museums Are Turning Up the Heat," *Washington Post,* 1 February 2008, T47.

16. "Campaign for Museums: Museums and Galleries Prepare for UK's Biggest Museum Promotion and Reveal Their Objects of Desire," *Presswire,* 21 April 2005, 1.

17. See Andy Johns, "More than 10,000 Students Scheduled to See T. Rex at Anniston Museum of Natural History," *Anniston Star,* 25 September 2007.

18. Gaile Robinson, "Museum School," *Fort Worth Star-Telegram,* 27 January 2008.

19. Deborah Ball, "A Stash of Stolen Art: Insurers, Investigators Work to Prevent Snatched Works from Being Resold, Ransomed," *Wall Street Journal,* 24 August 2004, B1.

20. Stevenson Swanson, "Loss Database One Answer to Art Thievery: Art Loss Register Has Helped in the Recovery of More Than $138 Million in Purloined Works," *Chicago Tribune,* 4 October 2006, 12.

21. See Mike Boehm, "Bowers Museum Didn't Need This Publicity," *Los Angeles Times,* 26 January 2008.

22. Joel Garreau, "Is There a Future for Old-Fashioned Museums?" *Washington Post,* 7 October 2007, R10.

23. Newseum, www.newseum.org.

24. See Garreau, R10.

8

Theme Parks ANDI STEIN

When Knott's Berry Farm unveiled its Silver Bullet roller coaster, dozens of coaster enthusiasts began lining up as early as 5 A.M., to be among the first to ride the park's latest attraction. Some had even bid hundreds of dollars in an online charity auction sponsored by the park to be among the first 60 people to inaugurate the high-speed coaster that featured an assortment of twists, curves, and loops and turned riders upside-down six times during its two-and-a-half-minute journey. While this may sound crazy to some, for die-hard roller coaster fans, the chance to be the first to try what *Orange County Register* reporter Michele Himmelberg called "the longest, fastest and tallest suspended coaster in the West"[1] was well worth the time and money.

Roller coasters and other thrill rides are an integral part of today's theme parks. They offer patrons an opportunity to live on the edge while dangling upside down or being tossed from side to side for a few frenetic minutes of adrenaline rush. But for many, theme parks represent more than just thrill rides. They give people a chance to leave their troubles behind for a few hours and escape into a simulated world where they can be entertained, amused, and even educated in a safe, family-friendly environment.

Whatever the draw, theme parks are indisputably a big part of today's entertainment industry. They include all-purpose parks such as Knott's Berry Farm and Disneyland, which are designed to appeal to all ages. They also encompass more specialized offerings such as Legoland and Sesame Place, which are aimed at specific market segments. In 2006, 335 million people visited the approximately 400 U.S. theme parks, resulting in revenues of

$11.5 billion, according to the International Association of Amusement Parks and Attractions (IAAPA).[2]

Although the theme park as we know it today is a relatively new phenomenon—largely thanks to Walt Disney and the establishment of Disneyland in 1955—the concept of a public place where people could congregate for amusement and entertainment is not new. In fact, the roots of the modern-day theme park can be traced to medieval times, when people gathered in large, open-air public spaces to enjoy games, refreshments, and other recreational diversions. Over the centuries, these primitive parks evolved into the highly structured, well-oiled amusement centers of the present, which accommodate thousands of visitors a day. The challenges of managing today's theme parks involve a constant attention to safety, a focus on creative marketing and promotional activities, the hiring and supervision of large numbers of employees, and the need to develop innovative rides and attractions.

This chapter will examine the origins of today's theme parks and how they have evolved over the years. It will also explore some of the issues and challenges that those working in the industry encounter on a day-to-day basis and the job opportunities available to those interested in working for a theme park.

History and Background

Early Amusement Parks

The amusement park industry can trace its beginnings to the pleasure gardens of medieval Europe, according to the National Amusement Park Historical Association (NAPHA).[3] These gardens served as a means for people to escape from the drudgery of their everyday lives and work. Although they lacked the finesse of today's theme parks, these pleasure gardens offered patrons an opportunity to enjoy live entertainment such as plays and puppet shows, fireworks, games, dancing, and, in some cases, even simple amusement rides. Some also gave people a chance to indulge at the drinking establishments that were often an essential part of the pleasure gardens. Many of the early pleasure gardens disappeared by the 1700s, but one still remains: Bakken in Denmark, north of Copenhagen, opened in 1593 and is considered the world's oldest amusement park still in operation.

Development of the Trolley Park

By the 1800s, the amusement park industry began to emerge in the United States as a result of a lifestyle change. As industrialization replaced agriculture, urban areas grew. People moved from farms to cities and relied on mass transit such as electric trolleys to get around. Ironically, one of the key developments in the growth of the amusement park industry can be attributed to the many electric trolley companies that existed in these cities.

Local utility companies supplied the electricity that enabled these trolleys to operate. They frequently charged the trolley companies a flat fee for this electricity, regardless of how many people used the trolleys. The trolleys had a high level of ridership during the week when people commuted to work, but they often sat idle on weekends, which ultimately cost the trolley companies money. The owners of these companies realized that if they built amusement parks at the end of their trolley lines, they could encourage people to ride the cars on weekends. Some of the best-known early U.S. amusement parks, such as Willow Grove Park, which opened outside Philadelphia in 1896, got their start this way.

Initially, these trolley parks, as they were known, were simply expansions of the medieval pleasure gardens, with picnic grounds, dance halls, food stands, etc. But, as Al Griffin explained, they were a great attraction for the people of that time who had "no television, no movies, no radio, or any other form of inexpensive entertainment. The appeal of picnicking in a shady grove after working in a dingy factory all week, plus the novelty of music and the thrill of rides, made the Sunday trolley excursion almost irresistible."[4]

Rides and Attractions

Rides became an important part of the landscape of the American amusement park toward the end of the nineteenth century. This was largely due to the success of the 1893 World's Columbian Exposition in Chicago. It was there that the public was introduced to the Ferris wheel, pioneered by George Ferris. The Exposition also featured the debut of the Midway, a stretch of rides, games, and concession stands that is often associated with the traditional amusement park. After the Exposition, many of the Midway rides were moved to Coney Island, NY, a seaside resort that became part of the amusement park scene in 1895. Coney Island quickly developed into one of the most famous amusement centers in the country and set the standard for many that followed.

By the early 1900s, the amusement park industry was flourishing. Sophisticated, thrill-oriented attractions such as roller coasters and water rides replaced the primitive rides of the early parks. According to the NAPHA, by 1919, at the peak of the industry, more than 1,500 amusement parks existed throughout the United States.[5]

Depression and Change

The heyday of the amusement park was short-lived. The Great Depression in the 1930s and the onset of World War II had a drastic impact on the amusement business, and the number of parks dropped significantly. Even after the war ended in 1945, people preferred to spend their leisure dollars on movies, theater, television, and other forms of entertainment.

Many of the original trolley amusement parks had aged considerably. They were no longer considered clean, safe recreational havens for visitors and their families. It was about this time that a man named Walt Disney realized the potential to create a new type of park, one that was designed to attract the next generation of amusement seekers.

Birth of the Modern-Day Theme Park

Walt Disney was already well established in the animated film industry by the 1940s. In the 1950s, he decided to use his creative talents to try and change the amusement park industry for the better. Disney had an initial vision to create a recreational environment that would appeal to adults as well as children. It would be based on the themes and characters he had made famous through his movies. As Disney's plans grew, it became apparent that Disneyland would be more than just a traditional amusement park: It was to become a collection of themed lands, each featuring rides and attractions that added an element of fantasy to the amusement park experience.

Disney used the relatively new medium of television to introduce the American public to his vision. Each week on his ABC-sponsored "Disneyland" television program, he offered viewers a chance to "preview" a different area of the park. He described the features of each section of the park and allowed viewers to follow the construction along with him. Soon after Disneyland officially opened in Anaheim, CA, on July 17, 1955, it didn't take long for the park to become a hit with the public. Disneyland ushered in the era of the modern-day theme park, and, more than 50 years later, it still serves as a model for the industry.

New Park Growth

The success of Disneyland inspired other theme-based parks. Six Flags over Texas opened near Dallas in 1961, followed by dozens of other parks that sprang up in the 1960s and 1970s. As the theme park industry grew, these began replacing the more traditional amusement parks that had been so popular at the turn of the twentieth century.

The Disney Company capitalized on the success of Disneyland with the opening of Walt Disney World in 1971, and Epcot Center in 1982, in Orlando, FL. Disney parks in Tokyo, Paris, and Hong Kong soon followed. Others jumped on the theme park bandwagon as well. The first Universal Studios park opened in Los Angeles in 1964, featuring a Hollywood theme. Sesame Place, a park geared toward young children based on the PBS hit *Sesame Street,* debuted outside Philadelphia in 1980. Six Flags over Texas grew into an organization that now includes 21 parks throughout the United States.

By the 1990s, the modern-day theme park was firmly entrenched in U.S. culture, offering exciting new opportunities for park visitors as well as some new challenges for those in the industry.

Figure 16: World's Most Visited Amusement Parks

Park	Number of Visitors (2007)
1. Magic Kingdom, Walt Disneyworld, Florida	16,640,000
2. Disneyland, Anaheim, California	14,730,000

3.	Tokyo Disneyland	12,900,000
4.	Disneyland Paris	10,600,000
5.	Everland, Kyonggi-Do, South Korea	7, 500,000
6.	Blackpool Pleasure Beach, Blackpool, UK	6,000,000
7.	Disneyland Hong Kong	5,200,000
8.	Tivoli Gardens, Copenhagen, Denmark	4,396,000
9.	Europa-Park, Rust, Germany	3,950,000
10.	Port Adventure, Salou, Spain	3,500,000
11.	Paramount Canada's Wonderland, Maple, Canada	3,230,000
12.	De Efteling Kaatsheuvel, Netherlands	3,200,000
13.	Gardaland, Castelnuovo del Garda, Italy	3,100,000
14.	Six Flags Mexico, Mexico City	2,054,000
15.	Playcenter, Sao Paolo, Brazil	1,600,000

Source: Forbes Traveler World's Most Visited Amusement Parks, www.forbestraveler.com

Challenges and Trends

Safety as Priority

Like many entertainment venues, theme parks present a set of management challenges for those involved in their day-to-day operations. No challenge is more important, however, than that of protecting the safety of patrons. And nothing brings more adverse publicity to a park than when this safety is compromised. In 2003, for example, an accident on Disneyland's Big Thunder Mountain Railroad made the front pages of both the *Orange County Register* and the *Los Angeles Times*. The accident involved a train car derailment that left one person dead and ten injured. Just as a plane crash or any other type of incident involving large numbers of injuries can make the public very uneasy, an accident at a theme park can do the same. An accident like the one on Big Thunder Mountain Railroad can stir up people's fears and make them leery about the overall safety of a park.

In reality, however, the number of fatalities and injuries caused by theme park accidents is surprisingly low, given the number of people who visit theme parks each year. The International Association of Amusement Parks and Attractions (IAAPA) partners with the National Safety Council (NSC) to collect information about theme park accidents. These organizations estimate that out of the more than 300 million people who attended theme parks in 2005, there were 1,713 injuries involving park attractions. Of these incidents, 132 required overnight hospitalization.[6]

But the statistics don't change the fact that safety comes first for those within the industry. Theme parks around the globe go to great lengths to ensure that their facilities are safe and well maintained in order to protect their guests and provide them with peace of mind.

Routine Inspections

Daily inspections are crucial to ensure that a park's attractions are running smoothly and safely. For instance, ride inspectors at Orlando's SeaWorld park begin inspecting rides each day at 4 A.M., well before the park opens, according to an article in the *Orlando Sentinel*. They not only check the mechanics of each ride but also test it by riding on it themselves to make sure everything feels normal.[7]

The Walt Disney Company has become a leader in park safety in recent years, in its quest to be number one in safe operations. Within the last few years, for instance, Walt Disney World has posted more than 10,000 signs containing safety instructions throughout the park to keep visitors informed about safety precautions and procedures.

Employee Training

Employee training is another way to ensure a safe environment in a theme park. Many parks incorporate training practices developed by their own facilities. In some cases, they also work in conjunction with IAAPA and the American Society for Testing and Materials (ASTM) to develop training programs. This safety training may encompass workshops and seminars. It also can include the creation of detailed operations manuals, which explain the safety procedures used for different rides. Training is provided to ride operators, maintenance personnel, guest relations managers, or anyone else whose job might involve the safety of a park's visitors.

Visitor Safety Education

Ironically, sometimes theme park patrons themselves may cause accidents to occur. This can happen when park guests, for example, ignore posted signs, fail to secure safety restraints properly, and act irresponsibly by standing up while a ride is moving.

To better educate theme park guests about safety procedures, Robert Niles, editor of the *Theme Park Insider* online newsletter (www.themeparkinsider.com), has come up with suggested guidelines for how to stay safe at a theme park. These include tips on obeying sign instructions, using safety harnesses properly, avoiding turbulent rides immediately after eating, and wearing protective gear to reduce incidences of heat stroke in hot weather. As Niles explained in his newsletter, "Almost all theme park accidents can be prevented."[8]

Marketing and Promotion

If safety is a top priority for theme park managers, marketing and promotion are not too far behind. Amusement and theme parks rely on well-planned marketing efforts to make customers aware of what they have to offer. They also use these promotions as a way to keep park guests interested in returning for follow-up visits. Today's theme parks use an assortment of marketing and promotional tools and techniques to encourage high rates of attendance and repeat business.

Customer Discounts

Many theme park marketers were put to the test after September 11, 2001, when terrorist attacks on the United States brought the travel and tourism industry to a virtual standstill. For several years following the attacks, attendance throughout the tourism industry plummeted, as people were reluctant to travel, particularly by airplane. For vacation destinations such as Florida and California, the attacks took a particularly harsh toll on tourism. Theme parks, too, were forced to step up their marketing and promotional efforts post-9/11.

One of the results of these marketing efforts was the increased number of park discounts, particularly those targeting local residents. Shortly after 9/11, for instance, Disneyland began offering discounted rates to Southern California residents, while Universal Studios in Los Angeles touted a promotion that allowed locals to buy a one-day ticket and get a year's pass for free.

Some of the promotions that were launched by theme parks shortly after 9/11 are still used today, as they have been so successful. As *Orange County Register* columnist Jonathan Lansner noted, "The truth is that competitive pressures keep discount deals plentiful and in fact, may have increased the scope and availability of these bargains."[9]

Corporate Partnerships

Corporate partnerships have been a long-standing way for theme parks to use their marketing muscle to make an impression on the public. According to Janet Wasko in *Understanding Disney,* "The original Disneyland involved 32 companies that sponsored exhibits or restaurants at the park, including Carnation, General Electric, and Monsanto."[10]

Corporate partnerships bring financial incentives and name recognition for both the theme parks and the corporations working with them. The website of Paramount's Great America in Santa Clara, CA, for example, features a page promoting the benefits of partnering with the park in ways that include "in-park sponsorship of rides and attractions, television and Internet exposure, retail sales, promotion, event sponsorship or sampling plus many other benefits."[11]

ConAgra Foods partnered with Six Flags Inc. to become the "Official Food of Playtime." The organization proceeded to add the names of some of its more popular brands to rides at various Six Flags parks. This resulted in the "Slim Jim Extreme Roller Coaster" and the "Orville Redenbacher Theater."[12]

Over the years, corporate partnerships have gotten more and more sophisticated and innovative. In England, for example, the Tussauds Group, which owns the Alton Towers Park in Staffordshire, partnered with the Flytxt mobile technology provider. Together, they created an interactive promotion, which included a combination of radio ads and cell phones. Radio listeners were encouraged to send a text message to Flytxt and were rewarded with a 2-for-1 ticket to the park. Those who responded then received follow-up reminder prompts on their cell phones, encouraging them to redeem the coupons over the weekend. This promotion was unique as it not only combined a typical partnership between a theme park and corporation but also got park patrons actively involved in the promotion itself.[13]

Advertising Campaigns

Print, radio, and television advertising are all a routine part of theme park marketing. Synchronized ad campaigns designed to reach large numbers of people have been used by venues such as the Disney and Six Flag parks as well as by smaller, regional parks.

In 1987, the Disney Company debuted one of its more famous, long-running ad campaigns. In a television advertisement, New York Giants football star Phil Simms was asked about his plans following his team's Super Bowl win. His reply: "I'm going to Disney World," became part of a 17-year advertising campaign for the company. The promotion subsequently featured sports greats such as Joe Montana, Michael Jordan, and Mark McGwire, who repeated the now-legendary phrase, according to a *Wall Street Journal* article.[14]

Six Flags, Inc. launched an unusual but catchy advertising campaign in 2004 featuring an elderly bald man wearing thick, black glasses. Dubbed "Mr. Six" by the company, he appeared in ads that ran for several years. In these television ads, Mr. Six danced feverishly while trying to round up bored youngsters and encourage them to hop on a bus to their local Six Flags park. The ad campaign was so offbeat that it resulted in some bonus publicity for the park, as Mr. Six was subsequently invited to appear on *Good Morning America.*

To celebrate the 50th anniversary of Disneyland, Disney ad executives implemented a global advertising campaign, inviting viewers to come join in "The Happiest Celebration on Earth." The initial television advertisement debuted during the Tournament of Roses Parade on January 1, 2005, where Mickey Mouse just happened to be the parade's grand marshall. In a strategically planned campaign, Disney used the promotional spot as a means to encourage attendance at all of its theme parks worldwide, not just Disneyland. The company ran local variations on the ad to suit each market.

Despite the high costs, even smaller regional parks frequently rely on advertising to boost their attendance figures. Western Playland Amusement Park in El Paso, TX, uses print and broadcast advertisements in English and Spanish to reach audiences in both the United States and Mexico. Woodland Park in Amarillo, TX, supplements its TV and radio ads with advertisements on billboards and bus benches. Pacific Park in Santa Monica, CA, relies on direct mail advertisements to promote its birthday party program to mothers of young children.[15]

Special Events

In recent years, a number of theme parks have used the sponsorship of special events as a way to attract visitors. These events often cater to specific target markets, especially in regional parks. This enables them to take advantage of what a particular region has to offer.

In the culturally diverse San Francisco Bay area, for example, Paramount's Great America has sponsored ethnic festivals such as a Carnaval en Verano Latin music fair, Japanese Festival of Anime, and Asian Heritage Festival. Six Flags Great Adventure in Jackson, NJ, kicked off its "Summer of Festivals" in 2002 featuring 10 different ethnic themes. One of the most successful, long-running theme park special events has been Knott's Berry Farm's Halloween promotion, "Knott's Scary Farm." Started in 1973, the event takes place in the evenings throughout the month of October when the park is transformed into a spooky setting of monsters, mazes, and mayhem.

Birthdays and anniversaries are a good way for theme parks to make the most of their marketing efforts. The 50th anniversary of Disneyland in 2005 became the focus of an 18-month celebration that encompassed a variety of marketing and promotional activities. Likewise, when Sesame Place in Pennsylvania turned 25, the park beefed up marketing activities to promote its "Summer Nights 25th Birthday Party." Milestone events such as these can frequently result in good financial returns for theme parks. The Disney Company's 50th anniversary celebration had a big payoff for both Disneyland and its sister park, California Adventure, which saw attendance increases of 8.5% and 3.6%, respectively, in 2005.[16]

Product Merchandising

Product merchandising can be an extremely lucrative aspect of a theme park's marketing efforts. Theme park managers count on patrons wanting to take a small piece of their experience home with them in the way of T-shirts, plush toys, magnets, keychains, etc. These souvenirs serve as long-lasting reminders of the fun that was had at the park and, ideally, provide an incentive to return for more.

Knott's Berry Farm has had a 20+ year licensing agreement with the estate of the late Charles M. Schulz, creator of the popular *Peanuts* characters. An area of the park is designated as "Camp Snoopy," and many of the products sold at Knott's feature *Peanuts* characters. According to an article in *Amusement Business*, products featuring the likeness of Snoopy account for 25% of the park's merchandise sales.[17]

Likewise, when the Het Land Van Ooit amusement park in The Netherlands introduced TV's *Sesame Street* characters into the park in 2001, the addition of the character's products in park gift shops increased merchandise revenues by 23%.[18] In short, within the theme park industry, marketing and merchandising go hand in hand.

Competition and Innovation

A good mixture of marketing and promotional efforts can often work effectively to draw customers into today's theme parks. But underneath all the sizzle and flair of these efforts, there needs to be one crucial element: something worthwhile to market and promote. The growing number of theme parks, particularly in California and Florida, has made for intense competition among park owners.

MICHELE WISCHMEYER

Marketing/Sales Manager, Knott's Berry Farm
www.knotts.com

Every workday for the past 24 years, Michele Wischmeyer has headed to Knott's Berry Farm. As the director of marketing and sales, Wischmeyer oversees a staff of 18 who do everything from handling media requests to approving all creative materials for commercials and print ads. "Every project is something new. Every event is different. Every day is exciting. It makes waking up and getting to work a lot of fun," she said.

Wischmeyer graduated from college and planned on entering the work force as a television reporter. But when the reality sank in that she would have to leave the Los Angeles area, she decided to try something else. She landed a job in television production at Knott's Berry Farm. That job required her to shoot and edit videotape and assist television reporters to get the material they needed for their stories. This first career stop showed her that her talents really lie behind the camera—organizing and planning stories and shoots—and not so much in front of the lens.

After several years of hard work, she was promoted to Media Production Manager at Knott's. Soon after, she was promoted again to include the public relations and marketing work as Creative Services Manager. Then, in 2006, she took over the entire department as the Marketing and Sales Director.

Wischmeyer loves her work, especially the creative assignments that allow her to plan extraordinary events like a recent World Championship Ping-Pong contest at the theme park.

In her current position, she said, every day is a whirlwind. She oversees the group sales staff, public relations team, development of the websites, tourism to the park, the company's three Soak City water parks, and youth sales. Wischmeyer is out of breath just going through her list of responsibilities.

The part of her job that she likes the least is managing people. "I love the creative. The step down to deal with the human side is hard."

Wischmeyer said the best way to succeed in your career is to find something that you are passionate about and stick with it. "If it's a passion, you will enjoy your job. Make sure it's your passion."

» » »

Today's theme park managers are constantly trying to come up with new and exciting attractions to entice visitors to come through their gates and remain loyal customers once they do.

Thrill-Packed Roller Coasters

Perhaps no attraction epitomizes the modern-day theme park experience better than the roller coaster. In recent years, technology has allowed for the creation of coasters that are higher, faster, and more adrenaline-pumping than ever before. For many theme parks, having at least a few exhilarating roller coasters is essential to provide enough marketing ammunition to attract visitors. Consequently, it seems that most major theme park operators try to introduce their version of the "latest and greatest" coaster every two or three years in order to stay competitive.

Six Flags Magic Mountain in Valencia, CA, is the place to go in Southern California for thrill rides. In 2008, the park had 15 coasters in place with names such as Scream, Viper, and Tatsu, which means "dragon" in Japanese. The company's sister park, Six Flags Great Adventure, is home to KingdaKa, which it claims to be the "tallest, fastest roller coaster on Earth,"[19] standing at 45 stories and racing along at 128 mph. Disney's newest coaster, Expedition Everest, which opened at its Animal Kingdom park in Orlando in 2006, combines traditional roller coaster thrills with robotics. As visitors wind through a 199-foot replica of Mount Everest, they have an unexpected encounter with the Abominable Snowman.

Roller coasters are such an integral part of amusement and theme parks that they have attracted their own loyal following. A Minneapolis-based nonprofit organization called American Coaster Enthusiasts (ACE) boasts 8,000 members who travel the world to ride as many coasters as humanly possible. Knott's Berry Farm hosts the group every year at its Winter Coaster Solace, giving group members access to the park's coasters for several hours before opening and after closing times. For parks wanting to beat the competition, a bigger, faster roller coaster is often the way to go.

Broadway-Style and TV-Based Shows

Roller coasters aren't the only innovations used by amusement and theme parks to keep up with competition. In recent years, parks have begun to add attractions designed for more sedentary guests (such as parents and grandparents) who want to be entertained in a less heart- and stomach-jolting manner. One of these innovations has involved adding a touch of Broadway to the theme park experience.

Disney's Aladdin, A Musical Spectacular premiered in 2003 at Disney's California Adventure, ushering in what one reporter referred to as "a new direction for theme park entertainment."[20] Based on the company's animated film *Aladdin,* the show featured costumes, staging, scenery, and special effects that equaled those seen in traditional Broadway productions. Disney followed its *Aladdin* show a year later at its Disneyland park with *Snow White—An Enchanting New Musical,* based on the company's first full-length animated feature.

Busch Gardens in Tampa Bay, FL, followed Disney's lead when it debuted *KaTonga, Musical Tales From the Jungle* in 2004, featuring large-scale puppets, elaborate costumes, and original music and choreography. When Hong Kong Disneyland opened in 2005, it featured a mini-version of the Disney Company's hit Broadway show, *The Lion King*.

Another innovation in theme park entertainment has been the creation of shows based on television hits. In 2001, Disney created a park version of its ABC mega-hit *Who Wants to Be a Millionaire?* for both its California Adventure park in Anaheim and Disney-MGM Studios park in Orlando. The show relied on volunteers from the audience to re-create the popular game show that captivated television audiences in the late 1990s and early 2000s. Universal Studios in Orlando followed suit with the introduction of *Fear Factor Live*, based on the NBC reality hit, *Fear Factor*. Audience members were invited to participate in a series of on-stage stunts that represented a scaled-down version of those depicted on the TV show.

Interactive, Technology-Based Attractions

Walt Disney pioneered the concept of audio-animatronics in the 1950s, using robotic technology to create 3-D, life-like animated figures. Today animatronics are a staple of Disneyland and other theme parks throughout the world. But for today's younger generations who have grown up with the Internet, cell phones, video games, iPods, and other, more sophisticated technologies, these animatronics are old fashioned and outdated. They are a form of entertainment that is too passive for today's youth who are used to more hands-on, interactive forms of entertainment.

Fortunately for the theme park industry, the swift development of new technologies has enabled many park owners and managers to create attractions that allow for more interactivity. They showcase the kinds of special effects today's younger generations have become accustomed to.

Disney's "Buzz Lightyear's Astro Blasters," inspired by the movie *Toy Story*, is an example of this trend. Riders occupy cars equipped with laser guns. They aim at flashing targets as the ride moves along its track, earning points for each target they hit. Disney first debuted the ride in its Magic Kingdom park in Orlando in 1998 and opened a version in Anaheim in 2005 as part of the park's 50th anniversary celebration. Quassy Amusement Park features an interactive water play area called "Saturation Station," where park patrons can play on slides, fire off water cannons, and cool off under a 300-gallon water-dumping bucket. The park also put in an attraction called the "Extreme Zone," featuring a 24-foot-high rock-climbing wall.[21]

Employment Opportunities

In an industry where thousands of customers are likely to walk through a theme park's gates in a single day, recruiting, hiring, and training the right people to provide service to these customers are absolutely crucial. If you are interested in seeking employment in this growing segment of the entertainment field, you need an understanding of how this employment process works because it is slightly different from that of the other fields covered in this book.

Recruitment Practices

Despite the broad scope and size of theme parks, in most parts of the world the amusement and theme park industry is a seasonal business. It is largely affected by weather and the available leisure time of visitors. While parks in warm weather locations are able to remain open throughout the year, those in less ideal climates are limited to a shortened season, generally between 3–6 months. Because of this, many theme parks rely heavily on part-time, seasonal employees to staff their facilities. Even those parks that are able to stay open year-round have definite high and low seasons that largely revolve around school vacation times.

From a hiring perspective, this presents certain challenges to park owners and managers who need to recruit employees who can work within this limited time frame. It is therefore no surprise that the majority of theme park employees tend to be high school or college students whose availability mirrors the high seasons of the parks. Since the potential employee pool is limited, many parks put a great deal of time and effort into recruiting their staffs, often starting the recruitment process months before a park's peak season begins.

Cedar Point in Sandusky, OH, is the fifth largest amusement park in the United States. Every summer the park hires close to 5,000 college students to run concession stands, operate rides, serve as retail clerks and wait staff, etc. Because of the park's Midwest location, Cedar Point is only open six months a year, from May to October, but the company begins its recruiting efforts in December by attending college fairs in six different states and occasionally recruiting workers from Europe through student exchange programs. The company also offers low-cost housing to many of its college-age staff as an incentive for those who are not within easy driving distance of the park.

Many amusement and theme parks now rely on the Internet to screen and hire job applicants. The Tussauds Group, which operates five theme parks in the United Kingdom and Germany, uses websites for each individual park to post job announcements and collect electronic applications, eliminating the need to process thousands of paper applications.

If you're interested in working for a theme park, find out what the company's recruitment practices involve. You may want to start out as a seasonal employee in a customer service job. This will give you an opportunity to learn the business from the ground up, which can be invaluable if you ultimately want to pursue a full-time career in the industry.

Advancement within the Industry

While working in a low-level customer service job at a theme park can be an adequate temporary job or provide a fun diversion for the summer, it may not be enough for those who are serious about the business as a long-term career option. So how can you make the transition from seasonal ride operator to a more permanent management position?

Because many parks do need full-time employees as well as seasonal staff, there are opportunities built into the theme park structure to help people move up in the ranks. The Tussauds Group, for example, offers a training and accreditation program that allows part-time, seasonal employees a chance to gain proficiency in leadership, customer service, and retail management. The program encourages those who want to stay in the business to expand their repertoire of skills, which can make them more marketable for the long term.

Once you've completed your college education, opportunities exist in management positions such as human resources, sales and marketing, public relations, engineering and design, and maintenance among other possibilities. Some theme park companies such as Universal Studios and the Walt Disney Company post full-time openings on their corporate websites. In an industry such as this one where the field is evolving, employment possibilities look promising.

Future Outlook

Interaction and Excitement to Engage Younger Customers

A survey of 122 general managers of North American theme parks and attractions indicated that

> People are turning more and more to interactive experiences in which learning and entertainment are blended. Technology has provided an opportunity to many operators in the attractions industry...to provide this type of experience.[22]

The movement toward increased interactivity is likely to play a big part in the future of the theme park. One trend may include the incorporation of cell phones into the theme park experience, where guests will be able to receive messages on their phones that give them clues about where to find special features hidden throughout a park.

Hand in hand with interactivity will be a focus on more excitement. The popularity of extreme sports such as bungee jumping, mountain biking, and snowboarding is likely to spill over into the theme park arena. The rock-climbing wall installed by Quassy Amusement Park a few years ago in its "Extreme Zone" is a good example of what promises to be a growing trend in more extreme sport attractions designed to appeal to a younger crowd.

ANN HOLBROOK

Production Coordinator, Guest Talent, Disneyland
www.disneyland.com

As production coordinator for guest talent at Disneyland, Ann Holbrook works primarily with youth groups to ensure their performance at the Happiest Place on Earth is the best it can possibly be. Holbrook has worked with singers, dancers, and high school bands. She's even helped organize 400 members of a baton-twirling group. "I coordinate all the details to make it a reality," she said.

A typical day for Holbrook might include preparing signs, coordinating costumes, or setting up a stage so that the space is right for a group. She also holds auditions for young people who want to perform at Disneyland. "I have to make sure the groups meet Disney's entertainment standards. Very young performers can be extremely cute, but if they can't get on stage and actually perform, it just won't work," she explained.

Holbrook also works with creative groups who attend one of many workshops at Disneyland. The workshops give the kids a chance to work with music directors or choreographers to fine-tune their performances. "I'm really proud of our program," she said.

Holbrook landed the job in Guest Talent after working as part of the events team that helped open the California Adventure Park and Downtown Disney. Her background in teaching and theater was a perfect fit for what she does now. She has a degree in musical theater and worked as a substitute teacher before landing the job at Disney. Holbrook still loves to teach and continues teaching musical theater at a public high school in Covina two nights a week.

If working at Disney and teaching weren't enough, Holbrook also performs on stage. She's been singing with the Mitch Hanlon Singers Group for 11 years and plans to continue. The group can be seen just about every summer when the Hollywood Bowl Orchestra features songs from theater productions.

» » »

Relaxation Options for Older Customers

On the flip side of the interests of the younger market, however, are the changing tastes of the largest segment of the population—the Baby Boomers. Members of this group are now the parents and grandparents of today's youth. By 2010, the oldest Baby Boomers will be 65. If theme parks hope to continue to attract this audience, they will need to add features that appeal to them as well.

The aging of the Baby Boomers is likely to result in a demand for more park comfort. This will include aesthetically pleasing surroundings such as gardens and fountains and a greater number of comfortable seating areas, according to an article in *American Demographics*.[23] This is likely to be accompanied by a growing interest in a greater variety of food venues. Boomers are likely to want sit-down restaurants where they can relax while their children play. They will want more sophisticated cuisine to supplement the traditional fast-food facilities found in many of today's parks.

Better Time Management for All Customers

Time management is another factor that could have an impact on the future of the theme park industry. As parks continue to add more and more attractions, it may become difficult for visitors to see everything they want to in a single visit. In addition, for an audience with a short attention span, having to wait in long lines can take away from the overall park experience. Some parks are already starting to take steps to tackle this growing customer interest in more efficient time management.

The Disney Company began to address this issue a few years ago when it implemented a "Fast Pass" system for park guests. Patrons can now obtain free passes that assign them specific times when they can ride some of the Disney parks' most popular rides such as Space Mountain and Big Thunder Mountain Railroad. This frees them up to do other things at the park. Then they can return at their designated time to ride these attractions without having to wait in long lines.

Many parks now encourage visitors to purchase their admission tickets online before coming to the park to avoid waiting in long lines at the gates. Some parks such as Kings Dominion have even offered discounted rates to those who buy their tickets online. With more and more park visitors now having access to the Internet, this trend is likely to grow in popularity.

A few theme parks have introduced the concept of a VIP pass. Customers are offered the option of purchasing an admission ticket at a premium, which allows them the privilege of bypassing long lines. Both Universal Studios Hollywood and Legoland have experimented with this in recent years, with other parks working on developing similar programs. As theme parks continue to grow and expand, programs and promotions designed to save guests time and make their experiences more enjoyable are apt to become routine parts of a park visit.

Summary

The amusement and theme park industry has seen a great deal of change and growth since its early beginnings in the pleasure gardens of medieval Europe. The U.S. trolley parks of the late 1800s gave way to the all-encompassing, modern-day theme park concept pioneered by Walt Disney in the 1950s. A period of growth and development in the 1980s and 1990s resulted in what is now an $11.5 billion industry.

Today's theme park owners and managers routinely grapple with a broad range of challenges and issues. These include keeping park visitors safe, marketing and promoting their attractions, coming up with new and innovative rides and shows, and recruiting, hiring, and training staff.

The industry was hard hit by the terrorist attacks of September 11, 2001, which impacted the tourism industry and resulted in lower attendance figures for many parks throughout the United States. But in recent years, the industry appears to have rebounded as park attendance has steadily increased in the years since 9/11. Analysts predict the industry will see growth in the area of attractions that feature more hands-on interactivity as well as those that address the needs and interests of the aging Baby Boom population.

As Don Mooradian and Matt Benz noted in an article in *Amusement Business,*

> The now multi-faceted amusement and theme park industry, like the roller coasters that have been its mainstay, has twisted, turned and learned how to adapt to the times. But the industry is sure to remain popular as long as people look for excitement and diversion, something not likely to change for a long time to come.[24]

ADDITIONAL RESOURCES

Associations and Organizations

American Coaster Enthusiasts (ACE): www.aceonline.org

International Association for Amusement Parks and Attractions (IAPPA): www.iaapa.org

National Amusement Park Historical Association (NAPHA): www.napha.org

Job-Hunting Resources

Theme Park Jobs.com: www.themeparkjobs.com

Theme Park Jobs and Careers Online: www.themedattraction.com/careers.htm

Books

Baine, Celeste. *The Fantastical Engineer: A Thrillseeker's Guide to Careers in Theme Park Engineering,* 2nd ed. Calhoun, LA: Bonamy Publishing, 2006.

Clave, S.A., and Andrew Clarke. *The Global Theme Park Industry.* Wallingford, England: CABI, 2007.

O'Brien, Tim. *The Amusement Park Guide,* 5th ed. Guilford, CT: Globe Pequot, 2003.

Samuelson, Dale, and Wendy Yegoiants. *The American Amusement Park.* Osceola, WI: MBI Publishing, 2001.

Magazines and Trade Publications

Amusement Business: www.amusementbusiness.com

Amusement Today: www.amusementtoday.com

Funworld: www.iaapa.org/funworld.html

Roller Coaster! Magazine: www.ACEonline.org/rcmag.htm

Websites

MousePlanet: www.mouseplanet.com

Theme Park Insider: www.themeparkinsider.com

DVDs / Videos

Sebak, Rick. *Great Old Amusement Parks.* WQED Pittsburgh, www.wqed.org

Young, Tim. *Life Was a Lark at Willow Grove Park.* Tim Young Productions, members.aol.com/taymed/catalog.htm

ENDNOTES

1. Michele Himmelberg, "Shot to the Heart," *Orange County Register,* 8 December 2004: B1.

2. International Association of Amusement Parks and Attractions, www.iaapa.org.

3. National Amusement Park Historical Association website, www.napha.org.

4. Al Griffin, *Step Right Up, Folks!* Chicago: Henry Regnery Company, 1974: 2.

5. National Amusement Park Historical Association, www.napha.org.

6. International Association of Amusement Parks and Attractions, www.iaapa.org.

7. Todd Pack, "Theme Parks Say Rides Are Safe," *Orlando Sentinel,* 13 September 2003: C1.

8. Robert Niles, "Theme Park Safety Tips," *Theme Park Insider,* www.themeparkinsider.com/reviews/theme_park_safety_tips.

9. Jonathan Lansner, "Playing the Price: Discounts Abound on Theme-Park Admissions," *Orange County Register,* 16 January 2005: D1.

10. Janet Wasko, *Understanding Disney,* Cambridge, UK: Polity Press, 2001: 160.

11. Paramount's Great America website, www.pgathrills.com/corporatepartners/corporatepartners.cfm.

12. "ConAgra Foods Adds Its Flavor to Fun of Six Flags, Sponsoring Rides, Theaters & More Enjoyed by Millions of U.S. Park Visitors," *Business Wire,* 2 May 2005, 1.

13. "Alton Towers Lures Visitors with SMS Drive," *Precision Marketing,* 1 July 2005, 3.

14. Suzanne Vranica, "Advertising: Disney Sets Global Parks Campaign—Move Is Aimed Particularly at Helping European Sites; 'The Happiest Celebration,'" *Wall Street Journal Europe,* 29 December 2004: A4.

15. See "Intelligent Marketing: Promotions at United States Amusement Parks," *Tourist Attractions and Parks,* September/October 2005.

16. See "Amusement-Park Attendance Rises for First Time Since 2001," *Wall Street Journal,* 27 December 2005, A9.

17. James Zoltak, "Snoopy & Pals Gave Knott's Marketing, Merchandising Muscle," *Amusement Business* 115:31 (August 4, 2003): 3.

18. See Tim O'Brien, "Sesame Street Characters, Show Big Hit at Dutch Park," *Amusement Business* 114:4 (January 28, 2002): 8.

19. See Six Flags Great Adventure, www.sixflags.com/greatAdventure/Rides/Kingdaka.aspx.

20. Natasha Emmons, "A 'Spectacular' Night: Disney's 'Aladdin' Posts Impressive Debut," *Amusement Business* 115:5 (February 3, 2003): 5.

21. Quassy Amusement Park, www.quassy.com.

22. Andy Milman, "The Future of the Theme Park and Attraction Industry: A Management Perspective," *Journal of Travel Research* 40:2 (November 2001): 139.

23. Christine Blank, "Parking It for Fun." *American Demographics* 20:4 (April 1998): 6.

24. Don Mooradian and Matt Benz, "What's Next for Parks?" *Amusement Business* 114:45 (November 11, 2002): 5.

Recreation as Entertainment

9

Sports   ANDI STEIN

The athletes file into the stadium, waving their hands at the crowd, clutching flags from their countries, and dressed in gear bearing the logos of their home teams. The people in the stands cheer, not only for the athletes but also for the event itself and what it represents. It is the opening ceremony of the Olympics, and the world is watching. For the next two weeks, people all over the globe will follow these athletes—the cream of the crop—as they compete in every sporting event imaginable. The athletes' achievements—and their failures—will be captured by international media and eagerly digested by an international audience.

Sports make up one of the largest components of the entertainment industry, from both the perspective of participants and spectators. The world of sports is complex, providing a source of fitness and recreation for some, a means of competition and achievement for others, and an endless source of enjoyment and entertainment for still others.

Sports transcend race, gender, and class. They offer activities for people of all ages, "from toddlers in infant swimming groups and teenagers participating in school athletics to middle-aged adults bowling or golfing and older persons practicing Tai Chi."[1] Professional sports entertain the masses with the assistance of the media, who have helped make the sports industry what it is today.

The sports industry is a billion-dollar business, almost too large to calculate. According to Plunkett Research,

The sports industry is so complex, including ticket sales, licensed products, sports video games, collectibles, sporting goods, sports-related advertising, endorsement income, stadium naming fees, and facilities income, that it's difficult to put an all-encompassing figure on annual revenue.[2]

The history of sports reflects a desire for competition and a passion for winning. It reveals the creativity behind the games and activities that have comprised the world of sports in various cultures and the process of change and refinement that has transformed these activities into what they have become today.

Because the nature of the business *is* so complex, the issues within it are as well. Challenges of modern-day sports pertain to marketing, media, and the management of crises and scandals. Employment opportunities in the industry are diverse and plentiful because the world of sports encompasses so many different elements.

This chapter will examine sports as an integral part of the entertainment industry. It will discuss the various components that make up the sports business and the challenges and trends inherent to the industry and explore some of the career options available.

History and Background

There are no existing records to indicate when sports officially became a part of everyday life. However, physical play and competition have long been considered a form of recreation dating back to ancient cultures.

The Beginning of Sports

Paintings found in Egyptian tombs from approximately 1800 B.C., for instance, suggest that physical contests such as wrestling, stick fighting, and stone tossing were types of recreational activities. Wrestling was also part of Asian culture, along with martial arts and archery. The Romans developed chariot races, which were an important part of their culture, and which have been depicted in Hollywood movies about ancient Rome.[3]

The Greeks are credited with the development of what has become the world's longest-standing sports competition—the Olympics. The first Olympics took place in Olympia in 776 B.C. They were conceived as a religious event to honor Zeus. Held every four years, they included contests such as foot races, chariot races, and equestrian events. These early Olympic games inspired the modern-day Olympics, which will be discussed later in the chapter.

Early European Sports

Sports in Europe in the Middle Ages largely consisted of archery matches and jousting tournaments, where two competitors on horseback would fight with lances and try to unseat one another. Fencing became popular during the Renaissance when grace and athleticism began to emerge as important elements of sports in addition to sheer physical strength.[4] By the late eighteenth and early nineteenth centuries, the concept of team sports began to take hold in England with the development of cricket, rugby, and soccer, known in Europe as "association football."

The Birth of Sports in the United States

Meanwhile, in the United States, organized sports began to take on a life of their own. The mid-1800s saw the development of the game of baseball, followed by basketball, American football, and hockey. Other organized sports such as volleyball, lacrosse, and water polo followed. By the mid-1900s, many of these sports were being played both at the professional and collegiate levels.

Professional League Sports in North America

Today four primary league sports are played professionally in the United States and Canada. They are: baseball, football, basketball, and ice hockey.

Baseball

Along with Mom and apple pie, baseball is considered one of the staples of American life. Professional baseball began with the formation of the eight-team National League in 1867. In 1869, the Cincinnati Red Stockings became the first of these teams to hire professional players. This development was followed by the establishment of the competing Western League, which eventually became the American League. In 1903, the two groups united and established an annual World Series, resulting in the baseball league structure used today. By 1954, players had formed an association, known today as the Major League Baseball (MLB) organization.

Today, there are 30 U.S. and Canadian teams in 28 cities, operating under the auspices of MLB. Baseball revenues total more than $6 billion, with the average worth of each team at approximately $472 million under a shared revenue system. In 2007, total attendance at major league baseball games was approximately 79.5 million.[5]

Football

American football grew out of the English game of rugby on Ivy League campuses and was refined by Walter Camp of Yale University in the late 1800s. The establishment of the Intercollegiate Football Association in 1896 led to the initiation of a Thanksgiving Day championship game between Yale and Princeton, launching an annual Thanksgiving Day college football tradition that continues to this day.

Football turned professional soon after, and in 1920, the National Football League (NFL) was established with 10 teams. Today, there are 32 teams in the NFL, divided into two conferences, the American Football Conference and National Football Conference.

The League's championship game is the Super Bowl, held each year at the end of January.

While baseball is considered the All-American sport, football is the moneymaker, with annual revenues of $6.5 billion. League teams have an average $957 million in net worth under a shared revenue system. In 2007, total attendance at NFL games was approximately 22 million.[6]

According to Plunkett Research, Ltd.,

> The NFL commands by far the greatest revenues, plays in the largest and most expensive stadiums and amasses more viewers in the United States than any other sport. This is all the more remarkable in light of the fact that that NFL plays far fewer games per season than does MLB (Major League Baseball) or the NBA (National Basketball Association).[7]

Basketball

A physical education teacher named James Naismith invented the game of basketball in 1891 as an indoor activity he devised for his students at the YMCA in Massachusetts. The game evolved into an outdoor amateur sport that was eventually adopted by a number of colleges and universities in the early 1900s.

By the mid-1940s, the game turned professional with the formation of the Basketball Association of America. That organization combined with the National Basketball League in 1949 to form the National Basketball Association (NBA).[8]

Currently, there are 30 NBA teams in 29 cities, divided into two groups—the Eastern and Western Conferences. Annual revenues total approximately $3.8 billion. Unlike baseball and football, NBA teams do not share revenues, which means that some teams are far more profitable than others. In 2007, for instance, the two revenue leaders were the New York Knicks (net worth of $608 million) and Los Angeles Lakers (net worth of $560 million). The Portland Trailblazers were at the bottom with a net worth of $253 million.[9] In 2007, total attendance at NBA games was approximately 21.5 million.[10]

Ice Hockey

The last of the four professional league sports is ice hockey, which made its official debut in Montreal in 1875. By the 1890s, the sport had spread throughout Canada. When Lord Preston of Stanley donated a cup to be awarded to the best Canadian hockey club, the "Stanley Cup" became the top prize coveted by teams across Canada.

By the early twentieth century, ice hockey had crossed the border into the United States, as teams formed in Pennsylvania and Michigan. The sport also began to take hold across Europe. The National Hockey Association, formed in 1908, became the National Hockey League (NHL) in 1924, and by 1967, the League had six teams in both Canada and the United States. By the end of the 1970s, there were 21 League teams. Today, there are 24 U.S. and six Canadian ice hockey teams in the NHL, playing in two conferences—Eastern and Western. League revenues are approximately $2.4 billion, with the average team net

JIM SALISBURY

Baseball Writer, Philadelphia *Inquirer*
www.philly.com/inquirer

When Jim Salisbury was just a kid, he knew he wanted to be a sportswriter. Today, Salisbury is the baseball writer for the Philadelphia *Inquirer,* where he covers the Philadelphia Phillies and writes about issues such as strikes, steroids, and the Baseball Hall of Fame. "I cover a lot of the baseball scene and also do columns with some commentary," he explained.

Salisbury got his start while majoring in English at Providence College in Rhode Island. "I had a student work study job in the sports information office," he said, and on the side, he started covering high school games for the *Providence Journal.* "It really sparked an interest in me."

After graduation, Salisbury went on to work for the *Pawtucket Times* as a general sports reporter. He loved the experience of working for a small paper because of what he learned from the job. "I did everything there. On Monday, I could be covering a Little League tournament, and on Friday, I could be covering the Boston Red Sox at Fenway Park," he said.

His ultimate goal was to get to a large metropolitan paper, and he eventually worked his way up to the *New York Post,* where he covered the New York Yankees, and then to the *Inquirer* in 1996.

His favorite part of the job is talking to people and helping them tell their stories. "It's always been a lot of fun telling a good story. If you write about people, you can't lose," he explained.

Salisbury recommends that those interested in sports writing pay attention to what makes for a good sports story. "Pick out writers you like—or even writers that are not your favorites—and see how they handle the story. Watch a ballgame really closely, and try to think how you might write that story. Then, read three writers you respect, and see how they wrote it." He also encourages aspiring sportswriters to do whatever they can to get published. "Write for school newspapers, town weeklies. Keep writing, keep improving, so someone eventually will notice you." Most importantly, he said, "Be yourself. When you write, you can't dazzle all the time. It's more important to write a complete and comprehensive story."

» » »

worth around $200 million.[11] In 2007, total attendance at NHL games was approximately 22.2 million.[12]

Minor and Independent League Sports

Minor league sports teams are generally affiliated with major league teams. In baseball, for example, minor league teams are used as training grounds for professional league teams, giving players an opportunity to develop their skills before moving up to the majors. Sometimes players who are recuperating from injuries or having subpar seasons may be sent back to a minor league team for a period of time to regroup and get back in shape.[13]

Independent leagues are not affiliated with major professional teams but may serve the same purpose in helping to prepare aspiring professional athletes for careers with the major leagues. The Independent Football League, for example, operates teams in inner-city neighborhoods in and around Philadelphia and is dedicated to "advancing players' level of performance in hope of being selected to play college or professional football."[14]

Non-League Professional Sports

In addition to professional league sports, there are many other non-league sports that attract audiences worldwide and generate millions of dollars in revenue. Auto enthusiasts, for example, follow Indy Auto racing and NASCAR (National Association for Stock Car Auto Racing) with unwavering devotion.

Professional golf has gained its share of fans in recent years, largely because of the popularity of Tiger Woods. The young African American player turned the sport on its head in the late 1990s and won his first career Grand Slam at the age of 24 in 2000 at the British Open. Woods's success has broken both age and racial barriers in what had previously been a sport dominated by older white males, noted Kathryn Jay.

> He created a new rainbow coalition of fans and sparked a renaissance of interest in the game. For any given tournament, 'how'd Tiger do?' has become the most interesting question at hand. His ability to hit the ball straight and far, his massive earnings, his talent for concentrating under extreme pressure, and his domination of the competition was more than enough to make him a hero to many.[15]

Likewise, the success of sister superstars Venus and Serena Williams has generated increased interest in the game of tennis. In 2007, for example, "Tennis had one of its strongest years in nearly two decades, setting records in event attendance, television viewership and recreational participation," noted Linda Frazier.[16] Other non-league sports with significant mass appeal are figure skating, boxing, wrestling, gymnastics, and soccer.

Collegiate Sports

Several of the world's most popular professional league sports originated at the college and university levels, first in England and later in the United States. As previously noted,

American football and basketball got their professional starts as college pastimes. In 1906, the Intercollegiate Athletic Association was formed to monitor and regulate college sports. It was renamed the National Collegiate Athletic Association (NCAA) in 1910.

To this day, football and basketball remain an integral part of the college experience, both for those participating in the sports as well as those in the stands cheering on their teams. This is evidenced by the proliferation of football "Bowl" games at the end of each season and the "March Madness" phenomenon that happens every spring as college basketball teams compete for the NCAA title.

At some colleges such as Ohio State University, the University of Texas, and the University of Virginia, sports generate huge revenues from ticket sales as well as donations from alumni.[17] This allows for the construction of new facilities and the purchase of uniforms, equipment, and other team resources. The revenues also may be used for the payment of extremely competitive salaries for coaches.

In 2005, for example, oilman T. Boone Pickens donated $165 to the athletic department of his alma mater, the University of Oklahoma.[18] Likewise, Phil Knight, CEO of Nike and a graduate of the University of Oregon, gave his school $35 million for the expansion of the football stadium in 2001 and pledged another $100 million for the construction of a new basketball arena in 2006.[19]

In addition to football and basketball, collegiate sports can include baseball and softball, lacrosse, field hockey, swimming and diving, volleyball, soccer, and wrestling, among others.

Women and Sports

While women have long participated in sports, it was not until the 1970s that women's sports were formally recognized as a part of American culture—and it took an Act of Congress to make that happen. Title IX of the Education Amendments Act of 1972 mandated that any federally funded schools providing resources for males had to provide equal resources for women. This opened the door for the expansion of women's sports programs and teams at the collegiate level as well as in primary and secondary schools.

As might be expected, Title IX was highly controversial and initially met a great deal of resistance from those who believed that the expansion of women's sports would come at the expense of men's. Even today, nearly 40 years later, some schools are not in full compliance with the law. Nevertheless, the passage of Title IX set in motion a tremendous change in the world of sports. At the high school level alone, for example, participation of girls in sports has increased from 2.7% in 1972 to 40% in 2008.[20]

Since Title IX, a number of efforts have been made to launch women's professional sports leagues similar to men's. Several of these—Ladies Pro Baseball and the Women's Professional Volleyball Association—were short lived because of inadequate sponsor support. However, two leagues—the Women's National Basketball Association (WNBA) and the Women's Professional Football League (WPFL)—have been in existence since the late 1990s with 14 teams in each league.[21]

In addition, women have made strides in individual sports that were once dominated by men. Tennis champions Venus and Serena Williams are among this group as well as golfer Michelle Wie and Indy racecar driver Danica Patrick.

International Sports

While many sports are regional to individual countries, several sporting competitions are considered international, as they attract athletes from all over the globe.

Olympics

The most renowned of these events is the Olympics. Held every four years and divided into summer and winter games, the modern-day Olympics were established in 1896 and patterned after the games of ancient Greece. Cities around the world vie for a chance to host the Olympics, and athletes come from all over the world to compete in a vast array of athletic events. At the Beijing 2008 Olympics, for example, more than 10,000 athletes from 205 countries participated in 300+ different competitions.[22]

Other International Events

Beyond the Olympics, numerous other international sporting events promote healthy competition among nations. The FIFA World Cup is an international soccer competition held every four years, taking place over the span of a month in the summertime and involving teams from 32 countries. The Tour de France is an annual, three-week bicycle race, where the world's top cyclists pedal through France. The Pan American Games bring together athletes from North, South, and Central America every four years to compete in more than 30 different sporting events. And the Maccabiah Games bring together Jewish athletes from all over the world to compete in a variety of competitive sports events in Israel.

Recreational Sports

Our discussion so far has focused on professional competition, but sports are also enjoyed as a form of recreation by millions of people throughout the world. Individuals of all ages engage in sports through schools, YMCAs and YWCAs, private gyms, Little League organizations, workplace league teams, etc. Sports offer people a source of exercise and a way to relieve stress in addition to providing fun, relaxation, and enjoyment. Among the most popular sports that people engaged in for recreational purposes in 2007 were: running and jogging (41,000); bicycling (39,000); hiking (30,000); basketball (26,000); swimming (18,000); and ice skating (11,000).[23]

Fantasy Sports

One aspect of sports that has gained a following in recent years is fantasy leagues. Individuals form fantasy leagues and put together their dream sports teams using real-life statistics. According to Plunkett Research, "Players contribute to a winning pot and then follow their chosen players' on-field statistics throughout the season. At the end of the season, the fantasy team with the best statistics wins the pot."[24] Fantasy sports leagues operators generally pay licensing fees to obtain the statistics used in the games.

Sports and Media

The popularity of organized sports can be largely attributed to the role of the media in helping to promote awareness of these sports. The media have transformed sports from mere physical activities into one of the largest sources of entertainment on the planet.

According to Joan Chandler's article in the *Encyclopedia of World Sport,*

> The relationship between the media and sport has always been symbiotic. Newspapers developed sports pages to sell more papers; sports organizations welcomed publicity because it brought more spectators to the games. As radio and television gave national exposure to local teams, the amount of money available to club owners and players vastly increased, turning professionals from often ill-paid journeymen into media celebrities.[25]

More information about the relationship between sports and media will be provided later in the chapter.

Challenges and Trends

Marketing and Promotion

One of the reasons sports have become such an integral part of public life is because of the marketing efforts behind them. Sports are big business, and the marketing, advertising, and promotion of sports generate billions of dollars each year. At the same time, sports provide an opportunity for marketers to cash in on the public's interest in them by linking their products to sports. As a result, companies are constantly trying to come up with new and innovative ways to capitalize on this.

Linking Products to Sports

Sports marketing encompasses a number of elements that involve making a connection between the experience of watching or participating in sports and purchasing products and services that enhance this experience. Consider, for example, the long-standing Nike campaign, "Just Do It," which links the concept of achievement to the company's products.

During the 2008 Beijing Olympics, Coca-Cola, a major sponsor of the Olympic Games, unveiled a television advertising campaign called, "Live Olympic on the Coke Side of Life," featuring Olympic athletes promoting Coke products, as if to suggest that anyone who drank these products could also be a champion.[26]

Courting Corporate Sponsorships

The flip side of this is the use of a company's products to boost the visibility of sports, often through corporate sponsorships. It's very common today to see arenas, stadiums, and other sports venues bearing the name of a corporate sponsor. Citizen's Bank Park in Philadelphia, The Honda Center in Anaheim, PetCo Park in San Diego, and Busch Stadium in St. Louis, are only a few of the sports venues with corporate names attached to them.

These sponsors often pay an annual fee to have their names displayed throughout these venues, according to Leah Boyd: "Corporations pay no less than $5 million to $10 million a year for arena naming rights, with some paying more than $20 million a year. About 10 or 15 years ago, $1 million to $1.5 million a year was the norm."[27]

One trend is for a sports team to find a corporate sponsor for the season as the Detroit Pistons did in 2003. This involves putting the corporate sponsor's name on everything from signage to game tickets to media guides to team letterhead—all for a hefty price.[28]

Preventing Ambush Marketing

One of the challenges for sports marketers is the prevention of what's become known as "ambush marketing." Generally, at a large-scale event such as the Olympics or the Super Bowl, companies can pay millions of dollars to become official sponsors of the event. However, "unofficial" sponsors can try to ambush these sponsored marketing efforts as an article in the *Economist* explained: At the Euro 2008 football tournament,

> Dutch buyers of Heineken beer were given green hats to wear. The hats were an "ambush marketing" campaign, in which companies try to promote their brands at sporting events without paying sponsorship fees. Heineken's rival, Carlsberg, was an official sponsor of Euro 2008, paying $21 million for the privilege. A few TV close-ups of fans wearing Heineken hats would have cost very little by comparison.[29]

To prevent this behavior, management of sports arenas and stadiums have begun policing spectators who are clearly attempting to ambush the paid corporate sponsors. In the Euro 2008 case, for instance, those trying to enter the stadium wearing green Heineken hats were asked by security guards to remove them.

Media Coverage of Sports

As previously noted, promotion of sports has been largely tied to the media's role in making sports accessible to the general public. Newspapers have included sports coverage in their pages since the 1800s, while radio play-by-plays have been a part of sports since the 1920s, but it is television that has had the most impact on sports coverage.

Using Television to Promote Sports

National programs such as ABC's *Wide World of Sports* and *Monday Night Football* brought sports into people's homes and made the names of sportscasters such as Jim McKay and Howard Cosell household names during the 1960s and 1970s. When ESPN (Entertainment and Sports Programming Network) made its debut on cable television in 1979, sports coverage became a 24/7 proposition.[30] As Kristian Jaime explained, "It is difficult to imagine modern sports coverage without the abbreviations ESPN or ABC Sports."[31]

Televised sports coverage is extremely lucrative for both the media and the sports organizations being covered. Consider the money paid for football alone:

> Current network deals to air NFL games amount to a $4.27 billion, eight-year package. Fox has a $4.27 billion extension through 2011; CBS a $3.73 extension through 2011; and NBC's extension through the same period amounts to $3.6 billion. In addition, DirecTV has a $3.5 billion, five-year extension through 2010. ESPN is currently in a $4.8 billion, eight-year agreement for rights to games other than *Monday Night Football.*[32]

Changing the Rules of Media Coverage

In the last few years, however, sports organizations have implemented changes that may have long-term effects on media coverage, particularly at the local level. In 2006, the National Football League (NFL) launched its own television network and began beefing up its website, www.nfl.com.

Then the league declared that it was going to limit the amount of game footage local media could use in their TV newscasts to 45 seconds—as opposed to the unlimited coverage previously allowed. They also put a limit on the amount of time that game clips could remain on a media outlet's website. The purpose was to encourage viewers to go directly to the NFL for game news rather than rely on their local media. Major League Baseball (MLB) plans to follow suit in the near future when it launches its own cable channel.

This change has not gone over well. For sports fans, it means more limited coverage from local stations. For local media, it restricts what they can offer the public in the way of game coverage. For the sports organizations themselves, however, it could ultimately be highly profitable, particularly as more and more fans go directly to the websites of the sports organizations for their sports news. As one reporter explained,

> The NFL's media strategies have drawn objections from a range of traditional media outlets and journalists, who have cast the efforts as a Big Brother-like move threatening to reduce unbiased coverage for fans. The change in policy indicates the NFL thinks there's ad money to be made from online video clips, and the league and its team owners want most of it.[33]

From an industry standpoint, this will certainly be something to keep a close watch on in the near future.

Making Use of Online Media

The use of online media for sports coverage is growing in the industry. A number of sports-oriented media outlets such as ESPN and FOX Sports now feature blogs and online video games on their websites. Some, such as CBS, even offer online resources for fantasy sports enthusiasts.[34]

As explained in the previous section, sports organizations are recognizing the escalating value of online media and how they can use it to attract fans. MLB, for example, was the first of the professional sports organizations to use streaming video to broadcast games on its website. "In 2007, the site attracted 62 million visitors per month to watch more than 12,000 streamed events through the year."[35]

A recent study by the European Interactive Advertising Association (EIAA) indicates that European sports fans are heavy users of the Internet, spending more than 13 hours online per week. The study showed that many of these fans are also regular users of social networking sites such as MySpace and Facebook.[36] Given that, it makes sense for those in the industry to continue to find new ways to tap into this market.

Crisis and Scandal in Sports

One of the challenges for those working in the industry in recent years has been dealing with the proliferation of crises and scandals that have routinely punctuated media headlines and cast a negative light on individual sports and players. The biggest scandal has involved the illegal use of performance-enhancing drugs, which has affected many different areas of the sporting world, including major league baseball, the Olympics, and the Tour de France.

Dealing with the Impact of Illegal Drugs

In 2007, a series of Senate hearings led by former Senator George Mitchell (D-Maine) investigated the use of steroids by major league baseball players. Some of the game's all-time greats such as Barry Bonds and Roger Clemens were put under the microscope for allegedly using the banned substances.

Other athletes have been affected by similar doping incidents. In 2007, Olympic sprinter Marion Jones was forced to give back the five gold medals she had won in the 2004 Sydney Olympics after admitting that she had used performance-enhancing drugs during the Games.[37] Tour de France cyclist Floyd Landis was stripped of his 2006 title after testing positive for illegal drugs at the end of the race.[38]

Managing Individual Scandals

For those working on the public relations side of the sports industry, managing crises brought on by individual players can also result in challenges, as when Atlanta Falcons football star Michael Vick was indicted by the FBI for conducting dog fighting in 2006. Although his actions had nothing to do with his team, the Falcons swiftly suspended him and then had to deal with the media aftermath resulting from the indictment and subsequent suspension. A betting scandal involving NBA referee Tim Donaghy in 2005 created similar public relations headaches for that league's management.[39]

Grappling with the Consequences of Scandals

Scandals like these can jeopardize lucrative corporate sponsorships for sports organizations. The Tour de France, for example, has been particularly hard hit by doping scandals in recent years. In addition, to the Landis incident in 2006, three cyclists were removed from the 2008 race before the end of the second week for illegal drug use. As a result, five major sponsors withdrew their sponsorships of the race.[40]

Sports scandals can also have an impact on public perception:

> Sports are rooted in time-honored tenets like sportsmanship and fair play. What separates them from other entertainment options like movies, video games and television is that they're supposed to be real. That trust has been violated, replaced by widespread public cynicism.[41]

Unruly Fan Behavior

Sports events attract large numbers of people who are eager to see "their" teams win and who may show their enthusiasm—or displeasure—through exuberant cheers and jeers. Sometimes, however, fans get carried away, and the results can be chaotic violence. This was the case in 2004 at a basketball game between the Detroit Pistons and Indiana Pacers. When an angry fan threw a beverage cup at Pacer forward Ron Artest, he responded by charging into the stands, followed by several of his teammates. An ensuing brawl between players and fans left nine people injured, several fans arrested, and Artest suspended for the rest of the season.[42]

Fan outbursts are not new—European soccer matches have been notorious in the past for eruptions of violent fan behavior,[43] but in recent years the trend has spread to sports that were previously considered immune from such outbursts, such as golf and tennis.[44]

This has led some sports organizations to implement more aggressive responses to unruly fan behavior. The Buffalo Bills football team, for example, began publicizing the names and addresses of fans arrested at games for bad behavior.[45] In Cincinnati, noted John Jeansonne in *Newsday,* "The NFL's Bengals felt a need to provide an in-stadium telephone hotline—call 381-JERK—as a way to anonymously protect fans against obnoxious behavior around them."[46]

The British have taken even more drastic steps, passing a law that requires soccer fans previously arrested for bad behavior to surrender their passports at least seven days before England competes in an international soccer match abroad.[47] It is likely that more sports organizations will start implementing sanctions if the trend of unruly fan behavior continues.

Employment Opportunities

Working in sports offers the potential to use many different skills and work in a variety of settings. Jobs may include participating in sports, managing and marketing sports-related organizations, and covering sports as a media professional, among other activities. Here are some of the job options available if you are interested in pursuing a career in sports.

Team Players

The prospect of becoming a professional athlete is something that many talented young sports enthusiasts dream about. In reality, however, competition is fierce, and the physical and emotional demands of being a professional athlete are numerous. If you don't have the talent and drive to be in this category, there are other ways to be part of the game. Jobs for coaches, umpires, referees, and managers exist at the professional level as well as on college and high school campuses. For those interested in coaching, previous experience in the sport of choice is helpful as are strong communication skills, a respect for the rules of the game, and the ability to motivate players and think strategically. A bachelor's degree in kinesiology or physical education is also useful.

Management and Administration

Many opportunities exist for those interested in the business and management side of the sports industry. Sports teams and other related organizations employ a variety of individuals to keep their day-to-day operations running smoothly. These include general managers, accounting and financial personnel, operations directors, equipment managers, statisticians, etc. Most of these jobs are likely to require a bachelor's degree in business, sports management, or a related field. For some positions, an advanced degree may be required.

Marketing and Promotion

As discussed throughout this chapter, marketing and promotion are key elements of today's sports industry. Independent agencies specialize in developing marketing, advertising, and promotional campaigns for sports teams and organizations as well as for products related to sports such as equipment and athletic wear. Teams and leagues hire public relations and marketing professionals to work with the media as well as special event coordinators who may be called on to organize sporting events such as tournaments or exhibition games.

In addition, colleges and universities with sports programs often employ sports information officers to promote their school programs to the public and media. For all of these jobs, a bachelor's degree and some experience in public relations, marketing, communications, or journalism is extremely helpful.

Sports Agents

The movie *Jerry Maguire* painted a Hollywood-style picture of the life of the sports agent. In reality, however, agents are very much a part of the industry. Today's high-paid athletes—and some not-so-well-paid ones—employ sports agents, according to Plunkett Research. "From contract negotiation to endorsement deals to special event planning to

ALEX GILCHRIST

Director of Media and Communications, Anaheim Ducks

http://ducks.nhl.com

Alex Gilchrist, Director of Media and Communications for the Anaheim Ducks, always has a front row seat at the team's hockey games—that is, if he has the time to sit in it. Gilchrist rarely has time to sit and enjoy the game. He's usually too busy making sure all the reporters covering the game have what they need to make their deadlines.

"I truly love everything about the job. I'd say the best time is playoff season. The drama and media attention are raised, and it's fun to be part of the team," Gilchrist said. He admitted the days are long and sometimes stressful, but he wouldn't have it any other way. "We host the media twice each game day during morning practice and game night, making all players and coaches available and handling whatever crisis comes up that day—hopefully, none!"

Gilchrist graduated from Loyola Marymount University with a degree in marketing. He got his start in public relations by working in sports information at the university. From there he landed an internship with the Los Angeles Angels of Anaheim baseball team. "For me, the critical step was landing the internship with the Angels. Breaking into the industry is the toughest part. Once you get there, it's up to the individual to take it from there," he said. Since both the Angels and the Ducks were owned by Disney, it was a fairly easy transition to move into media relations for the hockey team.

The most difficult part of the job for Gilchrist is handling the daily duties when a crisis or major trade occurs. "We can't just drop everything else—practices, meetings, interviews still need to take place as regularly scheduled," he explained. Gilchrist relies on his experienced staff to shift into over-drive when needed to get the job done.

Gilchrist admitted he's lucky to have a job he loves coming to every single day. "There is nothing I don't like about the job," he said.

» » »

investment planning to personal handling, agents have become indispensable to top athletes in every sport."[48]

If you're interested in a career as a sports agent, a background in business can be a plus, as well as a law degree. Both of these qualifications will be useful in the financial and legal aspects of the job.

Recreation/Fitness Specialists

Beyond the world of professional sports, there are numerous opportunities available for those who want to work on the recreation side of the industry. Health clubs, YMCAs and YWCAs, schools, and camps, are only a few of the organizations that employ people interested in sports. Many of the positions listed above are also available in these venues. While the pay may not be as high as on the professional sports side of the business, the job opportunities are likely to be more plentiful and far less competitive.

Sports Journalists

As previously noted, media coverage of sports makes up a large segment of the industry. Sportscasters, sportswriters, and online sports reporters provide the public with a steady stream of information about games, teams, players, issues, etc. Although today, opportunities for print journalists are limited because of the changing status of the newspaper business, the demand for broadcast and online media professionals is holding steady.[49] If you are interested in working in sports journalism, good writing skills and the ability to meet deadlines are a must. In addition, a degree in journalism, English, or some other area of communications is needed.

Education and Training

Many of the job opportunities discussed above require college degrees in fields such as business, communications, kinesiology, physical education, etc. In addition, the growing interest in sports marketing and sports management has resulted in the development of specialized programs in these fields. This reflects the increasing number of jobs in the industry and the need for adequate preparation for these jobs. According to an article in *University Business:*

> Pro sports are witnessing an economic rebirth. As a result, new pro sports career employment and marketing opportunities have grown exponentially. Today, college and university sports management and administration programs are proliferating—and creating more meaningful opportunities for students to engage in all aspects of professional sports management, athletic training, and sports medicine.[50]

Figure 17: U.S. Colleges and Universities Offering Programs in Sports Management/Administration and Sports Marketing

» Baylor University: www3.baylor.edu/HHPR/Graduate
» Bowling Green State University: www.bgsu.edu/colleges/edhd/hmsls

» Florida State University: www.fsu.edu/~smrmpe
» Indiana State University: www1.indstate.edu/rcsm
» Ohio State University: ehe.osu.edu/paes/sem
» Ohio University: www.sportsad.ohio.edu
» San Diego State University: www-rohan.sdsu.edu/~cba/sports/default.htm
» United States Sports Academy: www.ussa.edu
» University of Central Florida: www.bus.ucf.edu/sport/cgi-bin/site/sitew.cgi
» University of Kentucky: www.uky.edu/Education/KHP/smhead.htm
» University of Massachusetts: www.isenberg.umass.edu/sportmgt
» University of New Mexico: www.unm.edu/~sportad/
» University of Northern Colorado: www.unco.edu/nhs/ses/
» University of Oregon: lcb.uoregon.edu/warsaw
» University of South Carolina: www.hrsm.sc.edu/spte
» University of Washington: ial.washington.edu/ial
» Wichita State University: webs.wichita.edu/?u=spad&p=index

Future Outlook

Making Greater Use of Technology

Technology will continue to play a role in the delivery of sporting events and information about sports to the general public. Blogs, streaming video, and social networking sites such as eFans (www.efans.com) are likely to become regular features produced by sports organizations and media outlets covering sports. As this technology develops, sports organizations may well try to gain more control of the content of these websites, as has already been indicated by the actions of the NFL regarding media footage of game coverage.

The widespread adoption of high-definition television may prompt some sports fans to forego the in-person stadium experience for the luxury of being able to watch high-quality games from the comfort of their own living rooms. A recent study by the Consumer Electronics Association noted that "Three in 10 sports fans said watching sports in high-definition is better than attending. And of the 48 percent of those surveyed who plan to upgrade to high-definition sets within two years, more than half were sports fans."[51] This could have an impact on game attendance in the future.

Expanding into New Markets

The expansion of American sports to overseas markets is a trend that is expected to develop in the future, as several of the major sports leagues are attempting to make inroads into international territory, particularly in Asia. MLB, for example, previewed its 2008 season by sending the Los Angeles Dodgers and San Diego Padres to play exhibition games in China, while the Oakland As opened the season in Japan. In 2007, the NHL opened its season in London, while the NBA sent two teams to China and four to Europe. According to an article in the *Boston Globe,*

Pro leagues from the United States have been staging exhibitions in Europe and Asia for decades, but they have all become much more aggressive about their marketing. Owners of pro teams faced with the challenge of raising ever-more revenue to pay for ever-increasing salaries are eyeing new fans overseas and the big-money media and sponsorship deals they bring with them as their next frontier.[52]

Some of the leagues are also courting Asian sports fans by getting them into the game. Over the last decade, for example, the NFL has run flag football programs for children in China, while the NBA has unveiled plans to establish a basketball league there called NBA China.[53]

Targeting the Hispanic Market

On the sports marketing front, outreach to Hispanic sports fans will be a high priority in the near future. This reflects growth in a market segment that many in the entertainment industry are trying to tap into, explained Javier Erik Olvera:

> Latinos have…become a force to be reckoned with in the marketplace, controlling nearly one-quarter of the nation's total purchase power, annually buying more than $650 million in goods. That amount is expected to mushroom within the next few years, surpassing the trillion-dollar mark as early as 2010…. [54]

Some media outlets have already started trying to reach this market. In 2008, ESPN and Time Warner launched ESPN Deportes in the Los Angeles market, calling it a "multimedia, Spanish-language sports brand dedicated to providing the widest variety of sports to the U.S. Hispanic sports fan via television, online, print, radio, and wireless."[55] Meanwhile, FOX Sports en Español announced plans to expand its coverage of major league baseball and boxing on its Spanish-language network.[56]

Sports organizations are trying to capture this market as well. NASCAR, for example, began actively promoting Colombian driver Juan Pablo Montoya in 2007 and launched NASCAR.com en Español, a Spanish-language website for race car fans.[57] That same year, The San Jose Earthquakes, the city's soccer team, launched a campaign to reach out to the Latino market by promoting the team as "Los Terremotos" in advertisements throughout the San Francisco Bay Area, which has a 19% Hispanic population.[58]

Outreach efforts to Hispanic sports fans are predicted to escalate in upcoming years, as sports marketers try and come up with new and improved ways to target this booming market.

Summary

Sports are an integral part of society, providing recreation, competition, and an unending source of entertainment for those who participate in and watch them. They are also big business, generating billions of dollars in annual revenue.

International sporting events such as the Olympics bring people together to celebrate and showcase some of the outstanding achievements in the world of sports. The media have played a large part in helping the sports industry become what it is today by providing the world with access to these events.

Some of the current challenges faced by the industry are the marketing and promotion of sports and the management of crises and scandals within the business. Employment opportunities in the industry are healthy and are expected to remain that way, as the diversity of the field offers many different types of jobs and working environments for prospective employees.

Advances in technology will continue to impact the way sports information is delivered to the public. The industry will also see increased outreach efforts, as sports organizations attempt to broaden their reach to more of a global audience and try to make inroads into the growing Hispanic consumer market.

ADDITIONAL RESOURCES

Associations and Organizations

Fantasy Sports Trade Association: www.fsta.org
International Olympic Committee: www.olympic.org.
Major League Baseball: www.mlb.com
National Basketball Association: www.nba.com
National Collegiate Athletic Association: www.ncaa.org
National Football League: www.nfl.com
National Hockey League: www.nhl.com
North American Society for Sports Management: www.nassm.com
Women's National Basketball Association: www.wnba.com
Women's Professional Football League: www.womensprofootball.com
Women's Sports Foundation: www.womenssportsfoundation.org

Job-Hunting Resources

Sports Career Finder: www.sportscareerfinder.com
Team Work Online: www.teamworkonline.com
Work in Sports: www.workinsports.com

Books

Favorito, Joseph. *Sports Publicity: A Practical Approach*. Boston, MA: Butterworth-Heinemann, 2007.
Field, Shelly. *Career Opportunities in the Sports Industry*, 3rd ed. New York: Ferguson, 2004.
Heitzmann, William Ray. *Careers for Sports Nuts & Other Athletic Types*. New York: McGraw-Hill, 2004.

Levinson, David, and Karen Christenson, eds. *Berkshire Encyclopedia of World Sport*. Great Barrington, MA: Berkshire Publishing Group, 2005.

Graham, Stedman, Lisa Delpy Neirotti, and Joe Jeff Goldblatt. *The Ultimate Guide to Sports Marketing*. New York: McGraw-Hill, 2001.

Magazines and Trade Publications

Page 2 (ESPN publication): sports.espn.go.com/espn/page2

Sports Business Daily: www.sportsbusinessdaily.com

Sports Business Journal: www.sportsbusinessjournal.com

Endnotes

1. "Sports and Recreation," *MSN Encarta,* encarta.msn.com.
2. "Introduction to the Sports Industry," Plunkett Research, Ltd., 13 June 2008, www.plunkettresearchonline.com.
3. See David Levinson and Karen Christensen, eds., *Encyclopedia of World Sport: From Ancient Times to the Present*, Oxford, England: Oxford University Press, 1999: 75, 407, and 409.
4. See Allen Guttmann, "Sports in the Renaissance and Modern Periods," *Sports History*, www.britannica.com.
5. See "Revenue Sharing Boosts Major League Baseball," Plunkett Research, Ltd., 13 June 2008, www.plunkettresearchonline.com.
6. See "NFL Sets Attendance Record in 2007," www.nfl.com/news.
7. "NFL: The Biggest Money in U.S. Sports," Plunkett Research, Ltd., 13 June 2008, www.plunkettresearchonline.com.
8. See William J. Baker and S.W. Pope, "Basketball," in David Levinson and Karen Christensen, eds., *Encyclopedia of World Sport: From Ancient Times to the Present*, Oxford, England: Oxford University Press, 1999: 43.
9. "NBA Lacks Revenue Sharing," Plunkett Research, Ltd., 13 June 2008, www.plunkettresearchonline.com.
10. "NBA Attendance Report 2008," *ESPN,* sports.espn.go.com/nba/attendance
11. See "Canadian Hockey Teams Soar Thanks to the Weak U.S. Dollar," Plunkett Research, Ltd., 13 June 2008, www.plunkettresearchonline.com.
12. See "NHL Sets Attendance Record," *Reuters,* 7 April 2008, www.reuters.com.
13. See Joe Morgan and Richard Lally," *Baseball for Dummies*, 3rd ed. Hoboken, NJ: Wiley Publishing, 2005: 249.
14. Independent Football League, www.ifi-football.com.
15. Kathryn Jay, *More Than Just a Game: Sports in American Life Since 1945*, New York: Columbia University Press, 2004: 239.
16. Linda Frazier, "Tennis Maintains Growth in Popularity," *Tallahassee Democrat,* 25 January 2008.
17. See "NCAA Sports Are Big Business," Plunkett Research, 13 June 2008, www.plunkettresearchonline.com.
18. "Texas Businessman T. Boone Pickens Named Outstanding Philanthropist," *PR Newswire,* 19 March 2008.

19. Rachel Bachman and Brent Hunsberger, "Phil Knight's Influence Transforms University of Oregon Athletics," *Oregonian,* 4 May 2008, A1.

20. See "National Collegiate Athletic Association—Title IX," *Encarta,* encarta.msn.com.

21. See Women's National Basketball Association, www.wnba.com, and Women's Professional Football League, www.womensprofootball.com.

22. See "Official Site of the Beijing 2008 Olympics," en.beijing2008.cn/media/usefulinfo.

23. "Sports Participation Trends, U.S.: 2000–2007," Plunkett Research, Ltd., www.plunkettresearchonline.com.

24. "Fantasy Sports Take Off, Creating $500 Million in Revenues Online," Plunkett Research, Ltd., www.plunkettresearchonline.com.

25. Joan M. Chandler, "Media," in David Levinson and Karen Christensen, eds., *Encyclopedia of World Sport: From Ancient Times to the Present,* Oxford, England: Oxford University Press, 1999: 241.

26. See Natalie Zmuda, "Coke Unleashes Olympic Blitz," *Advertising Age* 79:27 (July 14, 2008): 6.

27. Leah Boyd, "High-tech, Niche Options Change Sports Marketing," *Crain's Detroit Business* 24:11 (March 17, 2008): 14.

28. See Keith Reed, "Brought to You By...," *Boston Globe,* 27 September 2007, D1.

29. "Playing the Game; Ambush Marketing," *Economist* 388:8587 (July 5, 2008).

30. See Barry Janoff, "ESPN Sports Marketing Walks the Walk, Talks the Talk," *Brandweek* 47:36 (October 9, 2006): 9.

31. Kristian Jaime, "ESPN and ABC Sports, Part of the Sports Culture," *La Prensa* 14:18 (January 23, 2008): 7.

32. "Lucrative Television Rights Bring in Big Bucks," Plunkett Research, Ltd., 13 June 2008, www.plunkettresearchonline.com.

33. Michael McCarthy, "NFL Taking Bold Steps to Control What Fans See," *USA Today,* 7 September 2007, A1. See also, Al Lewis, "Fans Should Boo NFL's Footage Grab," *Denver Post,* 10 September 2006, K1; and Adam Thompson, "Sports Leagues Impose More Rules on Coverage," *Wall Street Journal,* 16 July 2007, B1.

34. See, for example, Fantasy Sports at CBS Sports, www.sportsline.com/fantasy.

35. "Revenue Sharing Boosts Major League Baseball," Plunkett Research, Ltd., 13 June 2008, www.plunkettresearchonline.com.

36. See "Sports Fans More Likely to Embrace Web Activities Than Regular Surfers," *New Media Age,* 5 July 2008, 11.

37. See Michael O'Keeffe, "Jones Gives Back Gold, Returns Five Medals After Admissions," *New York Daily News,* 9 October 2007, 67.

38. See John Jeansonne, "Ruling Slaps Landis: 2–1 Vote Takes Away Tour de France Crown, Bans Him for Two Years," *Newsday,* 21 September 2007, A75.

39. See Paige Albiniak, "Sports and Scandal," *Broadcasting & Cable* 137:33 (August 20, 2007): 4.

40. See Christine Mattheis, "Amid Cycling Doping Scandal, New Sponsors Take the Lead," *Wall Street Journal,* 13 July 2008.

41. Jeff Duncan, "Sports Scandals May Be Unmatched in Intensity and Scope," *Times-Picayune,* 30 July 2007.

42. "Bill Saporito, "Why Fans and Players are Playing So Rough," *Time* 164:23 (December 6, 2004): 30.

43. Ibid.

44. See, for instance, Barker Davis, "Roaring to the Lead; Fans' Subpar Behavior Becomes Too Common," *Washington Times,* 15 July 2008, C1; and Nachman Shai, "Israeli Spoilsports," *Jerusalem Post* 12 February 2008, 16.

45. See Mark Yost, "Loutish Fans Disgrace the NFL," *Wall Street Journal,* 16 October 2007, D6.

46. See John Jeansonne, "Root, Root, Root for Whichever Team, but Act Like a Human Being," *Newsday,* 22 April 2007, B14.

47. Mark Yost, "The Goal? Keeping British Fans on Their Best Behavior," *Wall Street Journal,* 1 June 2005, D10.

48. "Sports Agents Become Indispensable," Plunkett Research, Ltd., www.plunkettresearchonline.com.

49. See Richard Perez-Pena, "The Top Player in This League? It May Be the Sports Reporter," *New York Times,* 24 December 2007, C1.

50. James Martin and James E. Samels, "Play Ball: Stepping Up to the Pro Sports Plate," *University Business,* www.universitybusiness.com.

51. Sarah Talalay, "Best Seats? In the House Some Sports Fans Giving Up Their Tickets in Favor of High-Definition TVs," *South Florida Sun-Sentinel,* 16 September 2007, E1.

52. Keith Reed, "Globalization: By Playing Regular-Season Games Abroad, American Professional Teams are Courting Worldwide Audiences and the Financial Boost These Games Bring," *Boston Globe,* 28 October 2007, E1.

53. See "NFL: The Biggest Money in Sports," and "NBA Lacks Revenue Sharing/Announces NBA China," www.plunkettresearchonline.com.

54. Javier Erik Olvera, "Quakes Look to Build Ties with Latino Community," *San Jose Mercury News,* 19 November 2007.

55. "ESPN and Time Warner Launch ESPN Deportes in LA," *Wireless News,* 13 March 2008.

56. "FOX Sports en Español Takes Content and Integration to the Next Level," *Business Wire,* 13 May 2008.

57. See Sarah Rothschild, "NASCAR Heavily Marketing Montoya," *Miami Herald,* 16 November 2007; Barry Janoff, "Can NASCAR Be *Numero Uno* With Hispanic Fans, Marketers?" *Brandweek* 48:29 (August 6–13, 2007): 10; and "NASCAR.COM Broadens Reach to Spanish-speaking Audience with the Launch of NASCAR.COM en Español," *Business Wire,* 17 September 2007.

58. Olvera, 19 November 1997.

10

Travel and Tourism

ANDI STEIN

With soaring gas prices and the U.S. economy teetering on the brink of recession, the head honchos at Visit Florida, the state's marketing organization, decided to take a new approach with their promotional efforts. In the midst of an especially cold and snowy East Coast winter, the agency launched an $8.65 million integrated advertising campaign called, "Sunshine," featuring a combination of television, online, and print advertisements promoting the Sunshine State. At the heart of the campaign was a fully integrated website—the first of its kind in state travel marketing—featuring videos, real-time weather updates, and blogs from local travel experts (www.visitflorida.com).

Scenes of pristine beaches and clear, sunny skies were broadcast throughout the winter in markets such as New York, Boston, Washington, DC, and Chicago to encourage those in cooler climates to venture south to experience some of the state's warm-weather attractions.[1] The results? Within the first three months of the campaign, more than 23.8 million people visited Florida, a 3.4% increase over the same time period of the previous year.[2]

Although Visit Florida's Sunshine campaign was deemed a success from a marketing perspective, it also showed how much appeal travel can hold for the general public, even in harsh economic times. Travel and tourism are among the largest segments of the entertainment industry and the largest service industries in the United States, accounting for 3% of the gross domestic product (GDP).[3] According to the Travel Industry Association (TIA) and the World Travel and Tourism Council (WTTC), money spent annually on leisure travel exceeds $700 billion in the United States and $2.97 trillion worldwide.[4]

For many, leisure travel holds the promise of excitement, adventure, and a chance to explore new places and try new things. Travel can come in a variety of forms—independent explorations, escorted tours, cruises, and all-inclusive vacation resort packages, to name just a few. Because of the tremendous popularity of travel as a form of entertainment, the tourism industry has grown by leaps and bounds, providing travelers with the necessary means of transportation, lodging, food, and attractions to enhance their travel experiences.

While the U.S. tourism industry was severely impacted by the September 11, 2001, terrorist attacks, in recent years the industry has rebounded and resurged, exceeding pre-2001 profits. Despite the rising cost of gasoline and the lowered value of the U.S. dollar against foreign currencies, people are still determined to spend their hard-earned cash on travel.

A variety of events in recent years have provided the industry with an array of challenges, as those within it strive to compete for consumer dollars. The struggling economy has led those in the business to try and come up with new and innovative ways to attract and please customers. Escorted tours, cruise-ship travel, and all-inclusive packages have surged in popularity, as travelers look for ways to get more mileage for their money. A growing interest in specialty travel such as adventure travel and volunteer vacations now offers new opportunities for those in the business.

At the same time, the aftermath of the 2001 attacks has also wreaked havoc on the ease of travel. Increased security regulations and tighter baggage rules have made the process of getting from one place to another far less appealing than it once was. This has had an impact on how and where people are traveling.

Nevertheless, despite these challenges, the travel and tourism industry is expected to continue on its growth course. According to Plunkett Research, Ltd., "Today's outlook for the travel industry is one of innovation, high occupancy rates, healthy competition and…returning profits."[5] This is likely to result in a variety of job opportunities for those interested in pursuing careers in the industry.

This chapter will explore the history of travel and provide background on the various enterprises that make up the tourism industry. It will examine some of the challenges facing the industry and the trends occurring in the business. Finally, it will take a look at what the future of travel is likely to bring as the industry continues to expand in the twenty-first century.

History and Background

The Beginnings of Travel

Early travel dates back to the Babylonians, who invented the concepts of money and the wheel around 4000 B.C.—two critical elements that have long allowed people to go places. The ancient Egyptians provided one of the early tourist attractions with the creation of monumental burial chambers for their Pharaohs, more commonly known as the Great Pyramids. As early as 1600 B.C., people began traveling to Egypt to see these man-made wonders.[6]

The construction of early roads around 2000 B.C. provided people with a way to move from one location to another. By 150 B.C., the Romans had started building more sophisticated roadways that made travel faster and more convenient. These roads contributed to the early development of the tourism industry, according to Goeldner and Ritchie in *Tourism: Principles, Practices, Philosophies*.

> The Roman combination of empire, roads, the need for overseeing the empire, wealth, leisure, tourist attractions, and the desire for travel created a demand for accommodations and other tourist services that came into being as an early form of tourism.[7]

Impact of Religion and Trade

Religious shrines provided reasons for people to make pilgrimages to places such as Delphi in Greece and Ephesus in what is now Turkey. Between A.D. 400 and 1300, expeditions to other religious sites such as Canterbury, England, had become commonplace.

In the Far East, the development of a trade route across Asia called the Silk Road enabled explorers such as Marco Polo (1254–1324) to venture across continents. Merchants traveling in caravans needed places to stay and food to eat as they sold their wares, leading to the development of roadside public houses and inns where travelers could stop to eat, drink, and rest.

The Grand Tour

European travel became more common during the seventeenth and eighteenth centuries with the development of the concept of the Grand Tour. As part of this tour, noted Goeldner and Ritchie, individuals would go to visit and study in some of Europe's major cultural centers, often for up to three years.

"A generally accepted itinerary included a long stay in France, especially in Paris, almost a year in Italy visiting Genoa, Milan, Florence, Rome and Venice, and then a return by way of Germany and the Low Countries via Switzerland."[8] The concept of the Grand Tour still exists today, "However: The tour is more likely to be three weeks, not three years."[9]

An Englishman named Thomas Cook is credited as one of the earliest travel agents. Cook began running train trips for groups across England in the mid-1800s, which expanded into a market for escorted tours. Cook's business eventually grew to be one of the largest travel organizations in the world.

Early Travel in the United States

An interest in travel and exploration led to the settlement of North America in the 1500s and 1600s as the Spaniards, English, and French made their way across the Atlantic Ocean. As the United States evolved, so did the opportunities for travel and the means to get places.

Impact of the Railroads

The development of railroads in the 1800s not only led to the expansion of the western United States. but also had an impact on the tourism industry, largely due to the efforts of a businessman named Fred Harvey. Realizing that cross-country train travelers would want food to eat and lodging along their journeys, he created a chain of Harvey House restaurants and hotels in conjunction with the Atchison Topeka & Santa Fe Railroad Company. "By the late 1880s, Santa Fe passengers could find a Harvey House every hundred miles along the entire line," according to the author of *The Harvey Girls,* Lesley Poling-Kempes.[10] In 1946, MGM made a movie called *The Harvey Girls,* which told the story of the impact these Harvey Houses had on the settlement of the West.

Establishment of the National Park Service

In 1872, U.S. President Ulysses S. Grant signed an Act of Congress creating the country's first national park, Yellowstone National Park. Then in 1916, President Woodrow Wilson authorized the establishment of the National Park Service (NPS).

Today, there are nearly 400 areas throughout the United States that fall under the NPS umbrella, including "national parks, monuments, battlefields, military parks, historical parks, historic sites, lakeshores, seashores, recreation areas, scenic rivers and trails, and the White House," according to the NPS. In 2006, more than 272 million people visited the nation's National Parks.[11]

Major Developments in Travel and Tourism

As the twentieth century unfolded, two major technological developments had a tremendous impact on travel and tourism: the invention of the automobile and the first airplane flight.

Impact of the Automobile

No one is certain exactly who invented the automobile, but it is believed to have been invented in Europe in the 1800s. However, thanks to American entrepreneur Henry Ford and the creation of his Model T, by the 1920s, automobiles were being mass produced at his Ford Motor Company factory in Detroit, making them affordable for many. As a result, automobiles eventually replaced both trains and horse-drawn carriages as the primary form of transportation and leisure travel for Americans. Today, more than 70% of leisure trips are made by car, according to the Travel Industry Association.[12]

The popularity of the automobile also paved the way for the establishment of the rental car business, largely pioneered by John Hertz in the mid-1920s. It also opened the door for the use of buses as a means of transporting people from place to place with the incorporation of The Greyhound Corporation in 1929.[13]

Development of the Airline Industry

The development of the airline industry grew out of the determination of brothers Wilbur and Orville Wright to conquer the sky, which they successfully did in 1903 at Kitty Hawk, NC. Their persistence eventually evolved into the country's first commercial airline, Varney Airlines in 1926. Many others soon followed—Western Airlines, Pan American Airlines, and Trans World Airlines, to name just a few.

As airplanes became larger and more technologically advanced, their ability to transport large numbers of passengers long distances afforded the industry rapid expansion and growth. In recent years, however, the airline industry has shrunk, as deregulation, mergers, and the high cost of fuel have had a severe effect on this segment of the travel and tourism business.

Travel and Tourism Today

Creation of State and City Tourism Bureaus

Over the years, individual states have established tourism bureaus to provide travelers with information about tourism within their areas. The purpose is to help boost state economies by encouraging tourism. Some states build "Welcome Centers" on highway exits strategically placed near their borders, so visitors can stop for information as they enter the state. There, visitors can pick up maps, lists of local attractions, special-interest guides, accommodation booklets, event calendars, and information about state parks.[14]

A number of cities have established Convention and Visitor Bureaus (CVBs) that serve a similar purpose. Often run as nonprofit organizations, these bureaus provide information to tourists as well as convention-goers. According to the Destination Marketing Association International (DMAI), "For visitors, CVBs are like a key to the city. They assist planners with meeting preparation and encourage business travelers and visitors alike to visit local historic, cultural, and recreational sites."[15]

Expansion of Lodging and Accommodations

The hotel/lodging industry as we know it has evolved since the early days when travelers sought out inns on their religious pilgrimages and exploratory journeys. In the United States alone, the industry has more than quadrupled. In 1910, there were an estimated 10,000 U.S. hotels; in 2006, that number was more than 47,500, according to the American Hotel and Lodging Association (AHLA).[16]

ELAINE CALI

Vice President of Communications Anaheim/Orange County Visitor and Convention Bureau

www.anaheimoc.org

Every year, an estimated 44 million visitors come to Orange County, CA. Elaine Cali's job as the Vice President of Communications for the Anaheim/Orange County Visitor and Convention Bureau is to make sure that those visitors have heard of and hopefully end up visiting one of the 800 businesses that belong to the bureau.

Cali never dreamed she would end up in tourism or public relations when she was a student at San Diego State University majoring in social welfare. "I graduated and was disillusioned with the industry, so I looked for other opportunities." She had taken several journalism classes and decided to put her strong writing skills to work. She landed a job with the County of Orange working in the Consumer Affairs department where she wrote speeches for the CEO, designed simple brochures, and pitched press releases to the media. "It was great fun. It was crazy. It could have been the screen-play for the show *The Office,*" she said.

In 1978, Cali moved to the Anaheim/Orange County Visitor and Convention Bureau as the Communications Manager. She and an administrative assistant were the only two in the office back then. Now, her office has five full-time managers. "Back then, I just figured it out as I went," she said.

A typical day for Cali starts with a list of to-do items. If she's successful, everything on the list is marked off by the end of the day. Her days are filled with internal meetings with the marketing and tourism teams to make sure they are all heading in the same direction. She also spends time meeting with businesses that belong to the bureau and helping them understand the business of tourism.

Cali said the most important skill in her business is writing. She spends approximately 70% of her time writing emails, letters, press releases, copy for brochures—the list goes on and on. "Students sometimes forget that a job in public relations involves a lot of writing. It's not all about talking and planning special events. Writing well is absolutely essential," she said.

» » »

Today, the hotel industry is dominated by large chains such as Hilton, Hyatt, and Sheraton, which are primarily owned by a handful of multinational parent corporations. Boutique hotels, bed and breakfasts, and timeshares also make up a segment of the lodging business.

Rise of the Cruise Industry

Travel by sea has been a way to get from one place to another ever since the Phoenicians began crafting large-scale water vessels in 800 B.C.[17] Ships were used by early explorers such as Christopher Columbus, who crossed the Atlantic Ocean and ventured into the New World in the fifteenth century. Ships ultimately carried thousands of immigrants from Europe and Asia to this New World, as the United States came into its own as a developing country between the seventeenth century and the turn of the twentieth century.

The concept of traveling by ship for enjoyment and relaxation, however, is relatively new, especially considering how long people have been traveling by sea. For many years, sea travel was simply used as a means of transporting people between continents. The first official leisure cruise set sail in December of 1966, when a company now known as the Norwegian Cruise Line launched its first cruise between Miami and the Bahamas, according to Kay Showker and Bob Sehlinger.

> The 1960s brought radical changes. New cruise lines…exchanged formality for fun and brought a new atmosphere to shipboard life…. Space was used for sports, recreation, and entertainment, turning ships into floating resorts. Getting there was no longer half the fun—it *was* the fun. New and younger passengers were attracted by the activity and informality. Families with children, too, were finding cruises to be ideal vacations.[18]

Today, cruising is the fastest-growing segment of the travel and tourism industry, according to the Cruise Lines International Association (CLIA), averaging an annual growth rate of 7.4% per year. The organization reports that 12.8 million people cruised in 2007, with numbers predicted to grow in the future.[19]

The size of the average cruise ship has grown over the years as well, with some ships now able to accommodate more than 3,000 passengers.[20] Amenities may include restaurants for fine dining, swimming pools, yoga and aerobics studios, rock climbing walls, ice skating rinks, bowling alleys, movie theaters, and an assortment of shopping venues. For many, cruising provides the convenience of having everything in one place—meals, accommodations, entertainment, and transportation, making it an ideal vacation choice that provides value for the money.

Growing Interest in All-in-One Travel

Two modes of travel that have picked up steam in recent years are the escorted tour and the all-inclusive vacation resort package. As noted earlier, Englishman Thomas Cook created the first escorted tour when he began arranging group train trips across England in the mid-1800s. Since then, numerous tour companies have offered travelers an easy means of travel by packaging motor coach tours that include accommodations, sightseeing, and meals while journeying to places all over the globe.

Although escorted tours may not appeal to everyone, they are becoming increasingly popular with aging Baby Boomers who are finding the all-in-one concept to be an easy way to travel. According to the United States Tour Operators Association (USTOA), more than 11 million Americans alone take an escorted tour each year.[21] Tour companies are capitalizing on the growing interest in escorted tours by coming up with new and innovative ways to package their tours, according to Carol Sottili in the *Washington Post:*

> The best-known larger companies that offer general tours designed to appeal to a wide-ranging demographic—including Globus, Collette Vacations, Trafalgar Tours and Tauck World Discovery—are finding more competition from smaller specialized firms that cater to a specific age group, a particular interest or an out-of-the-way destination.[22]

The all-inclusive vacation resort package, for example, a Club Med vacation, is similar to the escorted tour concept in that one fee covers a whole range of travel services. The main difference is that once a traveler arrives at the vacation resort, there is no additional travel involved; everything is available onsite—meals, lodging, entertainment, etc. Like a cruise or an escorted tour, this type of vacation holds great appeal for those who enjoy the idea of going someplace new without the hassle of having to plan the details themselves.

Changing Role of the Travel Agent

Travel agents serve as intermediaries between travelers and the companies that provide them with services needed for their trips—airlines, hotels, tour operators, car rentals, etc. Travel agents work closely with customers to help them plan, book, and get the most out of their trips. Traditionally, travel agents were paid for their work through commissions from travel service providers.

In recent years, however, the Internet has had a severe impact on the role of the travel agent, as more and more individuals are now booking their own trips online. In addition, many of the airlines that once paid agents commissions for handling customer bookings no longer do so. For a while, it appeared that the travel agent might become an extinct species.

However, like so many others affected by changes in technology, travel agents have made a few adjustments. Some agencies now charge clients small fees for their services to compensate for the loss of commissions—fees that many customers appear quite willing to pay, according to the American Society of Travel Agents (ASTA). "The job of a travel agent has grown and adapted to reflect the changes within the travel industry and difference in the way people think about travel."[23]

Challenges and Trends

Effects of an Unstable Economy

In recent years, skyrocketing fuel costs have plagued the travel and tourism industry as the price of crude oil has steadily increased. This has had a direct effect on airlines,

EMMA PITRE

Director of Operations
Destination America, Anaheim, Calif.
www.dest-amer.com

Emma Pitre's job has given her the opportunity to see America—from the front of a bus. As the Director of Operations for Destination America, she oversees many different aspects of the motor coach tour company, which encompasses Trafalgar Tours, Insight Vacations, Grand European Tours, and Brendan Worldwide Vacations.

"I have been in the travel business for 10 years and have taken on many roles: tour director, operations supervisor, reservation agent, director of reservations, just to name a few," Pitre said. Today, she is responsible for managing eight staff members who operate the company's North American tours as well as 65 tour directors who lead trips throughout North America.

With a B.A. from San Diego State University, Pitre hadn't planned on working in the travel industry. She credits a friend who was working for Contiki Holidays for helping her get started. "She convinced me to leave my corporate job where I had my own office and a pretty good view of the San Fernando Valley for two seats at the front of a motor coach with an amazing view of some great American destinations."

Pitre enjoys the opportunity to work with many different people, both in and out of the office, despite the occasional challenges that come with the job. "Every person who comes on tour comes for a different reason. It is our intention to meet each person's expectation, but sometimes this proves to be difficult. It is always so gratifying to accomplish this for each passenger who travels with us—and we do in almost all cases."

For those interested in working in the travel business, Pitre said, "Learn it from the bottom up. Whether you are starting with a hotel, a travel agency, or an air carrier, the travel business is best learned from the perspective of those who run the business each day. So if you have to start out at the front desk, the ticket counter at the airport, or be a customer service representative, this allows you the opportunity to see what happens on a day-to-day level. All that experience leads to acquiring both breadth and depth in a higher position."

» » »

which have been forced to raise their ticket prices to offset the high cost of fuel. In addition, a number of airlines have implemented other cost-cutting measures to compensate for high fuel prices—charges for checked baggage, for example, and the elimination of services such as in-flight movies and free beverages.

This has led a number of frustrated travelers to cut back on air travel—to the tune of $9 billion in 2007–2008, according to a survey conducted by the Travel Industry Association (TIA). These cutbacks have had an impact on other segments of the industry as well according to Anne Bond Emrich in the *Grand Rapids Business Journal.*

> The entire travel community took a hit in revenues as a result of travelers' cutbacks in flying. Hotels lost nearly a billion and restaurants more than $3 billion in revenues. Federal, state, and local governments lost more than $4 billion in tax revenue due to reduced spending by air travelers.[24]

Another issue that has affected the industry has been the weakening of the U.S. dollar against foreign currencies, especially the euro and the Canadian dollar. This has resulted in a reduction of numbers of Americans going abroad. However, from the standpoint of some areas of the U.S. travel market, business has improved slightly over previous years, as people in other countries such as Canada now find travel to the United States to be extremely affordable.[25]

Lingering Aftermath of 9/11

Since the terrorist attacks of September 11, 2001, safety and security have been high priorities for many segments of the tourism industry, particularly air travel. More stringent screening procedures at airports and strict regulations about what is and isn't allowed to be carried onto an airplane have resulted in longer security lines and pre-flight waiting periods. This situation, as well as the high cost of fuel, has contributed to the downturn in air travel in recent years.

In addition, federal regulations have resulted in tougher entry policies for those arriving in the United States from other countries. For the first time, international visitors must now be fingerprinted and photographed upon entering the country.

While many of these measures are designed to prevent the risk of future terrorist attacks, they have inadvertently resulted in a decline in the overall number of foreign visitors traveling to the United States since 2001. According to the Travel Industry Association, two million fewer international visitors came to the United States in 2007 (24 million) than in 2000 (26 million).[26]

From a public relations standpoint, the news is even grimmer. "In a study conducted by the Discover America Partnership, a travel-industry lobbying group, the United States. was rated by more than 2,000 foreign travelers as the most unfriendly, inaccessible destination in the world, with arduous procedures for entry and cheerless, arbitrary, and rude officials," noted an article in the *Columbus Dispatch.*[27]

As a result, legislation has been introduced in Congress to try and change this perception and ultimately combat the decline in international visitors. Called the Travel Promotion Act, the program would encompass a communication and marketing campaign designed to better explain U.S. security policies to international visitors and assure them that they are welcome in the United States.[28]

Impact of the Internet

Of all the topics covered in this book, travel and tourism may well be the most affected by changes in technology that have taken place in the past few decades. The creation of the Internet and World Wide Web, in particular, has turned the industry upside-down, taking control away from the travel agents and suppliers that sell travel services and giving it to the consumers. This has made travel easier for some and more affordable for many.

Travelers can now use the Internet to make reservations, purchase airline tickets, and check in online. They can read lodging and accommodation reviews on websites such as TripAdvisor.com and take virtual tours of hotels before deciding to book them on their home computers.

Online travel booking agencies such as Travelocity, Expedia, and Orbitz allow consumers to compare prices before making purchasing decisions. Many of these sites reserve airline seats and hotel rooms in bulk, enabling them to offer lower costs to consumers.

Travelers have responded favorably to these changes. A study conducted by market research firm Synovate in 2005 showed that, "Nearly half (47%) of Americans who travel prefer to use an airline's website to all other booking methods. Online travel agencies, such as Expedia and Travelocity, are preferred by 29% of travelers. Only 13% of travelers prefer to book air travel with traditional offline travel agencies. About one in ten travelers (11%) prefer to use an airline's reservations call center."[29]

As noted earlier in the chapter, the increased use of the Internet for individual travel bookings has had a tremendous effect on the role of the travel agent. The number of travel agencies has dropped from 35,000 to 15,000 since 1993, according to an article in the *Orange County Register*.[30] In addition, "The U.S. Department of Labor predicts the number of travel agents in the nation will drop by 6.1%."[31]

Some travel agents have had to reinvent their businesses, positioning themselves as travel consultants rather than booking agents. Despite the changes wrought upon this area of the industry by technology, it is likely that travel agents will survive by focusing on customer service, according to the American Society of Travel Agents: "There are some things technology cannot replicate, and personal touch is one of them. The Internet is a valuable resource, but it cannot replace the expertise, guidance, and personal service of a travel agent."[32]

Innovation in Accommodations

An increase in competition has led to innovative changes in some segments of the tourism industry, particularly in the area of hotels and accommodations. The last few years have seen some of the large hotel chains such as Hilton and Holiday Inn pour money into upgrading their facilities and adding amenities for customers in order to compete with smaller, sleeker, boutique hotels.

According to a survey conducted by Standard and Poor's,

Features found only in upscale properties a few years ago are more common in mid-scale properties; at economy chains, features such as spa-quality shampoos and lotions in bathrooms, high-speed Internet access in rooms and lobbies, flat-screen televisions, and docking stations for MP3 players are becoming more and more common.[33]

Hotels are also trying to design properties to attract niche markets, the survey revealed, such as Generation X and Y travelers who "prefer more modern hotel design, high-tech features in the rooms, and gathering spaces outside of rooms that are more functional than hotel lobbies."[34]

Rise of Specialty Travel

A growing interest in specialty travel has led tour operators to expand their package tour offerings. Traditionally, large tour operators have offered similar itineraries, covering the highlights of various major travel markets in Europe, Asia, the United States, and Australia/New Zealand. Today, consumers want variations in their package tours, prompting both large tour operators and smaller niche companies to come up with new and innovative ways to attract potential customers.

The president of the National Tour Association (NTA) was quoted in the *Chicago Tribune* as saying, "People no longer want to stop, stand, and stare, they want more hands-on, unique, and authentic experiences."[35] As a result, adventure travel has grown in popularity in recent years, according to the USTOA, where travelers can hike, bike, mountain climb, and participate in action sports as part of their trips.[36]

Volunteer vacations that allow travelers to donate some of their vacation time to helping others have also garnered interest, particularly with college students and retiring Baby Boomers. "These trips can include such things as caring for people affected by the AIDS pandemic in South Africa, working with sea turtles in Costa Rica, or helping children in China learn English."[37] Specialty travel may also encompass culinary tours, yoga retreats, and agritourism, where people spend time working on a farm.[38]

Some tour operators are finding it advantageous to develop package tours for specific groups such as women travelers or gay and lesbian travelers. Companies such as Gutsy Women Travel (www.gutsywomentravel.com) and Above and Beyond Tours (www.above-beyondtours.com) have developed specialty tours aimed at these growing segments of the travel market.[39]

Figure 18: 10 Most Visited Tourist Attractions

1. Times Square, New York
2. National Mall & Memorial Park, Washington, DC
3. Disney World's Magic Kingdom, Orlando, FL
4. Trafalgar Square, London
5. Disneyland, Anaheim, CA
6. Niagara Falls
7. Fisherman's Wharf/Golden Gate National Recreation Area, San Francisco
8. Tokyo Disneyland

9.   Notre Dame de Paris, France
10.   Disneyland Paris

Source: Forbes Traveler 50 Most Visited Tourist Attractions, www.forbestraveler.com

Employment Opportunities

Travel and tourism job opportunities are expected to be plentiful in upcoming years, as there are so many different facets to the industry. Some areas, however, are not likely to experience much growth in the near future—airlines, for example—as a function of competition and the state of the economy. Here is a sampling of the types of positions that exist within the travel and tourism industry.

Tour Operators

A number of opportunities exist for those interested in working in the package tour segment of the industry. Escorted tour operators employ guides to lead their tours. These guides are generally expected to learn about all aspects of specific destinations, so they can speak knowledgeably about them to those on tour. If you are interested in becoming a tour guide, it is important to be resourceful and to be able to handle the unexpected crises that are likely to occur during the course of a tour, such as a passenger illness or other emergency.

In addition to tour guides, package tour operators also employ reservations agents, salespeople, and public relations and marketing personnel who are responsible for preparing promotional materials.

Transportation Companies

Transportation companies such as airlines, railroads, and bus companies employ a variety of individuals for a wide range of jobs. There are those who operate the modes of transportation, such as pilots, engineers, and drivers as well as those who provide services onboard, such as flight attendants and conductors. Jobs in these segments of the industry are also available for ticket agents, traffic controllers, salespeople, engineers, and mechanics.

Lodging and Accommodations

Hotels and other types of lodging facilities offer travelers the comfort of a place to sleep as well as services such as food and entertainment to make them feel at home. Consequently, they employ large numbers of staff to provide these services—restaurant workers, housekeeping staff, maintenance personnel, etc. Hotels also hire reservations agents and desk clerks as well as managers and administrators responsible for keeping the day-to-day operations running smoothly.

Cruise Lines

Cruise lines need employees who can help customers feel comfortable during their stay on the ship just as hotels do. However, recreation and entertainment are also a big part of cruising. As a result, cruise lines employ performers, activity directors, instructors, and health professionals, among other positions.

Travel Agents

As previously explained, the market for travel agents has diminished in recent years as a result of the impact of the Internet on the travel business. However, even with these reductions, there are still approximately 101,000 people employed in travel agencies in the United States according to the Bureau of Labor Statistics.[40]

Education and Training

For some of the jobs mentioned above, a high school diploma may be the only degree required. If you have a bachelor's degree, you are likely to have more opportunities for advancement, particularly if you are interested in a pursuing a management track in one of the areas discussed. In addition, customer service is a key part of tourism and travel, and an interest in working with people is a trait many employers look for when hiring.

In some sectors of the tourism industry, additional certification or an advanced degree can be a big plus. As a result, a variety of colleges and universities offer specialized programs in travel and tourism. In addition, the National Tour Association (NTA) offers a travel certification program in conjunction with Temple University's School of Hospitality and Tourism Management for aspiring tour guides.[41]

Figure 19: U.S. Colleges and Universities Offering Programs in Travel, Tourism, and Hospitality Management

- » College of Charleston: www.htmt.cofc.edu
- » Cornell University: www.hotelschool.cornell.edu
- » Florida International University: hospitality.fiu.edu
- » George Washington University: business.gwu.edu/grad/mta
- » New York University: www.scps.nyu.edu
- » Pennsylvania State University: www.hrrm.psu.edu
- » Purdue University: www.cfs.purdue.edu/HTM
- » San Diego State University: htm.sdsu.edu
- » San Francisco State University: cob.sfsu.edu/hm
- » San Jose State University: www.sjsu.edu/hrtm
- » Temple University: www.temple.edu
- » University of Central Florida: hospitality.ucf.edu

» University of Hawaii at Manoa: www.tim.hawaii.edu
» University of Nevada, Las Vegas: hotel.unlv.edu
» University of South Carolina: www.hrsm.sc.edu/hrtm

Future Outlook

Reaching Out to Boomers and Xers

Niche marketing to different types of travelers is likely to be a big part of the agenda for those in the industry in upcoming years. The fastest-growing segment of the travel and tourism consumer market is the Baby Boomers. By 2011, the first of the Boomers will turn the traditional retirement age of 65. It is expected that many Boomers will use their retirement years and accumulated wealth to travel, and, according to Plunkett Research, many of them will not be willing to settle for the traditional, sedentary package tour.

> The exploding number of affluent, retired consumers will be looking for healthy activities and recreation on their travels. Tours that combine cycling, hiking, walking, and other activities of moderate intensity make sense in this market, and demand will grow sharply. Tours that combine hiking or cycling with luxury accommodations or unique lodging in pristine remote settings will find large numbers of customers.[42]

At the same time, as members of Generation X (those born between 1965 and 1981) are coming into their own as travelers, industry professionals will be working hard to reach out to them. "Generation Xers are traveling more than previous generations at the same age," reported the *Washington Times*.[43] They are extremely comfortable with technology and expect to find high-tech products and services like flat-screen, high-definition TVs and free high-speed wireless access in their rooms when they travel.

As previously noted, a number of hotels have already started catering to this new generation of travelers, and it is likely that in the near future, others in the industry will do the same.

Venturing into New Territory

Trips to what were once considered emerging travel destinations are expected to explode in upcoming years, according to the UN World Tourism Organization (UNWTO). This is already becoming evident in countries such as India, Malaysia, and, in particular, China.[44]

The 2008 Summer Olympics in Beijing gave China a chance to bask in the international spotlight. That, coupled with the current low cost of food and accommodations in China, will make the country a hot tourist spot in the near future.

"China soon will become the world's most popular destination," noted an article in the *Futurist*. "By 2020, China can expect 130 million international arrivals."[45] Other predicted emerging travel markets are countries in Eastern Europe such as Bulgaria and Romania as well as countries in Latin America and Africa.

Developing Smarter Travel Technology

Technology is likely to bring even more changes to the travel industry in future years. Some airlines already use self-service check-in kiosks, which allow travelers to check themselves in using only a swipe of their credit cards. These are expected to become commonplace in most airports in the next few years and are also predicted to be implemented by some hotel chains.

"Smart cards" containing passenger information will enable travelers to move more easily through airports, doubling as forms of identification and electronic boarding passes.[46] According to Plunkett Research,

> Luggage tags will also become "smart." Rather than bar-coded tags that are common today, the new tags will be embedded with radio frequency identification chips (RFID) containing information about the passenger and his or her flight. As luggage moves along the conveyor belt, scanners supplied with information about the airport's flight schedule will read the luggage and forward it to the correct plane or divert it if a flight is delayed or cancelled.[47]

The use of this technology could reduce one of the major hassles faced by travelers—lost luggage. "Industry analysts estimate that RFID systems could accurately identify bags at a 95% success rate, which would eliminate two-thirds of the lost bags problem."[48]

Summary

Despite an uncertain economy and the rising cost of fuel, travel and tourism remain among the top segments of the entertainment industry. With billions of dollars spent annually on travel, businesses within the industry are constantly coming up with ways to stay competitive and meet the growing, changing needs and interests of travel consumers.

In recent years, the travel and tourism business has been beset by a number of challenges. The high cost of fuel, threats of terrorism, and the impact of the Internet on the way business is done has caused those in the field to rework their approach to some of their basic core services. This has resulted in innovations on the part of hotel and tour operators and cost-cutting measures on the part of airlines as they struggle to remain competitive without alienating consumers.

In the future, it is expected that travel and tourism will continue to grow and flourish. Job opportunities in many sectors of the field look promising. As Baby Boomers reach retirement age and prepare to start spending some of their hard-earned cash on travel, and Generation Xers look to spend more time traveling, companies are gearing up to meet their travel needs and expectations.

Technology will continue to bring changes to the industry, and new emerging markets will provide greater opportunities for exploring more sites and destinations. In general, the outlook for the travel and tourism industry is healthy and is expected to remain that way for several years to come.

ADDITIONAL RESOURCES

Associations and Organizations

Air Transport Association: www.airlines.org
American Automobile Association: www.aaa.com
American Hotel & Lodging Association: www.ahla.com
American Society of Travel Agents: www.asta.org
Cruise Lines International Association: www.cruising.org
Destination Marketing Association International: www.iacvb.org
National Tour Association: www.ntaonline.com
Travel Industry Association: www.tia.org
Travel & Tourism Research Association: www.ttra.org
UN World Tourism Organization: www.unwto.org
United Motorcoach Association: www.uma.org
United States Tour Operators Association: www.ustoa.com
World Travel & Tourism Council: www.wttc.org

Job-Hunting Resources

GetATravelJob.com: getatraveljob.tia.org
Travel & Tourism Research Association Career Net: www.ttra.org/jobs.asp
Travel Industry Jobs: www.travelindustryjobs.com

Books

Eberts, Marjorie, Linda Brothers, and Ann Gisler. *Careers in Travel, Tourism, and Hospitality,* 2nd ed. New York: McGraw-Hill, 2005.

Milne, Robert Scott, and Backhausen, Marguerite. *Opportunities in Travel Careers.* New York: McGraw-Hill, 2003.

Magazines and Trade Publications

Group Tour Magazine: www.grouptourmagazine.com
Lodging Magazine: www.lodgingmagazine.com
Packaged Travel Insider: www.serendipitypublishing.com
Travel Agent: www.travelagentcentral.com
Travel Weekly: www.travelweekly.com

Online Travel Resources

Expedia: www.expedia.com

Hotels.com: www.hotels.com

Orbitz: www.orbitz.com

Priceline: www.priceline.com

Railpass.com: www.railpass.com

Sidestep: www.sidestep.com

Professional Travel Guide: www.professionaltravelguide.com

Travelocity: www.travelocity.com

ENDNOTES

1. See Linda Rawls, "Ads Tout Sun, Surf to Lure Northerners to Florida," *Palm Beach Post,* 12 February 2008, D1.

2. See Douglas Hanks, "In-state Trips Boost Tourism," *Miami Herald,* 16 May 2008.

3. "TIA Co-Hosts Congressional Roundtable on $1.6 Trillion U.S. Travel Economy," Travel Industry Association, www.tia.org.

4. "Introduction to the Travel Industry," Plunkett Research, Ltd., 29 August 2007, www.plunkettresearchonline.com.

5. Ibid.

6. See Charles R. Goeldner and J.R. Brent Ritchie, *Tourism: Principles, Practices, Philosophies,* 9th edition, Hoboken, NJ: John Wiley & Sons, 2003: 43.

7. Ibid, 46.

8. Ibid, 52.

9. Ibid.

10. Lesley Poling-Kempes, *The Harvey Girls: Women Who Opened the West,* New York: Paragon House, 1991: 37. See also, Victoria E. Dye, *All Aboard for Santa Fe,* Albuquerque, NM: University of New Mexico Press, 2005.

11. National Park Service, www.nps.gov/faqs.htm.

12. See "Domestic Travel Fast Facts," www.tia.org/pressmedia/domestic_activities.html.

13. "Brief History of Buses and Rental Cars in the U.S.," www.library.duke.edu/digitalcollections/adaccess/carandbus.html.

14. See State and Local Government on the Net, www.statelocalgov.net/50states-tourism.htm.

15. Destination Marketing Association International, www.iacvb.org.

16. "History of Lodging," American Hotel and Lodging Association, www.ahla.com.

17. See Goeldner and Ritchie, 50.

18. Kay Showker and Bob Sehlinger, *The Unofficial Guide to Cruises,* 10th ed., Hoboken, NJ: John Wiley & Sons, Inc., 2007: 5.

19. "Profile of the U.S. Cruise Industry," Cruise Lines International Association, www.clia.org.

20. See "Cruise Industry Bookings Are Strong, Including Berths on Luxury Liners," Plunkett Research, Ltd., 29 August 2007, www.plunkettresearchonline.com.

21. "Italy, Eastern Europe Named Top Destinations for Packaged Travel," United States Tour Operators Association, www.ustoa.com.

22. Carol Sottili, "If the Group Tour Fits…," *Washington Post,* 3 April 2005, P1.

23. "Frequently Asked Questions," American Society of Travel Agents, www.asta.org.

24. Anne Bond Emrich, "Flyers Sour on Air Travel," *Grand Rapids Business Journal,* 9 June 2008, 11.

25. See Cameron Ainsworth-Vincze, "Canadians Leave Home in Droves," *Maclean's* 121:22 (June 9, 2008):52; and Kyle Stock, "Purchasing Power: Dollar's Weakness Makes U.S. Travel a Bargain for Foreigners," *The Post and Courier,* 14 January 2008, E18.

26. "Significant Decline in Overseas Travel to the United States Persists Through 2007," Travel Industry Association, www.tia.org.

27. "The Cost of Security: Anti-terrorism Efforts Have Taken Toll on U.S. Tourism Industry," *Columbus Dispatch,* 11 May 2007, 10A.

28. "United States Welcomes Two Million Fewer Overseas Visitors in 2007 Than in 2000," *PR Newswire,* 11 March 2008.

29. "Does Technology Change Americans' Travel Options for Better or Worse?" *Business Wire,* 6 September 2005, 1.

30. See Jan Norman, "Innovate or Stagnate," *Orange County Register,* 28 January 2008, 1.

31. See Chris Churchill, "Not Packing Their Bags Just Yet," *Times Union,* 31 July 2007, C1.

32. "Frequently Asked Questions," American Society of Travel Agents, www.asta.org.

33. "Lodging & Gaming Industry Profile," Standard & Poor's, 2008.

34. Ibid.

35. "A Tour for Everyone with Every Special Interest," *Chicago Tribune,* 17 August 2005, 49.

36. See "Adventure Travel Gains in USTOA Poll," United States Tour Operators Association, 2 December 2007, www.ustoa.com.

37. "Volunteer Vacations: For Some, Better Than a Day at the Beach," *Lesbian News,* 32:11 (June 2007): 47.

38. See Kara Keeton, "Growing Agritourism," *The Lane Report* 23:4 (April 2008): 32.

39. See, for example, Deanna MacDonald, "Who Needs a Man to Travel With?" *Vancouver Sun,* 4 March 2006, D8.

40. Bureau of Labor Statistics, "Travel Agents," *Occupational Outlook Handbook 2008–2009,* www.bls.gov/oco.

41. See National Tour Association, www.ntaonline.com.

42. "Aging Baby Boomers Will Cause Significant Changes in the Leisure Sector, Including Sports and Activity-Based Travel," Plunkett Research, Ltd., www.plunkettresearchonline.com.

43. Jen Haberkorn, "Travel Industry Woos Boomers; Tourism Face Poised to Change with Generation X," *Washington Times,* 12 April 2006, C10.

44. See "Emerging Tourism Markets—The Coming Economic Boom," UN World Tourism Organization, 24 June 2008, www.unwto.org.

45. Marvin J. Cetron and Owen Davies, "Trends Shaping Tomorrow's World," *The Futurist* (March–April 2008): 43.

46. See "The Future of Travel," Plunkett Research, Ltd., 29 August 2007.

47. "Self-Check-In Kiosks, RFID and Other New Technologies Save Labor Costs for Airlines and Hotels," Plunkett Research, Ltd., 29 August 2007.

48. Ibid.

11

Shopping
BETH BINGHAM EVANS

An afternoon at the mall just might also include a quick run down a man-made ski hill and a trip to the ball field to catch a minor league baseball game. Sound impossible? Not if you are in New Jersey at the Meadowlands Xanadu shopping and entertainment complex, which opened in late 2008. The massive five-story, 4.8 million-square-foot complex is being billed as the largest shopping mall and entertainment complex in the United States. Meadowlands Xanadu offers visitors everything from the latest in fashion at 200 stores to a 30-lane bowling alley, from fly-fishing demonstrations to a 287-foot-high Ferris wheel. The massive $2 billion structure also houses the Xanadu Snow Dome complete with a half-pipe for snowboarders and snow play area for children. And if that's not enough to keep everyone in the family busy, next door there is a luxury hotel, and eventually there will be a new football stadium for two professional teams, the Jets and Giants, to call home. The shopping experience has certainly evolved into an entertainment experience.

The shopping centers of today are literally blowing the lids off what used to be considered "the mall." Retailers are banking on the idea that consumers want more than a sterile traditional mall. Shoppers today are looking for more than a new pair of shoes—they are looking for an entertainment experience along with their new purchase. In the case of the Meadowlands Xanadu center, shopping is just one small part of the experience. Consumers can find a pair of shoes, but they can also bowl, learn to cook, visit an amusement park, and catch a ball game—all without moving the car. In locations where the weather is nice, malls are morphing into lifestyle centers. Lifestyle centers are usually open-air malls that also encourage catching up with friends and neighbors. In addition to offering plenty of stores to find the latest in fashion, they give visitors a sense of community similar to what they used to find in city downtown areas.

This chapter will explore why entertainment is king when it comes to luring retail customers. It will take a look at the history of malls and the shopping experience and try to explain why these so-called power towns and lifestyle centers are becoming so popular. The chapter will also take a closer look at how technology is changing the shopping experience by promoting E-commerce.

History and Background

For hundreds of years, merchandise was sold primarily in marketplaces. Before the Renaissance in Europe, most peddlers traveled from location to location setting up their wares in the city's center or the village marketplace. In Europe around the fourteenth century, some peddlers tired of traveling from village to village and opened market stalls that became permanent and ultimately evolved into stores and business districts.[1] The Grand Bazaar of Istanbul was built in the fifteenth century and is still in existence today. It is one of the largest covered markets in the world with more than 4,000 shops.

The first modern-day retail chain store was what is now the Great Atlantic and Pacific Tea Company based in New York City.[2] The company's history goes back to 1859, when its founders, George F. Gilman and George Huntington, started the business to buy and sell tea. It began as a mail-order business and eventually added permanent retail stores in the 1860s. At the turn of the 20th century, nearly 200 stores were in business selling everything from tea and coffee to spices and extracts.

The first department stores date back to Europe and Asia during the seventeenth century. "The famous 'Bon Marché' in Paris grew into a full-fledged department store in the mid-1800s," according to *Britannica Online Encyclopedia*.[3] By the middle of the twentieth century, department stores were seen in almost all major cities and towns in the United States.

Shopping Malls

Shopping malls came into existence as early as the 1800s. The Galleria Vittoria Emanuele II in Milan, Italy, opened in the 1860s, and the spacious outdoor mall is still in business today. The Lake View Store at Morgan Park, one of the first indoor shopping malls in the United States, opened in Duluth, MN, in 1915.

But the shopping mall really flourished in American suburbs in the 1950s and '60s as more and more people moved out of the cities and bought cars to get around. The original point of building malls in the suburbs was to provide the consumer with many options for shopping and services in a single, self-contained location. The malls offered the convenience of a city's downtown area outside of town.

As more and more malls were built, shopping in downtown areas declined. By the 1970s, malls were everywhere. A change in the tax code "allowed investors to write down a large proportion of a new building's cost as a loss. That made malls more profitable," according to an article in the *Economist*.[4]

Location-Based Entertainment

One of the best ways to increase sales in a mall is to increase traffic. "With more than 70% of shopping trips and purchase decisions being made by women, it is important to meet a woman's needs at shopping destinations," according to the White Hutchinson Leisure and Learning Group.[5] So, to help meet a mother's needs, many malls added areas designed specifically for children. Sometimes a mall added a carousel or a play area, but it was the larger destination entertainment facilities such as family and children's entertainment centers that became all the rage in the 1990s.

An example of a family entertainment attraction at a shopping mall today is Nickelodeon Universe at the Mall of America in Minneapolis, MN. It's the nation's largest indoor family theme park and has 30 rides and attractions including roller coasters.

Mega Park at Les Galeries de la Capitale in Quebec, Canada, is another popular family entertainment center that includes bumper cars, a skating rink, and an IMAX theater. Another example of a family entertainment center is the T-Rex at The Legends at Village West in Kansas City, KS, which is billed as a destination restaurant: a place to shop, eat, and explore dinosaurs as they come to life.

And it appears that family entertainment centers have worked to get people to the mall. The next time you are at the mall take a look around—it's likely you will see kids, parents, grandparents, couples, and teens. The mall has been transformed from a place to shop to a place for the whole family to be entertained.

Shopping Vacations

Shopping has become the number one activity on vacation. Americans on average spend 21% of their vacations shopping, according to America's Research Group, a consumer behavior research firm.[6] So, it's no surprise to see clusters of shopping areas at the point where tourists disembark from a cruise ship in an exotic location such as the Caribbean. Retailers have realized the potential of the shopper on vacation. We now see shopping centers built right next to popular travel destination locations such as casinos, amusement parks, and historical sites. Even the ski area of Mammoth Mountain in the Sierras in central California has lots of boutique shopping on the ground floor and condominiums on the upper floors right next to the gondola entrance in town.

Some vacations are built completely around shopping. The online travel site Vacations Made Easy now offers shopping vacation packages, where you can "shop boutiques, outlets and craft malls with shopping vacation packages that will help you shop 'til you drop," according to the organization's website, www.vacationsmadeeasy.com. Some of the most popular shopping destinations include: Boston, MA; Branson, MO; and Los Angeles, CA.

DOUG KILLIAN

Director of Tourism
Mall of America
www.mallofamerica.com

Doug Killian loves to travel. On his company's dime, he has traveled to China, Iceland, and Germany. It's all part of his job as the Director of Tourism for the Mall of America in Minneapolis, MN. Killian visits travel shows around the world for work. "Traveling is one of the side benefits of the job," he said.

He landed the job at Mall of America seven years ago. Before that, he worked almost two decades for Northwest Airlines. He loved his work in public relations at Northwest, but after the tragic events of September 11, 2001, and the economic hardships the airline industry faced, Killian decided to make a change. Now he is so glad he did. His job at Mall of America requires him to plan travel shows, design tourism brochures, write budget reports, and answer lots of questions from visitors interested in traveling to Minnesota. "It's a fun job, and every day is different," he said.

Killian also works with partners such as car rental companies, hotels, and convention and visitor bureaus to help plan travel packages for many of the tourists who travel to Minnesota to visit the Mall of America.

"Forty million visitors come to Mall of America every year. That's more people than the combined populations of Canada, North Dakota, South Dakota, Wyoming, and Montana," Killian said. Mall of America is one of the most popular tourism sites in the country.

Killian never dreamed he'd be working for one of the largest shopping malls in the country when he was studying journalism at the University of Minnesota. When he interviews young people just out of college, he encourages them to pursue jobs in tourism and shopping. "It's a great industry," he explained.

When Killian interviews candidates to work in his office, he said he looks for people with good verbal and written skills. Candidates must understand the purpose of a marketing plan, and he emphasized that prospective employees must be willing to be part of a team.

» » »

E-Commerce / Online Shopping

Retail spending on the Internet continues to grow. In 2007, online sales of everything from cars to clothing reached an all-time high of approximately $131 billion.[7] As more and more people get high-speed Internet connections, growth is expected to continue. Another contributing factor to the increase is more tech-savvy Americans. At least 72% of American adults surf the Internet on a regular basis.[8]

Online sales started with the World Wide Web. Once the coding language of HTML was introduced in 1989, people could connect to the Internet. Retail sales boomed in the mid-1990s as shopping online was a convenient novelty. The Internet industry entered a bleak period around 2000 as many Internet-based companies failed to make a profit. Thousands of people were laid off, and thousands of Internet companies closed their doors. By 2003, some of the easy-to-navigate and easy-to-shop Internet-based businesses started showing a profit. Consumers liked buying products over the Internet. Two very popular Internet-based retail companies are Amazon and eBay.

eBay started in 1995 as a website where online visitors could trade or buy antiques or other collectible goods—similar to an auction house. eBay is now one of the largest retail websites in the United States, with 4% of the market share in 2007.[9]

The giant in terms of retail websites is Amazon. Amazon is a more traditional store than eBay. It also started in 1995, primarily as a place to buy books. Online customers can now find DVDs, electronics, jewelry, toys, and much more at the Amazon website. Amazon has 11% of the market share and has more than $10 billion in annual sales.[10]

Online shopping and in-store shopping are not mutually exclusive. Many shoppers who browse a retailer's website are doing research and end up inside the store to buy. "For every dollar spent by consumers online, an additional $6 is spent in stores as a result of Internet research," according to Plunkett Research.[11]

Power Towns

The huge growth of shopping over the Internet has caught the attention of shopping center developers in a big way. Brick and mortar retailers have found they need to offer a lot more than just merchandise if they want to lure shoppers from behind their computers and into the retail store. "New shopping centers, especially those in urban areas, are devoting up to 40% of gross leasable area to entertainment, restaurants and movie theaters," according to Plunkett Research.[12] Some of these new shopping centers are so large they are being called "power towns."

Power towns are likely to include big anchor stores, small specialty stores, dozens of entertainment options, a multiplex movie theater complex, and lots of restaurants in a visually pleasing atmosphere. Desert Ridge in Scottsdale is a good example of a power town. Desert Ridge is home to 110 retailers and is spread out over 1.2 million square feet of retail space. Shoppers can find everything from a full-service bank to a billiards room, from an 18-screen movie theater to a dentist and even a dry cleaner. Desert Ridge brings people in from a 15-mile radius. And a lot of those shoppers drive right past other shopping malls to get to Desert Ridge.

Figure 20: 20 Largest Shopping Centers in the United States

(Ranked by Gross Leasable Space)

Rank	Name	Location	Size (square feet)	Number of Stores
1	Eastwood Mall Complex	Niles, OH	3,200,000	200
2	King of Prussia Mall	King of Prussia, PA	2,793,200	400
3	Mall of America	Bloomington, MN	2,768,399	522
4	South Coast Plaza	Costa Mesa, CA	2,700,000	280
5	Millcreek Mall	Erie, PA	2,600,000	241
6	Grand Canyon Parkway	Las Vegas, NV	2,500,000	10
7	Aventura Mall	Aventura, FL	2,400,000	275
8	Sawgrass Mills	Sunrise, FL	2,383,906	350
9	The Galleria	Houston, TX	2,298,420	375
10	Roosevelt Field Mall	Garden City, NY	2,244,581	294
11	Woodfield Mall	Schaumburg, IL	2,224,000	300
12	Palisades Center	West Nyack, NY	2,217,322	400
13	Tysons Corner Center	McLean, VA	2,200,000	300
14	Plaza Las Americas	San Juan, PR	2,173,000	300
15	Del Amo Fashion Center	Torrance, CA	2,100,000	300
16	Lakewood Center	Lakewood, CA	2,092,710	255
17	Oakbrook Shopping Ctr.	Oak Brook, IL	2,018,000	175
18	Westfield Gard. State Pla.	Paramus, NJ	2,000,000	369
19	NorthPark Center	Dallas, TX	2,000,000	235
20	Jordan Creek Town Ctr.	W. Des Moines, IA	2,000,000	160

Source: International Council of Shopping Centers. November, 2007

Lifestyle Centers

Another way shopping center developers have lured people back to the brick and mortar stores is by building "lifestyle centers." These attract customers by raising the roof—literally taking the roof off existing shopping centers and completely rebuilding the new center as an open-air entertainment and shopping destination.

One example of a "lifestyle center" is the Bella Terra Center in Huntington Beach, CA. The former shopping mall, the Huntington Center, was built in 1966 and looked like a traditional mall with anchor department stores on either end and an enclosed walkway connecting smaller stores inside the mall. In the 1990s, the mall was showing its age, and many retailers had moved out.

In 2003, builder J.H. Snyder tore the roof off the center and knocked down walls to build what is now the Bella Terra Center. The open-air center looks more like city streets with an emphasis on restaurants, shopping, and benches for people watching. The idea behind the lifestyle center is that if it offered more than just a shopping experience, the visitor might stay longer and visit more often. It's estimated that in 2002 there were just 30 lifestyle centers in the United States. By 2006, there were more than 130.[13]

The newest trend in shopping centers is to build residential units along with the retail and entertainment venues. Some of these new centers are building condos above the retail space or including town homes right next door. Ridge Hill Village in Yonkers, NY, is one example. The development is underway and calls for 1.3 million square feet of retail space, 1,000 apartments, a hotel and conference center, a grocery store, a Costco, and 160,000 square feet of office space. Ridge Hill Village is slated to open in the fall of 2009 and will encompass a massive 2.5 million square feet of development just 18 miles from midtown Manhattan.[14]

Challenges and Trends

Weak American Economy

Naturally, shopping and money go hand in hand. One of the biggest challenges in the retail industry is the stagnant economy in the United States. As confidence in the economy declines, more and more Americans are reluctant to spend money on non-essentials. The mortgage crisis and slowdown in the housing market in 2007 and 2008 forced many Americans to put the brakes on spending money on entertainment and shopping. While entertainment spending might have declined, competition among discount retailers has been very fierce. As Americans look for ways to make their dollars stretch further, discount chains like Wal-Mart have become very attractive.

While the troubled economy is creating apprehension among Americans, many people in other parts of the world see the weak dollar as an opportunity to get a bargain. Many Asians and Europeans are buying American products because their currency has more buying power than in recent years.

In an effort to lure tourists to shopping centers, some mall developers are doubling as tour operators. These developers are offering discounts and package deals including airline fares to get foreign tourists to the mall. One of the advantages of luring tourists to the mall, according to an article in the *Christian Science Monitor,* is that they "spend four to 10 times more than local shoppers, and they rarely return what they buy."[15]

Another challenge facing the retail industry is high consumer debt. It is estimated that the average American household has over $9,000 of credit card debt.[16] Combine that with a lack of faith in the economy, and many people will choose to curb their spending. So, the challenge for retailers is not only getting visitors to the mall but also getting them to spend money.

Online Shopping

Buying products online is going to continue to be popular as people look for ways to use their time efficiently and to find the best price, but, the biggest growth area for online shopping is expected to be China. The number of people who have access to the Internet in China grew by 50% in 2007.[17]

Although the Chinese people may want to buy American products, their government is hesitant. The Chinese government doesn't want to hand over control to foreign companies and is quick to ban websites that may have what the government considers "sensitive content." Google has encountered problems in China: It launched a different version of its website just for its Chinese audience after the international version was banned in China. eBay is also having trouble becoming successful in the Chinese Internet market. The issue with eBay is less about the Chinese government and more about the Chinese people. The Chinese are skeptical about buying items from unknown individuals on the Internet.

Online shopping helps promote in-store shopping, and that will continue to be a growing trend. The most successful companies will find a way to provide customers with many options when buying either at the physical store or on the website.

Retailer J.Jill has incorporated a system where buyers can return merchandise bought online to any J.Jill store. And inside the stores, shoppers can browse on the store's computers to find different sizes and colors on merchandise in the warehouse and have it shipped to the shopper's home free of charge. Bloomingdales tried something even more innovative in its stores. Shoppers could use their "interactive" mirror to send an image of the customer wearing a particular outfit to friends or relatives and get instant feedback from loved ones at home.

Figure 21: Top 20 Retail Websites in the United States

Rank	Name	Domain	Market Share
1	Amazon.com	www.amazon.com	11.08%
2	Wal-Mart	www.walmart.com	7.20%
3	Target	www.target.com	4.86%
4	Half.com (eBay)	www.half.ebay.com	4.03%
5	Yahoo! Shopping	shopping.yahoo.com	3.50%
6	Best Buy	www.bestbuy.com	2.91%
7	JC Penney	www.jcpenney.com	2.48%
8	Overstock.com	www.overstock.com	2.39%
9	Bizrate	www.bizrate.com	2.36%
10	Circuit City	www.circuitcity.com	2.34%
11	Toys 'R Us	www.toysrus.com	2.32%
12	Sears	www.sears.com	2.16%
13	Shopzilla	www.shopzilla.com	2.08%
14	QVC	www.qvc.com	2.07%
15	Smarter.com	www.smarter.com	2.01%
16	Dell	www.dell.com	1.90%
17	Ticketmaster	www.ticketmaster.com	1.61%
18	Kohl's	www.kohls.com	1.39%
19	Lowes	www.lowes.com	1.29%
20	Home Depot	www.homedepot.com	1.29%

Source: Hitwise (www.hitwise.com). November, 2007

Next Generation of Shoppers

The next generation of shoppers might be looking for something different from their parents. The Generation-X consumer group is characterized as having a love of technology and being computer savvy. The Gen-X group tends to be less swayed by advertising claims and less impressed with designer price tags. Generally speaking, this group likes extreme sports and adventure vacations. So, shopping centers that also offer entertainment and extreme rides or sports just might appeal to this group. Shopping malls with lots of choices from discount stores to higher-end stores might also be what the Gen-X generation is looking for.

Security and Theft Prevention

It might seem obvious, but it is worth mentioning that security is and will remain a top concern for shopping mall executives. A very popular entertainment event, whether it's a singer or an author signing books, could attract thousands of people to a power town or shopping mall. If that happens, security is going to have to be beefed up. Visitors need to feel safe at the shopping mall if they are to return. Theft prevention inside stores will also continue to be a big problem. Most department stores have employees who do nothing but monitor shoppers to limit theft of merchandise.

Deadmalls.com

Some people just don't like change. Or maybe it's hard to let go of the past. Whatever the reason, retail historians Peter Blackbird and Brian Florence decided to take their fascination with dead malls to a website, www.deadmalls.com. News outlets from the *Sacramento Bee* to National Public Radio have reported on the website and its list of dying malls. The website has a map that shows dead or dying malls, a blog where readers can relive their memories of mall life, and a dictionary of dead mall jargon.

For instance, you may not find the word "labelscar" in the dictionary, but according to deadmalls.com it means "fading or dirt left behind from a sign on or in a mall. Labelscars leave a readable marking, which is very helpful when identifying former stores."[18]

Employment Opportunities

The employment opportunities in the area of shopping and retail are as diverse as the shirts on a rack at your favorite department store. Here's a look at some of the most popular and visible jobs currently in demand at shopping malls and retail stores across the country.

Administration

Shopping malls of the 1960s needed a group of people to manage the center, and the new power towns and lifestyle centers are no different. General managers are needed at centers across the country. The GM's primary responsibilities include: keeping the mall running efficiently and safely day after day and increasing sales and traffic. The GM is also expected to be an excellent negotiator and have a professional image. Most job openings require a B.A. or B.S.

Mall Designers / Architects

Architects and designers continue to be needed to conceptualize, design, plan, and build new shopping centers or to redevelop existing centers. As malls have moved away from a cookie-cutter look, more creativity will be required to design centers based on land availability and potential usage.

One look at the artist's sketches of the Meadowlands Xanadu project, and it's obvious some very creative engineering and designing were utilized. Corners of the Meadowlands Xanadu structure jet out into the air. Bold, bright colors of the outside of the structure are visible for miles in every direction. For projects like Meadowlands Xanadu, interior designers will also be needed once the structures are complete to design sitting areas conducive to people watching and relaxing. Degrees in construction, engineering, or architecture will be required.

Marketing

Shopping areas need a marketing team to coordinate public relations, coordinate promotions and events, manage advertising and gift card programs, and help support the tenants so that they see sales increase. Most marketing managers have a degree in marketing or public relations. Positions in marketing require strong writing skills and the ability to coordinate many projects happening simultaneously. The marketing team might also be responsible for coordinating tourism programs in an effort to bring visitors to the shopping center.

Security

As mentioned previously, security at the shopping areas and inside the stores will remain a constant challenge. Therefore, there will continue to be a need to hire people with security, criminal justice and law enforcement backgrounds.

Store Managers / Employees

As malls get larger there will be a growing need to employ people to work inside each individual store. Some of the largest shopping centers in the United States have hundreds of stores. The Mall of America in Minneapolis, Minn., has more than 400 stores. That translates into lots of jobs for retail managers and sales associates. A sales associate might be the perfect job for a college student. Many associates move into management and find the work very rewarding.

Personal Shopper

Large department stores like Nordstrom have employed personal shoppers for years. The personal shopper works with clients to pull together clothing or outfits before the client comes into the store to try on the clothes. As more and more Americans find themselves overwhelmed with their "to-do" lists, there is an opportunity for the personal shopper to take over some of the chores, including shopping.

All Around Town Concierge & Errand Service in New York does just that. Personal shoppers can be hired for $150 an hour to run errands, do shopping, wrap gifts, send out cards, pick up dry cleaning, do grocery shopping, and decorate homes for a party or during the holidays.

Future Outlook

The retail industry is the second largest industry in the United States. Americans love to shop, and that isn't likely to change anytime soon. But as long as the economy remains uncertain, Americans will have less disposable income, and that will curb retail sales.

But the power of entertainment will continue to attract customers to shopping centers that offer a variety of things to do. We will continue to see power towns built with many options for entertainment including family entertainment centers. We will also continue to see power towns with ski runs, Ferris wheels, roller coasters, ice skating rinks, lots of shopping—the variety of options as extensive as the designer's creativity.

Lifestyle centers will continue to be popular, offering the shopper the feel of a downtown village. Open-air shopping centers that incorporate small streets, beautiful landscaping, and wicker lounge chairs will continue to offer the visitor a place to connect with friends and to do some boutique shopping. The future may bring more lifestyle centers that incorporate residential units, so that people can shop and be entertained right outside their front doors.

Internet shopping will remain popular. It's easy, doesn't require hunting for a parking spot, and makes comparison shopping a virtual sport. But many stores have found that integrating the store and the website is really what consumers want. Shoppers like to do research online and then buy in a physical store. That trend is likely to continue.

ALEXIS MCKINNIS

Personal Shopper
Owner, Personal Touch,
Errands & Assistance

www.personal-touch-errands.com

If there are more errands and shopping to get done than there are hours in the day, Alexis McKinnis might be able to help. McKinnis runs the Personal Touch, Errands and Assistance Company in the Minneapolis, MN, area. McKinnis started her company in 2001 and has been helping clients finish their to-do lists ever since.

This former executive assistant has been known to find the perfect gift for a business partner and shop and deliver groceries to a client all in the same day. Almost nothing surprises McKinnis anymore. She's baked homemade cookies for a client trying to say he's sorry to his girlfriend. She's also met a client at a restaurant to get $40 cash to be delivered to the client's babysitter who ordered a pizza at home. No two days are ever the same. McKinnis said it's not uncommon for a client to hand her thousands of dollars in cash to shop for a new wardrobe.

McKinnis estimated that 50% of her time is spent running errands. The other 50% is shopping. "I still like shopping. I'm an expert at shopping," she said. Most of her clients are men who don't live with a wife or girlfriend. She also gets a lot of business from clients who live outside of the Twin Cities who don't know where to turn to find a perfect outfit or gift.

The need for personal shoppers appears to be growing. McKinnis said when she started her company in 2001, there was no one offering the same kinds of services in Minneapolis. Now, there are at least six businesses in the area that do similar work.

McKinnis frequently reads résumés from personal shoppers who want to work for her. She said she won't even consider someone if he or she can't write and has trouble constructing a complete sentence. Also, she is surprised when prospective employees show up dressed unprofessionally. In this business, she said, image is everything.

» » »

Summary

Shopping may not be a competitive sport, but it's certainly become a favorite pastime for Americans. We shop to buy staples; we shop when connecting with friends, and we shop on vacation. But the retail experience has changed over the past 50 years. No longer are shoppers content with a windowless, nondescript suburban shopping mall. They now want to be entertained while they shop.

Location-based entertainment venues started popping up near or in shopping malls in the 1980s and '90s, and shoppers liked them. Storeowners and managers also liked the entertainment. With entertainment came more business in the form of tourists and repeat customers. So, power towns started appearing throughout the United States.

The power town can be thought of as a shopping mall on steroids, offering visitors enough shopping and entertainment to keep them busy for several days. Add a professional sports team, a hotel, and some residential units nearby, and you have a combination that is sure to attract people wanting to live, visit, and spend money.

Boutique shopping by way of the "lifestyle center" also gained in popularity after the turn of the twenty-first century. Visitors wanted the feel of an urban downtown with small shops, plenty of places to eat, and lots of comfortable seating to visit with friends or to people watch.

In summary, shopping is here to stay, but we want it spiced up a bit…with a bit of an adrenaline rush via the roller coaster on the side.

ADDITIONAL RESOURCES

Associations and Organizations

International Council on Shopping Centers: www.icsc.org
National Retail Federation Inc.: www.nrf.com

Job-Hunting Resources

All Retail Jobs: www.allretailjobs.com
Shopping Center Jobs: www.shoppingcenterjobs.com
Work in Retail: www.workinretail.com

Books

Beyard, Michael D. *Developing Retail Entertainment Destinations,* 2nd ed. Washington, D.C.: Urban Land Institute, 2001.
Moss, Mark H. *Shopping as an Entertainment Experience.* Lanham, MD: Lexington Books, 2007.
O'Malley, Stephanie. *Start Your Retail Career.* Newburgh, NY: Entrepreneur Press, 2008.

Magazines and Trade Publications

Chain Store Age: www.chainstoreage.com

Retail Merchandiser: www.retail-merchandiser.com

Retailing Today: www.retailingtoday.com

Retail Traffic: www.retailtrafficmag.com

Stores: www.stores.org

WWD (Women's Wear Daily): www.wwd.com

Government Agencies

U.S. Bureau of Labor Statistics: stats.bls.gov

U.S. Department of Commerce: www.commerce.gov

ENDNOTES

1. "The History of Retailing," *Britannica Online Encyclopedia,* www.britannica.com.
2. Ibid.
3. Ibid.
4. "Birth, Death and Shopping; Retailing," *The Economist* 385:8560 (December 22, 2007): 104.
5. *Shopping Centers & Retail Projects,* White Hutchinson Leisure and Learning Group, www.white-hutchinson.com
6. America's Research Group, www.americaresearchgroup.com.
7. "Brick, Clicks and Catalogues Create Synergies While Online Sales Boom," Plunkett Research, Ltd., www.plunkettresearchonline.com.
8. Ibid.
9. "Top 20 Retail Websites, U.S.," Plunkett Research, Ltd., www.plunkettresearchonline.com.
10. Ibid.
11. Ibid.
12. "Entertainment-Based Retailing, including Power Towns," Plunkett Research, Ltd., www.plunkettresearchonline.com.
13. Andrew Blum, "The Mall Goes Undercover," *Slate Magazine,* April 6, 2005, www.slate.com.
14. Ridge Hill Marketing Brochure, www.ridgehill.com.
15. Suzi Parker, "Have Visa Will Travel: Tourists Flock to the Mall," *Christian Science Monitor,* 18 August 1998, 3.
16. Liz Pulliam Weston, "The Big Lie About Credit Card Debt," www.msn.com, 30 July 2007.
17. "US E-Commerce Companies Expand Overseas, China to Become World's Largest Online Market," Plunkett Research, Ltd., www.plunkettresearchonline.com.
18. Deadmails.com, www.deadmalls.com.

Interactive Entertainment

12

Gambling
and Casino Gaming   ANDI STEIN

When a fire broke out on the rooftop of the Monte Carlo casino in Las Vegas on a wintry January afternoon, guests rapidly evacuated and escaped to safety. One woman, however, was reluctant to leave the penny slot machine she had been playing. The reason? Only minutes before the fire alarm sounded, she had hit a $1,577 jackpot that she had been unable to collect before the evacuation.

Fortunately for her, a quick-thinking security guard notified the casino's surveillance team, and he and the woman waved at a nearby video camera where they were captured on tape to verify that she had won. The next day, she returned to the casino to collect her winnings.[1]

While this might seem a bit over the top, it serves as a prime example of the public's fascination with gambling and casino gaming and the allure that the possibility of "winning the jackpot" can hold. Whether the pastime be rolling the dice at a glitzy casino on the Las Vegas strip or betting on the NCAA "March Madness" playoffs in the office basketball pool, the promise of instant riches has a strong pull for many.

Gambling and casino gaming comprise a billion-dollar piece of the entertainment industry. According to the American Gaming Association, in the past 12 years, revenues from commercial casinos alone have doubled from $16 billion in 1995 to $32.4 billion in 2006.[2] And casino gaming is only one part of the legalized gambling industry in the United States. Lotteries, Indian gaming, pari-mutuel wagering such as horse and dog racing, and charitable gaming like church bingo games and PTA raffles are also included among legal-ized gambling activities.

In the United States alone, commercial casino gaming is legal in 12 states, while Indian gaming has been quietly growing in another 28 states. Thirty-seven states and the District of Columbia have lotteries, and 43 have legalized pari-mutuel wagering. Only two states—Utah and Hawaii—prohibit gambling altogether.

Gambling and gaming are also popular at an international level. Since 2002, the development and growth of the casino industry in Macau, a Special Administrative Region of China, for example, have resulted in revenues that have surpassed those of Las Vegas.[3]

These figures don't even include the assortment of unauthorized gambling activities that take place on a regular basis, such as chipping into the office Super Bowl pool or taking a chance on gambling websites on the Internet, an activity that has sparked great debate and controversy over the past 10 years.

For those working in the industry, the popularity of gambling and casino gaming has led to tremendous growth, presenting an assortment of challenges for those in the business. Keeping up with the competition and managing risks such as employee theft or potential acts of terrorism provide everyday trials and tribulations for those in the industry.

In addition, while gambling and casino gaming offer the potential to win big, they also offer the opportunity to lose big—something that is far more common for the average gambler than winning the jackpot. Because of this, overcoming negative perceptions about the downsides of gambling and the potential for patrons to develop gambling problems can also be a challenge for those in the business.

This chapter will explore some of the allure that gambling and casino gaming hold for the public. At the same time, it will examine the day-to-day activities faced by those working in the industry who are responsible for keeping this allure alive.

History and Background

Early Beginnings

Despite a recent surge in popularity, the practice of gambling is not new. In fact, it dates back thousands of years, according to the American Gaming Association.[4] In ancient Egyptian tombs, for example, 4,000-year-old dice have been discovered, while evidence of games of chance can be traced to China and Japan in 2300 B.C.

In the Middle Ages, soldiers and merchants often engaged in drinking and gambling while stopping off at inns for the night in their travels. By the early 1500s, lotteries had become popular in Europe as a means of raising money for royalty—a form of "voluntary taxation."

During the early years of the American colonies, some of the Founding Fathers such as Ben Franklin and George Washington ran lotteries to raise money for new construction. Even schools got in on the action: Ivy League colleges such as Yale, Harvard, and Dartmouth relied on lottery funds to help build dormitories for their students.

By the nineteenth century, gambling establishments had become quite popular in Europe in places such as Great Britain and Monte Carlo in Monaco, a site still renowned for its casino. By the twentieth century, gambling was formally sanctioned in the United States, and in 1931, Nevada became the first state to legalize casino gambling, which led to Las Vegas becoming the gambling capital of the world.

The Rise of Gambling in the United States

In the early years of Las Vegas, casinos were operated by individuals with ties to the Mafia, such as Bugsy Siegel. By the late 1960s, however, legislation designed to oversee the industry led to a change in ownership, as two Corporate Gaming acts opened the door for corporations to launch casinos. Harrah's Entertainment became the first corporate gambling establishment traded on the New York Stock Exchange in 1973, ushering in a new era in the casino business.

When casino gaming was legalized in New Jersey in the mid-1970s, opportunities suddenly became available for those on the East Coast of the United States to get into the market. The first casino opened in Atlantic City in 1978, and a scenic seaside resort was slowly transformed into a strip of hotel/casinos similar to those in Las Vegas.

A New Kind of Casino

By the late 1980s, the concept of the casino as a destination resort began to emerge in Las Vegas with the construction of the Mirage by Steve Wynn. The hotel/casino featured more than 3,000 hotel rooms, headline entertainers, and a property that had a resort-like quality—unlike anything that had been seen before in the gambling capital. Over the next decade, the Mirage was followed by the construction of other resort casinos, some of them with prominent "themes"—the Excalibur, Treasure Island, the Venetian, and the Bellagio, to name just a few.

Growth and Expansion of the Industry

While the casino gaming industry in Las Vegas was exploding, other states began to see the value of permitting gambling. In 1989, South Dakota and Iowa voted to legalize gambling, and other states such as Rhode Island, Delaware, and West Virginia soon followed.

At the same time, the legalization of casino gaming on U.S. Indian reservations in 1988 opened doors for states to develop casinos on federally owned Indian territories without formally approving gambling on non-federal lands. This legislation has had a great impact on the expansion of casino gaming throughout the United States.

Figure 22: Top 10 U.S. Casino Markets

1. Las Vegas Strip
2. Atlantic City, NJ
3. Chicagoland (Indiana/Illinois)
4. Connecticut
5. Detroit
6. Tunica/Lula, Mississippi
7. St. Louis, MO
8. Reno/Sparks, NV
9. Boulder Strip, NV
10. Shreveport, LA

Based on 2006 data from the American Gaming Association.

Other Types of Gambling

Casino gaming was not the only form of legalized gambling to develop and grow in the United States during the twentieth century. In 1964, New Hampshire introduced the first formalized state lottery, and many other states subsequently implemented their own lotteries over the following two decades.

Interest in the development of pari-mutuel wagering also grew in the twentieth century with the establishment of legalized horse racing in the late 1800s and greyhound racing tracks in the 1920s. By the 1970s, off-track betting and the simulcasting of races had become a part of the industry. A twist on the racetrack concept developed in the early 1990s when the first "racino" opened in Rhode Island in 1992, combining traditional horse racing tracks with casino slot machines.

In 1995, the American Gaming Association was created to represent the commercial casino industry. This was followed by the National Center for Responsible Gambling as a means of addressing the growing issue of problem gambling.

The Impact of Electronic Media

The establishment of the World Wide Web in 1995 offered the potential for a whole new dimension of games of chance with the introduction of Internet gambling. While this area of the industry has grown tremendously, so has the controversy surrounding it. Many traditional gambling establishments have protested the existence of online gaming, while the U.S. government has struggled to determine how to regulate it. The debate remains unresolved.

In 2003, a cable television show called "World Poker Tour" had an impact on the casino gaming industry, as it brought poker to the forefront of people's consciousnesses, resulting in a surge of interest in the game at gambling establishments throughout the world.[5]

Modern-Day Gambling and Gaming

Today, casino gaming in Las Vegas continues to grow. Mergers of corporations such as Harrah's Entertainment and Caesar's Entertainment as well as the MGM-Mirage Group's acquisition of the Mandalay Resort Group have led to a handful of corporate owners controlling the Las Vegas Strip's major resorts. Construction is booming in Las Vegas, and it is expected that the next decade will see the development of at least three major casino properties.

On an international scale, interest in casino gaming has also made a dramatic shift to the east with the expansion of the industry in Macau, a Special Administrative Region of China. Not wanting to be left out of the international equation, Las Vegas moguls such as Steve Wynn and Sheldon Adelson, owner of the Venetian, have had a hand in the development of this market, which is predicted to eventually displace Las Vegas as the gambling capital of the world.

In short, the popularity of gambling and casino gaming continues to flourish and is expected to do so for many years to come. As a result, the industry offers many challenges to those already working in the business as well as opportunities for those seeking careers in the field.

Types of Legalized Gambling

There are five types of legalized gambling in the United States: commercial casino gaming, Native American Indian gaming, lotteries, pari-mutuel wagering, and charitable gaming.

Commercial Casino Gaming

As mentioned above, commercial casino gaming is a billion-dollar industry that encompasses major markets in Las Vegas ($6.7 billion) and Atlantic City ($5.5 billion) as well as smaller markets in other parts of the country. Riverboat gambling is the norm in states such as Illinois, Indiana, and Missouri, for example. The Gulf Coast of Mississippi is populated with nearly a dozen casinos, many of which were destroyed by Hurricane Katrina in 2005, were subsequently rebuilt, and are thriving once again.

Commercial casinos offer a variety of gambling options including slot machines, table games such as poker, blackjack, roulette, and craps, and, in the state of Nevada, sports wagering.

Native American Indian Gaming

Since 1988, when the Indian Gaming Regulatory Act legalized casino gaming on American Indian reservations, a number of tribes throughout the United States have partnered with commercial casino corporations to develop casino gaming on their lands. According to the National Indian Gaming Association, of the 562 federally recognized

Indian tribes, 225 are currently involved in some sort of casino gaming. In 2005, Indian gaming generated $22.6 billion for these tribes.[6]

Currently, 28 states offer Indian gaming. This has resulted in the development of Las Vegas-style casinos on Indian lands, which include many of the same amenities offered by their commercial counterparts. In California, the legalization of Indian gaming has had an impact on Nevada casino revenues, as the proliferation of casinos on Indian lands, particularly in Southern California, has made it easier for local residents to satisfy their gambling urges without straying far from home.

Lotteries

As already noted, the first legalized state lottery took place in New Hampshire in 1964. Today, 37 states and the District of Columbia have lotteries, offering a range of games that include quick-pick, instant scratch-off tickets, and weekly "Big Spin" drawings.

A number of states have also banded together to form the Multi-State Lottery Association (MSLA), which sponsors the Powerball game that enables people to compete for jackpots that can sometimes consist of hundreds of millions of dollars. According to the MSLA, 29 states, the District of Columbia, and the U.S. Virgin Islands participate in Powerball.[7] One of the largest Powerball jackpots to date was $365 million, won by a group of eight co-workers at a food processing plant in Nebraska in 2006.[8]

Pari-Mutuel Wagering

Pari-mutuel wagering is similar to the structure of a lottery in that the total amount of the prize money is based on the amount of money bet. In the United States, three different types of activities fall under the guise of pari-mutuel gambling: horse racing, greyhound racing, and jai-alai.

Horse racing in particular has had a long-standing following in the United States, and approximately $20 billion are bet on horses each year, according to the National Thoroughbred Racing Association.[9] The granddaddy of all horse races is the Kentucky Derby, held the first Saturday in May in Louisville.

Today, there are more than 100 racetracks in 32 states. Races are also simulcast through closed-circuit television, enabling patrons to bet on races without being physically present at a specific track to do so. Eleven states also have "racinos," which complement their traditional tracks with Las Vegas-style slot machines.

Greyhound racing also falls into the category of pari-mutuel wagering, and while it is not nearly as popular as horse racing, it still generates revenues in the billions. According to the Greyhound Racing Association of America,

> The sport reached its peak in 1992, when attendance approached 3.5 million, and nearly $3.5 billion was bet on 16,827 races at more than 50 tracks. Since then, revenue has dropped by nearly 50 percent, and 13 tracks have closed. Other forms of legalized gambling have been the major problem, but pressure from animal rights groups has also hurt.[10]

LIZ FURTADO

Senior Marketing Specialist
California Lottery
www.calottery.com

As an employee of the California Lottery, Liz Furtado and anyone living in her household are forbidden from playing. So, when Furtado was in Maryland at a conference, she took the opportunity to play the state lottery there and was thrilled when she won $20 dollars. "It's nice to get to see the game as the player does," she explained.

Furtado oversees development of all the scratcher games. That involves coming up with the creative ideas, ticket design, and prize structure as well as making sure the tickets are secure and that there are no misprints. She also implements the new scratchers across the state. Furtado and her team design 45 games a year.

Furtado started as an office clerk with the California Lottery right before the kickoff date in 1985. She's held several jobs within the office, including serving four years as the producer of the Big Spin television show. She landed with the scratchers' product development team 12 years ago. "I love it. Every game is different. It never gets old or redundant," she said.

As a student at Sacramento City College, Furtado began working for the state. Her goal was to work her way up to an analyst in the government hierarchy. She said she quit college when her career started to take off.

The advice she offers to young people who are hoping to work in a similar field is that "math is so much more important than I ever thought." She said she was never fond of math but has found it essential to what she does. Furtado also recommended that students be "well balanced in all their subjects." What students learn in school will come in handy in the job eventually, she explained.

The best part of the job, according to Furtado, is the fact that what she does has the opportunity to be life-changing. "Growing up, I didn't have much. If I can't win, I like to see someone win big. There's nothing like seeing someone get a big check from the California Lottery."

» » »

Today there are 46 greyhound tracks in 15 states, according to the organization, but the popularity of the sport is clearly waning. Some states ban this type of racing outright, claiming it is inhumane to the dogs.

Jai-alai is a game played with a ball and glove attached to a wicker basket that originated in the Basque regions of Spain and France. Although it is considered a legalized form of pari-mutuel wagering, it is far less popular than horse or greyhound racing. While the game was once played in several states including Connecticut and Rhode Island, today, betting on jai-alai is only available at a handful of establishments in Florida.

Charitable Gaming

The last type of legalized gambling in the United States is designed for nonprofit organization fundraising purposes. Charitable gaming encompasses activities such as church bingo games, school raffles, and Las Vegas nights. While some state governments have established charitable gaming divisions, in general these types of activities are not heavily regulated, as the proceeds are intended to benefit the nonprofit organizations that sponsor them.

Challenges and Trends

Competition

Upgrades and Expansion

Because gambling and gaming have grown by leaps and bounds in the last few decades, one of the biggest challenges faced by those in the industry is keeping up with the competition, particularly in the area of casino gaming. In Las Vegas, for example, there has been a major construction boom as older, long-established casinos are being replaced with sleek, upscale mega-casinos that place as much emphasis on dining, shopping, and entertainment as they do on gambling.

In 2005, the ultra-modern Wynn casino was built on the former site of the Desert Inn, one of the original Las Vegas casinos. Two others, the Stardust and Frontier, were demolished and replaced by large-scale hotel/casino/condominium complexes. One of the reasons for this shift is the change in the Las Vegas clientele.

> The demographics of the Las Vegas tourist are shifting towards the younger and wealthier, which is stimulating the demand for higher-end lodging and retail. As a result, the existing properties that currently serve this segment...may soon find themselves overshadowed by upscale mega resorts that are in the development or planning stages.[11]

Other indications of this shift in demographics have been the proliferation of trendy nightclubs, gourmet restaurants, and high-priced entertainment acts that have sprung up in the Strip's casinos in recent years.

Increased Global Competition

The threat of Macau as a gambling destination for international tourists is also likely to have an impact on the Las Vegas market. According to the *New York Times,* "Booming property and stock markets in mainland China and Hong Kong, along with the opening of resorts that adopt the style of Las Vegas, like the Venetian, are drawing wealthy gamblers from around the world."[12] A casino consultant with PricewaterhouseCoopers was quoted in the same article as saying, "The implications are that some of the focus that has traditionally been on Las Vegas might shift further to Macao."[13]

Planned Growth for Atlantic City

The legalization of gambling in Pennsylvania in 2006 has had an impact on business in Atlantic City, which is the second largest casino gaming market in the United States. In 2007, Atlantic City casino revenues dropped 5.7% shortly after the first casinos opened in nearby Philadelphia.[14] A recently approved ban on smoking inside Atlantic City casinos is expected to have a negative impact as well.

To combat these potential threats, casinos in Atlantic City are exploring their own options for expansion. "Virtually every casino is either in the midst of an expensive expansion or renovation, has just completed one or is planning one soon," according to the Bergen County *Record:*

> The building boom is adding thousands of new hotel rooms and investing billions of dollars in a resort struggling to remake itself as a national destination where visitors stay for three or more days instead of a place for bus-riding day-trippers to linger for a few hours before hitting the buffet and heading home.[15]

Indian Casino Development

Commercial casinos are not alone in repackaging themselves to keep up with the competition. Indian casinos are also taking steps to enhance their existing facilities in order to make themselves more attractive as vacation destination resorts rather than spots for one-day outings. In California, for example, a number of casinos such as Pechanga, Morongo, and Cache Creek have built high-rise hotels to complement their casinos.

In Connecticut, the two major Indian casinos, Foxwoods and Mohegan Sun, have suffered as a result of the expansion of legalized gaming in nearby Rhode Island and New York. Consequently, Foxwoods has partnered with the MGM Grand to open a second casino on its property, while Mohegan Sun is in the midst of a $925 million expansion that will include the opening of a 39-story hotel.[16]

A Merger of Casinos and Racetracks

The development of the racino concept is also having an impact on the casino gaming industry. As more and more horse racing tracks are adding slot machines into the mix, they are pulling customers away from established casinos in states such as Indiana and Michigan.[17]

For some of these tracks, however, the addition of slot machines may be just what is needed to inject some new life into a sagging business. In California, which does a large share of its racing business through the summertime county fair circuit, attendance figures have dipped significantly, resulting in shortened seasons and the consolidation of racing venues.[18] States such as Pennsylvania and New York are hoping the addition of slot machines will draw more customers to the track and rekindle an interest in live racing.[19]

Risk Management

In addition to keeping up with the competition, managers of casino gaming establishments are finding risk management to be a big part of their jobs.

> Gaming resorts today are self-contained living and entertainment environments operating 24 hours a day, seven days a week. Including staff, most large resorts contain more people at any given time than most towns.[20]

Consequently, the potential for problems is high, and casinos are continuously developing new techniques for managing risk.

Video Surveillance

A typical casino is rigged with a sophisticated surveillance system, often referred to as the "eye in the sky," to keep constant tabs on what is happening inside the casino and to cut down on theft and fraud, among other uses.

With money flowing freely, temptation is constant inside a casino environment. As a result, casinos are constantly on the lookout for indications of employee theft. According to an article in the *Las Vegas Sun,*

> Employee theft—sometimes as simple as pocketing cash or chips—is a recurring problem in the cash-rich industry, which can corrupt the most trusted employees. Most crimes are not publicized by casinos, and regulators are reluctant to discuss them for fear of tipping thieves to new techniques.[21]

Sometimes, however, incidences of employee theft do make the news. In 2006, a woman was arrested for stealing more than $50,000 from a Louisiana casino after surveillance cameras caught her emptying cash from 30 slot machines into a garbage bag.[22] In Chicago, a group of 19 employees and players were charged with a card-shuffling scam that involved one of the players paying off a dealer to improperly shuffle cards at a minibaccarat table. This, too, was caught on tape by casino video cameras.

Surveillance cameras sometimes serve as a means of reducing customer fraud as well. Personnel at Harrah's Entertainment have reported that occasionally, customers will try to cheat the organization by claiming their cars were damaged in casino parking lots or while being parked by valets when, in fact, videotape shows that the cars already appeared to be damaged when they were driven onto the lots. One man claimed that he was bitten by a snake that crawled out of a toilet at a Harrah's casino, but a security camera revealed the man carrying the snake into the bathroom in a burlap sack.[23]

Casinos also use other means of technology to cut down on theft and fraud. Some gaming establishments have begun embedding their casino chips with radio frequency identification (RFID) tags, which allow for the monitoring of the chips' location. This helps security personnel keep track of each chip and alerts them to any chips that are removed from the casino floor.

Preventing Terrorism

Another risk management issue that has taken precedence in recent years is the threat of terrorism. Since September 11, 2001, security has been upped in all kinds of environments that attract large numbers of people—airports, theme parks, theaters, etc. Casinos have not been exempt from this increase in homeland security.

Some casinos have installed metal detectors, which screen casino employees and guests for guns, knives, and other weapons. Casinos have also taken more precautions with their hotels, according to an article in *Security Management:*

> Many hotels now require that guests present a photo ID when they check in, and many establishments also run a check of the guest's name against those on the government's terrorist watch list. Many establishments also have a security officer posted around the clock at the elevators to check guestroom keys.[24]

As a result of this increased emphasis on security, some casinos have implemented employee-training programs to educate security personnel on the implementation of these policies. The Barona Valley Resort in Southern California, for example, has employed a full-time security trainer since 9/11.[25]

Crisis Management

Dealing with unexpected crises can also be a part of a casino's risk management activities. When Hurricane Katrina struck the Gulf Coast in 2005, it virtually destroyed the casino industry in Mississippi and Louisiana. Until that point, gaming in Mississippi had only been allowed on barges situated offshore, largely in Gulfport, Biloxi, and Tunica. The hurricane blew some of these barges to bits or uprooted them from their foundations. The Grand Casino in Gulfport, for instance, was tossed by the wind onto a local highway.

While situations like this are extreme, it is not uncommon for casino personnel to have to deal with unexpected turns of events. Consequently, they need to develop solid crisis management plans and employ specialists to implement these plans.

Crises can also come in the form of unexpected customer health issues such as patrons suffering strokes or heart attacks while on the casino floor or in the resort hotels. A number of Las Vegas casinos have invested in automatic external defibrillators, which can be used to provide what can be a life-saving jolt to a patron whose heart has stopped.

According to an article in the *Wall Street Journal:*

> Medical research shows that casino visitors whose hearts suddenly stop survive at higher rates even than people who happen to go into cardiac arrest while visiting a hospital.... Casinos' security officers have become so adept with them that they usually decline offers of aid from physician bystanders.[26]

The presence of video cameras throughout casinos helps security personnel easily identify those in medical trouble, which allows them to get help from security officers quickly.

Overcoming Negative Perceptions of Gambling

One of the more difficult challenges those in the industry face on a routine basis is the process of overcoming some of the negative perceptions commonly affiliated with gambling and casino gaming. Opposition to gambling can come from a variety of sources, including religious organizations and community groups that claim gambling is detrimental to society.

It's no secret that gambling involves taking risks with money—sometimes large amounts of money—and the odds of losing are much greater than the odds of winning. Some people may also fear that such facilities as racetracks and casinos will attract a wide demographic of people, including unsavory or potentially threatening individuals. Groups may mobilize to protest the legalization of gambling in certain states or the opening of new gaming facilities on the premise that such facilities will lead to an increase in crime or personal bankruptcy.

When the state of Kentucky debated the expansion of gambling at racetracks, an organization called the Family Foundation of Kentucky led a movement to formally oppose the idea.[27] Likewise, when casino gaming was legalized in Pennsylvania in 2004, a number of community groups in Philadelphia banded together to protest the development of a casino in the heart of the city's downtown waterfront area. These objections were ultimately overruled, and the casino was approved.[28]

In 2008, a survey of Massachusetts residents about the possibility of opening three casinos in that state revealed that residents were split on the issue, with 41% in favor, 42% opposed, and 17% neutral.[29] This type of public response reflects the attitudes that those in the gambling and gaming industry face on a continual basis. Despite the vast amount of dollars spent on gambling and gaming, the public perception about whether it is a suitable form of entertainment is still a matter for debate.

Problem Gambling

Directly related to the negative perceptions of gambling is the idea that the availability of gaming facilities can lead to an increase in problem gambling. According to the National Coalition on Problem Gambling, problem gambling is "gambling behavior which causes disruption in any major area of life: psychological, physical, social or vocational."[30] On a practical level, this can lead to an inability to meet financial obligations or prioritize day-to-day responsibilities because of the uncontrollable urge to gamble. Just as with any other type of addiction—alcohol, drugs, sex, etc.—the urge to gamble compulsively can wreak havoc on people's lives.

A number of industry organizations offer programs to educate people about the hazards of problem gambling and the resources that are available to help them. The American Gaming Association funded the National Center for Responsible Gaming in 1995 to promote research and education pertaining to the issue.[31] The National Council on Problem Gambling and the Association of Problem Gambling Service Administrators co-sponsor Problem Gambling Awareness Week in March: "The goal of the grass-roots public awareness and outreach campaign is to educate the general public and health care professionals about the warning signs of problem gambling and raise awareness about the help that is available both locally and nationally."[32]

Individual casinos mount their own campaigns to try to reduce problem gambling as well. In conjunction with Problem Gambling Awareness Week, for example, the Foxwoods Casino in Connecticut created a 30-minute educational video called "21" and distributed pamphlets to patrons that provided a list of treatment resources for problem gambling.[33] The San Manuel Casino in California makes a concerted effort to encourage responsible gambling by "posting signage and placing brochures in highly visible locations throughout the property and directing patrons to the 24-hour confidential Problem Gambling Hotline."[34] Even states themselves are participating in the education process. The state of Kansas, for instance, designates 2% of the taxes collected from state-owned casinos to be used for the treatment of addiction, including drug and alcohol abuse and problem gambling.[35]

Online Gaming

One industry trend that has emerged in recent years is the popularity of online gaming and the impact this will have in the long run on the legalized gambling industry. Since the public debut of the Internet and the World Wide Web in 1995, online gaming has made the ability to wager from the comfort of one's own home a reality for anyone with a computer—even those not legally old enough to gamble.

The controversy over online gaming, however, has been fierce. Public debate over how to regulate it, how to tax it, and whether it should even be legally permitted has raged since its inception. Nonetheless, online gaming websites are widespread. The American Gaming Association estimates that there are more than 2,000 online gaming websites, offering everything from lotteries to casino games to sports wagering.[36]

The majority of these sites are located outside the United States because of the ongoing debate over whether online gambling is actually legal in the United States. The U.S. Department of Justice claims that online gambling is illegal under the provisions of the U.S. Wire Act of 1961, which prohibits gambling "over the wires."[37] However, the U.S. Circuit Court of Appeals for the Fifth Circuit has disagreed.

Several attempts have been made by the U.S. Congress to pass legislation banning gaming over the Internet, including the Unlawful Internet Gambling Enforcement Act in 2006. According to the American Gambling Association, "The bill makes it illegal for banks, credit card companies or similar institutions to collect on a debt incurred on an online gambling site."[38] Implementation of this legislation has proven difficult, however, because it puts the burden on financial institutions rather than on online gamblers or owners of online gambling websites.[39]

It is likely that the debate over the legality of online gambling will continue for several years to come. Meanwhile, the popularity of online gaming shows no signs of letting up.

Employment Opportunities

Because the gambling and casino gaming industry has grown so much in the past two decades, the opportunities for employment are plentiful, especially in those states that are developing or expanding their gaming options. According to the American Gaming Association and the National Indian Gaming Association, commercial casinos alone employ more than 350,000 people, while Indian casinos provide another 670,000 jobs.[40]

Casino Employment

Within the casino industry, jobs fall roughly into two categories—casino floor positions and corporate and hotel/entertainment-related jobs.[41] Casino floor jobs are those that encompass hands-on activities pertaining to the day-to-day operations of the casino. These can include dealers, cashiers, floor managers, pit supervisors, and security personnel, among other jobs. Many of these jobs do not require a college degree, although some, such as dealer positions, may require special training. Employees working on the floor are generally paid an hourly wage.

Most casinos today consist of more than just gambling venues and may include hotels, restaurants, entertainment, and retail outlets. As a result, there are a number of job opportunities on the corporate and hotel/entertainment side of the business. Positions in this segment of the industry can include marketing and sales, public relations, human resources, accounting and finance, and hospitality management, to name just a few. These jobs are more likely to require a college degree and, in some cases, an advanced degree such as an M.B.A. They are more likely to be salaried positions and, in some cases such as sales, may include bonuses or commissions.

Employment in Other Industry Sectors

Job opportunities also exist within the racetrack and lottery businesses. Racetrack jobs often consist of positions that involve working with animals—such as groomers, trainers, jockeys, and veterinarians—and jobs on the business side for those with backgrounds in communication, finance, and sales and marketing.

State lotteries, too, employ people with good business and communication skills. Although lotteries don't employ as many people as casinos, given the smaller size of that segment of the industry, they can offer good opportunities for those with training in accounting, computer science, public relations, human resources, and sales and marketing.

Education and Training

A few universities around the United States have started casino training programs to prepare potential employees for management careers in the industry. Richard Stockton College in New Jersey offers a certificate program designed to train future industry executives.[42] Tulane University of New Orleans started a program at its Mississippi Coast campus to educate those interested in gaming industry careers.[43] And the University of Southern Mississippi recently launched an online course for students aspiring to management careers in the business.[44] As the gambling and casino gaming industry continues to grow, it is likely that more and more programs like this will develop at colleges located in states with legalized casino gambling.

In general, if you aspire to work in the industry, you will be expected to have good customer service skills because of the vast numbers of people you will come into contact with on a regular basis. When the Foxwoods casino advertised for employees to staff its new MGM Grand facility, for example, the casino specifically sought out applicants with a knack for customer service. The company used behavioral assessment as part of the screening process to determine if applicants had personalities that were compatible with the jobs for which they were applying.[45]

Future Outlook

As more and more states legalize gambling, it is predicted that the gambling and casino gaming industry will continue to expand accordingly. Here are some things to look for in the future:

Growth of the Mega-Casino

The mega-casino concept was introduced to Las Vegas in the 1990s, and other gaming venues are starting to jump on the bandwagon. Atlantic City, in particular, is moving in that direction, as nearby Pennsylvania and New York impinge upon the monopoly it once held on the East Coast gaming industry. At present, three mega-casinos are under development in Atlantic City and are expected to include luxury hotel rooms, spas, upscale retail

READ SCOT

Director of Entertainment
Caesars Palace, Las Vegas
www.caesarspalace.com

A typical day for Read Scot, the Director of Entertainment at Caesars Palace in Las Vegas, just might include finding the perfect décor elements for *America's Next Top Model* to be used during a taping of an episode inside the hotel. It could also involve supervising the unloading of Cher's 15 semi-trucks filled with items for her headliner show or casting for actors to serve as Roman ambassadors who wander through the facility. Scot admitted his days are long, usually 10 to 12 hours, but he loves what he does for a living. Every day his work includes "lots of challenges, but that's what makes it interesting and rewarding."

Scot started from the bottom and worked his way up to his current position. His first job at Caesars Palace was as an actor working in the position of the Roman Caesar. He loved interacting with the guests. "I literally started at the ground level and worked my way up the corporate ladder. I earned my toga," he said.

Scot was a dance and theater major at Southern Methodist University in Dallas. After graduation, he went on the road touring with various musicals. One show made a stop in Las Vegas, and Scot knew that was where he wanted to live. But it would take several years before he landed a job in Las Vegas. He worked as an actor in commercials, sitcoms, and several movies. Then, he decided to try his luck in Las Vegas, and that's when he landed the job as a Roman at Caesars Palace. He's been there every since.

"I am passionate about the industry. I like the creative process. At the end of the day, the guest knows it's Caesars Palace, and it doesn't get any better than this," he said.

Scot's advice to others wanting to follow in his footsteps is to be as diverse as possible. He feels it is just as important to know the technical elements as well as the creative elements of a show. "Don't hide behind the creative. It's called show business for a reason," he explained. "If you can't run it as a business, you won't be around for long."

» » »

outlets, and fine dining venues. The city hopes the expansion will help extend its reach beyond the local market it currently serves.[46]

Indian casinos are also beginning to adopt a mega-casino mentality. The new MGM Grand at Foxwoods has plans for a 4,000-square-foot theater and "the largest ballroom in the Northeast"[47] in the works to complement its gaming and hotel facilities. Foxwoods' prime competitor, the nearby Mohegan Sun, is making plans for its own mega-casino to be completed in 2010.

Meetings and Conventions

The future will also see a greater focus on the convention business in major casino markets like Las Vegas and Atlantic City. Although the convention trade has long been a part of the Las Vegas scene, it has taken a backseat to other revenue-generating activities. However, according to the *Wall Street Journal,* in the last few years, the number of conventioneers has steadily increased. In 2006, "6.3 million business travelers visited Las Vegas for conventions or business meetings, up from 5.7 million.... Those visitors spent $8.2 billion."[48] The 2008 opening of Sheldon Adelson's Palazzo hotel and casino, which is linked to the Sands Expo and Convention Center along with its sister hotel, the Venetian, is expected to lead to an even greater increase in Las Vegas convention visitors.

Other gaming venues are hoping for the same. Atlantic City and the Mississippi Gulf Coast are looking to the convention business to bring in added revenues, and plans for the two Indian casinos in Connecticut—Foxwoods and Mohegan Sun—include the construction of convention space.[49]

Casinos in the Sky

The rapid development of the gaming business in Macau has led to a proposal that could put a new twist on the industry. The Las Vegas Sands Corporation has plans to equip private jumbo jets with gaming facilities and use them to fly high-roller gamblers between the company's casinos in Asia and the United States. "In addition to the typical luxury items found on a casino company's private aircraft, customers would also have an amenity at their disposal—high-limit baccarat tables to pass the time during the 14-hour direct flights."[50] This could open a whole new window of possibilities for reaching out to the international gaming market.

Racinos and Greyhound Racing

On the racetrack front, the growth of racinos is expected to continue to breathe new life into the horse racing market. Already, racetracks with slot machines in states such as Pennsylvania are seeing an increase in track profits. According to the *Pittsburgh Business Times,* "Harrah's total purses increased from $3.4 million in 2006 to $21.7 million in 2007 due to the infusion of slot revenue." Betting on horses was up 20% as well.[51] Other states with legalized racinos are expected to see similar results.

Prospects for greyhound racing do not look as promising. Low track attendance and protests from animal rights groups have led to the closure of a number of tracks in Florida, which is the top market for greyhound racing.[52] The declining numbers suggest that this type of pari-mutuel wagering, like its counterpart jai-alai, may be on the way out.

Summary

Gambling and casino gaming make up a sizable chunk of the entertainment industry, as the promise of winning big motivates consumers to spend billions of dollars each year on commercial casinos, Indian gaming, horse and greyhound racing, and state lotteries.

Some of the challenges faced by those in the industry include keeping up with the competition, managing risk, dealing with negative perceptions of gambling, and addressing the issue of problem gambling. The advent of new technologies has also led to the development of Internet gaming, resulting in controversial debates over the legalization of online gambling.

Employment opportunities are expected to be plentiful within the industry over the next few years, as more and more states are taking steps to legalize gambling, particularly in the areas of Indian gaming and racinos—racetracks with slot machines. This will result in the construction of new gambling facilities and the potential for the creation of hundreds of jobs.

It is predicted that competition will lead to the expansion of mega-casinos, where customers can find a vast array of dining, entertainment, and shopping options to complement their gaming activities. The industry also is likely to see an increase in the convention trade in sites such as Las Vegas and Atlantic City as more and more casinos add convention space to their facilities.

In short, the gambling and casino gaming industry is one of the fastest-growing segments of the entertainment industry. As David C. Wyld has noted, "Gambling has moved from being a subject of taboo to becoming a major, mainstream industry in the United States."[53]

ADDITIONAL RESOURCES

Associations and Organizations

Casino Gaming

- » American Gaming Association (AGA): www.americangaming.org
- » Global Gaming Expo (G2E): www.globalgamingexpo.com
- » National Indian Gaming Association: www.indiangaming.org

Horse and Greyhound Racing
» Greyhound Racing Association (GRA): www.gra-america.org
» National Thoroughbred Racing Association (NTRA): www.ntra.com

Lotteries
» Multi-State Lottery Association (MUSL): www.musl.com
» North American Association of State and Provincial Lotteries (NASPL): www.naspl.org
» World Lottery Association (WLA): www.world-lotteries.org

Problem Gambling
» National Center for Responsible Gambling: www.ncrg.org
» National Council on Problem Gambling: www.ncpgambling.org

Job-Hunting Resources

Casino Careers Online: casinocareers.com

Casino & Gaming Jobs: www.jobmonkey.com/casino

Casino Jobs Network: www.casinojobs.net

Books

Earley, Pete. *Supercasino: Inside the "New" Las Vegas.* New York: Bantam, 2001.

Field, Shelly, and Brian Vargas. *Career Opportunities in Casinos and Casino Hotels.* New York: Facts on File, 2000.

Kilby, Jim, Jim Fox, and Anthony F. Lucas. *Casino Operations Management, 2nd ed.* Hoboken, NJ: Wiley, 2004.

Wiesenberg, Michael. *The Ultimate Casino Guide.* Naperville, IL: Sourcebooks, Inc., 2005.

Magazines and Trade Publications

Canadian Gaming News: www.canadiangaming.com

Casino Enterprise Management: www.casinoenterprisemanagement.com

Casino Life: www.casinolifemagazine.com

Gaming and Leisure: www.gamingandleisuremagazine.com

Gaming Today: www.gamingtoday.com

Indian Gaming Business: www.indiangamingbusiness.com

Inside Asian Gaming: www.asgam.com

Inside the AGA: www.americangaming.org

Native American Casino: www.nacasino.com

Responsible Gaming Quarterly: www.americangaming.org

Websites

American Quarter Horse Racing: racing.aqha.com/racing

Indian Gaming: www.indiangaming.com

ENDNOTES

1. Howard Stutz and Benjamin Spillman. "Monte Carlo Guest Flees Fire, Keeps Slot Jackpot," *Las Vegas Review*, 24 February 2008, E1.
2. American Gaming Association, www.americangaming.org
3. Geoffrey A. Fowler, "Casino Brings Vegas to Macau," *Wall Street Journal*, 29 August 2007, D9.
4. "Early History of Gaming," American Gaming Association, www.americangaming.org.
5. "Feeling Flush: Hugely Successful World Poker Tour TV Series Features Richest Buy-In in Poker History," *Business Wire*, 13 April 2003, 1.
6. National Indian Gaming Association, www.indiangaming.org.
7. Multi-State Lottery Association. www.musl.com.
8. North American Association of State and Provincial Lotteries, www.naspl.org.
9. National Thoroughbred Racing Association, www.ntra.com.
10. Greyhound Racing Association of America, www.gra-america.org.
11. "Competition Heats Up in Vegas," *Real Estate Finance and Investment*, 20 August 2007, 1.
12. Donald Greenlees, "Americans in the Action as Macao Casinos Soar," *New York Times*, 18 January 2008, C4.
13. Ibid.
14. Sharon Smith, "Competing for Customers; Area Slots Enthusiasts Can Play Closer to Home," *The Patriot-News*, 7 February 2008, A13.
15. Wayne Parry, "A.C. Casinos Gamble on Expansion," *The Record*, 23 July 2007, A11.
16. Mark Peters, "Betting That If They Build It...," *Hartford Courant*, 24 February 2008, L3.
17. "Erika D. Smith, "If Track Slots Hit Jackpot, Casinos Could Feel the Pinch," *Indianapolis Star*, 28 January 2008.
18. Debbie Arrington, "Summer Circuit Used to Be Robust but Now It's.... in Fair Condition: The Days of Packed Grandstands Are Over, and Some Are Trying to Make Changes," *Sacramento Bee*, 17 July 2007, C1.
19. Sharon Smith, "Off-track Wagering Operations Fade Fast," *Patriot-News*, 3 May 2007, C1.
20. Diana R. Cook, Alan E. Meyer, Ruthanne Murray, David A. Skup, and Nicholas P. Thilges, "Place Your Bets: Risk Management and the Gaming Industry," *Risk Management*, October 2004, p. 42.
21. Liz Benston, "Thieves inside the Machine," *Las Vegas Sun*, 6 December 2007, A1.
22. "Casino Theft Suspect Caught in Virginia," *Times-Picayune*, 31 October 2006.
23. Roberto Ceniceros, "Casino Cameras Lower Odds on Fraud," *Business Insurance*, 41:18, April 30, 2007, p. 22.
24. Derk Boss and Ann Longmore-Etheridge, "Casinos Strengthen Their Security Hand," *Security Management*, 50:9, September 2006, p. 78.
25. Ibid.
26. Kevin Helliker, "Las Vegas Wins Big with a Bet on Defibrillators," *Wall Street Journal*, 31 January 2006, p. 27.
27. James Mayse, "Analyst Calls for Casino Resistance," *Messenger Inquirer*, 8 March 2006, p. 1.
28. Jeff Shields, "Philadelphia Casino May Proceed, State Supreme Court Says," *Planning* 74:2 (February 2008): 56.
29. Stephanie Vosk, "New Poll Finds State Residents Split on Casino," *Cape Cod Times*, 18 March 2008.

30. National Council on Problem Gambling, www.ncpgambling.org.

31. American Gaming Association, www.americangaming.org.

32. Gale Courey Toensing, "Foxwoods Announces Initiatives to Address Problem Gambling," *Indian Country Today,* 12 March 2008.

33. Ibid.

34. "San Manuel Indian Bingo & Casino Named Certified Responsible Gaming Establishment by California Council on Problem Gambling," *PR Newswire,* 16 July 2007.

35. Rick Alm, "Kansas Fights Problem Gambling," *Kansas City Star,* 11 March 2008.

36. American Gaming Association, www.americangaming.org.

37. Ibid.

38. Ibid.

39. Cindy Skrzycki, "Internet Gaming Rules Face Long Odds," *Washington Post,* 4 March 2008, D2.

40. See www.americangaming.org and www.indiangaming.org.

41. Casino Industry Jobs, www.jobmonkey.com.

42. Victoria Hurley-Schubert, "A New Program to Make Casino Careers a Sure Thing," *NJBIZ,* 19:4 January 23, 2006, 11.

43. Lynn Lofton, "Tulane Sees Success with Gaming Program on the Coast," *Mississippi Business Journal,* 26:13 March 29, 2004, 25.

44. "USM Unveils Gaming Program," *Mississippi Business Journal,* 29:23 June 4, 2007, 8.

45. Mark Peters, "Casino Hiring at Fast Pace: Foxwoods Needs to Add Thousands," *Hartford Courant,* 24 January 2008, A1.

46. Suzette Parmley, "Atlantic City Is Wagering on Mega-Casinos: Luxury Rooms and Fine Dining Are the New Trend." *Philadelphia Inquirer,* 14 October 2007, D1.

47. John Christoffersen, "Competition Pushes Casinos to Hike the Glitz Ante," *Providence Journal,* 8 September 2007, F1.

48. Tamara Audi, "Betting Big on Conventions in Vegas," *Wall Street Journal,* 28 November 1007, B1.

49. Gary Tufel, "Soon…A Casino Near You," *Tradeshow Week* 38:6, February 11, 2008, 10.

50. Howard Stutz, "LV Sands Hopes Gaming Revenue Will Soar," *Las Vegas Review-Journal,* 9 February 2008, D1.

51. Erin Lawley, "Slots Boosting Pennsylvania Horse Racing Industry," *Pittsburgh Business Times,* 26 February 2008.

52. Nicola M. White, "Bettors Lament End of Dog Races," *Knight Ridder Tribune Business News,* 13 August 2007, 3.

53. David C. Wyld, "The Ace in the Hole: How Smarter Chips—and Cards—Can Enable Casino Management to Gain Insights into Player Behavior and Better Compete in Today's Increasingly Crowded Entertainment Marketplace," *Competition Forum* 5:1, 2007, 166.

13

Video Games

GENELLE BELMAS

The stereotypes are familiar and spoofed in comedies from *South Park* to *The Simpsons*: A long-haired, pockmarked teenager or overweight, greasy-haired, middle-aged man huddles over a keyboard, surrounded by empty soda cans and crumpled snack food bags, hand on his mouse, staring blearily at the screen. Or the junior-high boys at the arcade after school, zapping aliens or bad guys with oversized guns and joysticks. The world of video games was boys only, a phase that parents expected their sons to outgrow, or a sad commentary on a hopelessly geeky nerd.

Fast forward a couple of decades: Video games have grown up. And video games are big business. Blizzard Entertainment, creator of the wildly popular online game *World of Warcraft,* announced in July 2007 that *World of Warcraft* had surpassed 9 million total subscriptions[1]—more than the population of New York City (about 8.2 million). The Entertainment Software Association (ESA) reported that 65% of American homes play video games.[2] According to researchers the NPD Group, the video game industry generated $6.6 billion in sales in the first half of 2008 and was likely to have total 2008 revenues of $21–$23 billion.[3]

With increases in gaming popularity comes the need to push the envelope, to create edgy new content. In June 2008, Rockstar Games settled a class-action suit against its 2004 video game *Grand Theft Auto: San Andreas* with 2,676 customers offended by hidden sexual content. A previously inaccessible minigame inside the main application, dubbed "Hot Coffee," permits the main character to join his girlfriends in their apartments for "coffee." Players control the main character's sexual actions during the "coffee" encounter. A "mod" (modification) published online in 2005 allowed anyone to access the minigame.

The Entertainment Software Rating Board (ESRB), in charge of assigning ratings to video games, reclassified *GTA: SA* in 2005 with an "adults only" rating.[4] The code was removed from future editions, allowing those editions to retain the original "mature" rating, but the minigame caused a furor in both Congress and the video game industry.

But there is a softer side to video gaming. Just ask a six-year-old about her Webkinz and watch her wax rhapsodic about her stuffed pet's online life. Sold by toy manufacturer Ganz, a Webkinz stuffed animal comes with a secret code that children may use to access games and activities online. Children can earn virtual money, called KinzCash, by playing games to spend on improvements to their pets' homes, clothing, or food.[5]

Millions, both young and old, log in daily to solve crossword puzzles or play bridge, mah-jongg, or card games on Yahoo! Games and other gaming sites. And entire families gather around their Nintendo Wii consoles, playing virtual golf, bowling, fishing, and more. In April 2008, Nintendo announced that it had sold over 24 million Wii systems worldwide since the console's November 2006 launch.[6] Perhaps it's no surprise that Nintendo brags, "You don't just play Wii, you experience it."[7]

This chapter will explore the history of the video game industry from its earliest incarnations to its current technology. It will examine the challenges and opportunities faced by professionals who create, program, market, and support the games to not only beat the competition but capture the minds, hearts, and flying fingers of video gamers everywhere.

History and Background

Early Beginnings

In his history of the early video game industry, *Supercade,* Van Burnham credits programmer William Higinbotham of Brookhaven National Laboratory with the first video game.[8] Higinbotham created *Tennis for Two* in 1958, a precursor to the famous *Pong.* By the 1960s, programmers had developed a "TV game" concept, leading to the development of the "Brown Box," a home game system sold in the 1970s by Magnavox as the *Odyssey.* The *Odyssey* featured overlays to be placed on TV screens to simulate backgrounds for games like football, hockey, and Simon Says.

Thirteen years after *Tennis for Two,* Nolan Bushnell introduced the first coin-operated video game to arcades: *Computer Space* was too complex for most players, but a simplified version became *Pong.* The success of *Pong* funded Bushnell's company, Atari, which released the home version of *Pong* in 1975.

Golden Age of Arcades

Burnham credits the Apple II and the arcade game *Space Invaders* for ushering in the golden age of arcades. The Apple II, released in 1977, was widely accessible and used by many would-be game creators to learn how to program; it was also chosen as the "Greatest PC of All Time" by *PC World* in 2006.[9] In 1978, Japanese game company Taito Corporation released *Space Invaders,* a simple arcade game by today's standards that catapulted arcade games into a cultural phenomenon. The game featured a movable laser cannon at the bottom of the screen that destroyed waves of advancing aliens. In 2008, the 30th anniversary of *Space Invaders,* Taito announced new versions of the game for several popular consoles.

Arcade titles such as *Asteroids, Defender,* and *Galaxian,* now classics, formed the foundation of the golden arcade age. An unlikely game featuring a ghost-gobbling creature that became a major sensation, *Pac-Man,* was released by Midway for the Japanese company Namco in 1980 and was soon followed by Nintendo's first major arcade offering, *Donkey Kong.* In the 1980s the first video game sequels appeared such as *Ms. Pac-Man* and *Galaga,* the sequel to *Galaxian.* Versions of many of these games are now available for home console systems.

In 1981, American arcades hit their highest revenues, topping $5 billion. Moreover, video gaming had found an audience: Americans spent over 75,000 hours in 1981 playing video games.[10] On the home gaming front, by 1982 there were several popular systems, including Intellivision, Colecovision, and Atari 5200, each with its own games and graphics. Coleco got a boost from Nintendo, which licensed *Donkey Kong* and *Donkey Kong Jr.* to Colecovision, while Namco provided the *Pac-Man* titles to Atari.

One other arcade game deserves mention: the 1983 Cinematronics title *Dragon's Lair* in which players followed Dirk the Daring on his quest to save Princess Daphne from the evil dragon, Singe. The game was revolutionary in its use of a laserdisc system, greatly enhancing the graphic and sound quality. Former Disney animator Don Bluth (who also animated the Disney movie *Pete's Dragon*) created the animations, and the characters had a decidedly Disney flavor. Actual voices spoke to the players. However, the laserdisc technology often did not hold up to the constant strain required in an arcade console, and laserdisc players had to be frequently replaced. *Dragon's Lair* has been released in many other formats, most recently on Sony's Blu-ray high-definition disc.[11]

The Video Game Crash

But it has not been all upward trends for video gaming. An insider-trading controversy in 1982–83 culminated in an industry crash best summed up by Gamespot's analysis:

> With too many products on the shelves from a multitude of publishers, many third-party companies go out of business. The games from these companies are then discounted heavily. Companies that are still in business cannot compete against the cheap games, so they wind up losing money because of unsold inventory.[12]

Moreover, the entry into the market of inexpensive home computers that could also do word processing and spreadsheet management, and the diversification of companies like Atari and Coleco into areas like toys and personal computers, weakened the already-staggering market.[13]

The Rebound: Console Wars

By 1985, video gaming companies were slowly recovering from the crash. Nintendo introduced its Nintendo Entertainment System (NES) successfully to a limited New York market and then nationally by 1986. Following Nintendo's lead, Sega released its Sega Master System (SMS) and Atari released the Atari 7800 in the United States. Several software publishers emerged that would become household names such as Electronic Arts and Sierra.

The 1980s and onward have been marked by strong competition between several major video gaming companies. By 1989, Nintendo had introduced the first GameBoy and had a $2.5 billion income. Both Sega's and Atari's attempts at handheld systems were unsuccessful. In 1990, Nintendo released *Super Mario 3*, the all-time best-selling video game cartridge. But 16-bit systems had been introduced by Sega (the Genesis) and other companies and promised better gaming quality and advanced graphics, sound, and memory. Once Nintendo entered the 16-bit race, the console wars were truly on. By 1991, Nintendo had announced the Super NES and another Mario title, and Sega shot back with the endearing *Sonic the Hedgehog* title for the Genesis that it hoped would seriously compete with Mario.

As the technology improved, Nintendo and Sega released more sophisticated systems with better graphics and sound. By 1993, both Sega and Nintendo had announced plans for 64-bit systems, and the violence in titles such as *Mortal Kombat, Doom,* and *Night Trap* drew the ire of several senators and culminated in a congressional investigation and the creation of an industry-wide rating system. In 1994, the Entertainment Software Rating Board was established to rate video games and to provide information on the amount of sexual or violent content.

Figure 23: Top 10 Selling Console Games of 2007 by Units Sold

Rank	Title	Platform	Rating
1	*Halo 3*	Xbox 360	Mature
2	*Wii Play with Remote*	Wii	Everyone
3	*Call of Duty 4: Modern Warfare*	Xbox 360	Mature
4	*Guitar Hero III: Legends of Rock*	PlayStation 2	Teen
5	*Super Mario Galaxy*	Wii	Everyone
6	*Pokémon Diamond Version*	Nintendo DS	Everyone
7	*Madden NFL 08*	PlayStation 2	Everyone
8	*Guitar Hero 2*	PlayStation 2	Teen
9	*Assassin's Creed*	Xbox 360	Mature
10	*Mario Party 8*	Wii	Everyone

Source: Entertainment Software Association, "Essential Facts About the Computer and Video Game Industry 2008," http://www.theesa.com/facts/pdfs/ESA_EF_2008.pdf

32 Bits, 64 Bits, and Beyond

The Sony PlayStation, the Sega Saturn, and the Nintendo N64 hit store shelves in 1996. The PlayStation and Saturn were CD based, while the N64 was cartridge based—a feature critics thought was on the way out. These systems feature improved graphics and game play as well as more violence and sex (think Lara Croft of *Tomb Raider*). In addition, third-party "hacks" could render characters like Lara Croft naked.

By 1996 the prices of consoles had dropped, and, with the news of sluggish Saturn sales in the United States, rumors circulated that the end of Sega was near. Atari had closed its hardware manufacturing doors that same year, merging with a computer hard drive producer. In 1997, Sega announced plans to merge with Bandai, a Japanese toy company, but the merger fell through (Bandai marketed the very successful Tamagotchi virtual pet, which was also introduced in GameBoy and PC versions). In 1999, Sega released its final console, the Dreamcast.

In 1998, Nintendo announced *Pokémon* (short for "pocket monster") for the United States. Two editions of the games were released for the GameBoy (by then color) and became Nintendo's fastest-selling games ever. Although 1998 was a banner year for home video gaming, arcades were not faring as well despite the efforts of some gaming companies to bring back versions of classic arcade games like *Asteroids*.

By 1999, Nintendo and other companies had announced plans for cell phone games, and in 2000, Sony released the PlayStation 2, followed by Microsoft's Xbox and Nintendo's GameCube in 2001. Today's video game market is considered to be the seventh generation,[14] beginning in 2005 with the Xbox 360 and continuing with the PlayStation 3 and the Wii. These systems provide the opportunity for players to play with or against each other online.

Arcades today focus on physical games like *Dance Dance Revolution,* where players physically mirror dance moves displayed on the game screen, or *Whac-a-Mole,* which has players hitting moles that pop up at random. Light gun games like *House of the Dead,* where players use light guns to shoot zombies, are also popular, as they have large equipment not generally available to the home player.

Personal Computer (PC) Games

As long as there have been personal computers, there have been personal computer games. In 1962, in the first computer game with graphics, *Spacewar!,* players controlling two armed space ships could fire at each other while in the gravity well of a star.[15] The game was played on a Digital Equipment Corporation machine.[16] The first widely sold consumer personal computer, the Altair 8800, sold as a mail-order hobbyist's kit through the magazine *Popular Electronics* in 1975, was itself a game to assemble and could flash blinking lights when programmed (it had no keyboard or screen). By the 1980s, players of text-based games like *Zork* relied on typed commands like "open mailbox" or "go west" to interact with the game environment. The lack of graphics required *Zork* players to simply imagine the unfolding plot.

PC games have come a long way since the Altair, *Spacewar!* and *Zork*. There are two general types of PC games—standalone games that are played by one player either with or against the computer without any connection to an online environment, and Massively Multi-Player Online Role-Playing Games (MMORPGs) that are played with or against other players in an online setting. It would take a book much longer than this one to describe the multitude of PC games, both standalone and MMORPG, that have entertained and delighted players over the years, but several titles deserve special mention. The dates below are the debut dates; most of the titles continue to have sequels and be released for multiple platforms.

Tetris (1984)

The addictive puzzle game *Tetris* was created by Russian programmer Alexei Pajitnov in 1984 for his workplace computers at the Academy of Sciences in Moscow.[17] Despite the then-Soviet Union's strict licensing requirements, *Tetris* made its way to Europe and the United States in 1986 and now appears on nearly every gaming platform.

Sims Series (1987)

Created by Maxis, early *Sims* titles in the franchise include *SimCity,* where players can create their own cities and communities, and *SimLife,* where players populate their own ecosystems. But the most popular and many-sequeled series *The Sims* (debuted in 2000) lets players create their own individual characters (called "avatars"), homes, families, jobs, vacations, and more. Called a strategic life-simulation game, *The Sims* continues to be a best-selling PC game. A MMORPG version, *Sims Online*, debuted in 2002 and ended in 2008. Maxis was acquired by Electronic Arts in 1997.

Sid Meier's Civilization Series (1991)

Inspired by the turn-based strategy board game, MicroProse released a computer version of *Civilization* in which the player creates an empire in competition with other civilizations. Players choose a historic civilization (such as the Romans or the Aztecs) and select paths and technologies to pursue. They can also declare war on other civilizations. The game is won either by destroying all other civilizations, by winning the space race to Alpha Centauri, or by accruing the most points.

Myst (1993)

Brøderbund's original *Myst* began with the player opening a book and being whisked away to a fantasy world in which there are puzzles to be solved and a beautifully designed environment to be explored. One of the first PC games to use CD-ROM technology, *Myst* was a surprise hit given that there were no preset goals, no violence, and no enemies to kill—players must explore to find out what to do in the game.

Doom (1993)

Doom, released by id Software, is a "first-person shooter," in which the action takes place from the player's point-of-view. The game had revolutionary 3D graphics and could be played against other players in a network setting. The unnamed "Doomguy" must kill demons and zombies that have overrun his space base. The game's level of violence and satanic imagery, coupled with the fact that Columbine High School shooters Eric Harris and Dylan Klebold often played *Doom*, have made it a target of controversy. *Quake* and *Duke Nukem* followed the first-person shooter trend as well as *Half-Life*.

Ultima Online (1997)

Generally considered to be the first major and longest-running MMORPG, Origin Systems' *Ultima Online* allows many players to interact with each other in a fantasy setting. A new game engine in 2007 enhanced the graphics and made the game competitive against more recent MMORPGs. Electronic Arts acquired Origin Systems in 1992 and currently manages the *UO* world.

StarCraft (1998)

Released by Blizzard (also creator of *World of Warcraft*), this real-time space strategy game pits the player against other intergalactic species in the struggle for resources to engage in military conquests. The player builds an infrastructure from which attacks on the enemy species can take place. *StarCraft* is widely credited to be one of the best real-time strategy games and can also be played against other players.

Half-Life (1998)

This Sierra title won awards for being a first-person shooter with a storyline. The game has been hailed for its innovative use of scripted sequences, which advance the plot and give the game additional depth. Players follow Dr. Gordon Freeman as he fights his way out of Black Mesa, a secret underground laboratory in which teleportation experiments have failed, by completing puzzles and killing imported aliens. The 2004 sequel, *Half-Life 2*, again featured Dr. Freeman in his fight for survival in a post-Black Mesa world.

World of Warcraft (2004)

Blizzard's blockbuster MMORPG, *World of Warcraft*, boasts the lion's share of the current MMORPG subscription base—over 10 million of the 16 million total MMORPG subscriptions.[18] Innovations included many quests that players complete to gain experience and advance their avatars (more fun than "grinding" or "farming"—repetitively killing the same monsters over and over for experience), high-quality graphics and soundtrack, and a wide variety of equally interesting character races and classes. Activision Blizzard merged with Vivendi in July 2008.[19]

Figure 24: Top 10 Selling Computer Games of 2007 by Units Sold

Rank	Title	Rating
1	*World of Warcraft: Burning Crusade Expansion Pack*	Teen
2	*World of Warcraft*	Teen
3	*The Sims 2 Seasons Expansion Pack*	Teen
4	*Call of Duty 4: Modern Warfare*	Mature
5	*Sim City 4 Deluxe*	Everyone
6	*The Sims 2*	Teen
7	*Command & Conquer 3: Tiberium Wars*	Teen
8	*The Sims 2 Bon Voyage Expansion Pack*	Teen
9	*MS Age of Empires III*	Teen
10	*The Sims 2 Pets Expansion Pack*	Teen

Source: Entertainment Software Association, "Essential Facts About the Computer and Video Game Industry 2008," http://www.theesa.com/facts/pdfs/ESA_EF_2008.pdf

Challenges and Trends

Competition and Marketing

Big Companies

While the "console wars" continue to rage, the contest is down to three major competitors: Sony, Nintendo and Microsoft. According to U.S. sales figures released at the July 2008 industry-wide E3 (Electronic Entertainment Expo) Media and Business Summit, based on figures from the NPD Group, the Nintendo Wii had sold 10.9 million units as of July 1, 2008, while the Microsoft Xbox 360 came in second at 10.5 million units, and Sony PlayStation 3 came in last at 5 million units.[20] Sony has trailed its competitors for several years, and it needs success with the PS3 to support its Blu-ray disc format.[21] The Wii's focus on a family gaming experience has supported much of the growth of the console.

Small, Independent Companies

While it may be difficult to break into the Big Three console wars, the way is clear for smaller companies to make big splashes. The Wii Ware, the PlayStation 3 Network, and the Xbox Live services allow players to download games and content online.[22] Small game developers can easily enter the big gaming markets with relatively low costs. And the potential payoff is substantial: a 2007 report by financial analyst IDC predicted online console revenue in North America—including downloadable software sales—to total $583 million in 2007.[23]

For example, thatgamecompany, started by two recent University of Southern California graduates, released the very successful title *flOw* for the PlayStation 3 Network (it can also be played for free online at the company's website). Bucking the trend of traditional strategy or first-person shooter games, the object of *flOw* is, according to thatgamecompany's website, "piloting an aquatic organism through a surreal biosphere where players consume other organisms, evolve, and advance their organisms to the abyss."[24]

Beyond the Boys

The success of *flOw* points to the potential market in non-traditional gaming cohorts. Many titles are targeted toward the teenage boy market, but according to Plunkett Research, 82.5 million people in the United States play "simple" online games like bridge and checkers, earning game companies $450 million a year, primarily through advertising (less than 2% of players pay to play).[25] The Entertainment Software Association reports that 40% of all gamers are female; the average gamer is 35 years old and has been gaming for 13 years, and 26% of Americans over the age of 50 played video games in 2008.[26]

While women play in large numbers, research suggests that they look for different things in their gaming experiences: they value problem-solving, dialogue, and interaction, and the ability to personalize the game experience, and they are not as willing to commit large chunks of time to gaming.[27] As one female gaming executive and gamer explained, "From a publishing angle, I think there's a better understanding that if we build games for women, they will come—not just 'Let's put a pink wrapper on what we've already got and they'll come.'"[28]

Some companies are responding: Buena Vista has published *Disney Princess* titles for young girls and has targeted the older female audience with a game based on the TV show *Desperate Housewives*.[29] But some female gamers don't want to be perceived as just "girl gamers" interested in female titles—as the critically acclaimed website WomenGamers. com proclaims, "WomenGamers.com—Because Women DO Play."

Multi-Platforms

The Entertainment Software Association reported that gaming companies sold over 13.4 million portable game units in 2007.[30] Moreover, 36% of heads of household reported in 2008 they played games on wireless devices (such as cell phones or personal data assistants), an increase of 20% over 2002.[31] There is a market potential for games to be either created for or ported to handheld and wireless devices.

As more players move between platforms or onto mobile or handheld devices, gaming companies often create games that can be played on different platforms. For example, Blizzard's smash MMORPG *World of Warcraft* can be played on either Macintosh or Windows machines. Ubisoft's 2007 *Assassin's Creed,* an adventure game where the player is an assassin exploring and adventuring in twelfth-century Jerusalem, Damascus, and Acre, is available for the PC, Xbox, PS3, handheld, and mobile formats.

MEAGAN VANBURKLEO

Associate Editor
Game Informer Online
www.gameinformer.com

Meagan VanBurkleo was packing for a trip to Japan. This wasn't a vacation—it was work. VanBurkleo said traveling is the best part of her job as an associate editor for one of the most popular web online sites for people who love video games, *Game Informer Online.*

VanBurkleo landed what she called her "perfect job" right out of college. She majored in graphic design with a minor in journalism at the University of Minnesota. After graduation, she wasn't sure which discipline to pursue. When she found out that the magazine she read all the time was in her backyard, she applied at *Game Informer* as both a graphic designer and as a writer. Because there were no jobs available in design, the company offered her a position with the online website as an editor.

A typical day in the office involves doing interviews for news pieces about the industry or playing a new video game to write a review. She also travels extensively to cover the industry. She's been to Los Angeles several times, San Francisco, and Las Vegas. She's spent two weeks in Japan for work and is likely to travel to Germany and England as well. It's the perfect work schedule for a twenty-something who loves everything about video games. "I live, eat, and breathe geek," she said.

VanBurkleo admitted that often she is the only female covering an event. "I don't even notice that I'm the only girl besides the fact that I have my own bathroom," she said.

She believes she owes her success so far partly to her passion about the career and her ability to network successfully. "Networking is huge," she said. "You've got to get yourself out to meet people and to cover events."

And just in case you were wondering—VanBurkleo said her favorite game is Fatal Frame 3. It's a survival horror game, and she said it's great fun to play with a group of friends.

» » »

Regulations and Community Outreach

Although American courts have never limited the First Amendment protection of video games, these games have long been targets of public concern about violence and sexual content delivered to minors. In 1976, inspired by the movie *Death Race 2000*, Exidy released an arcade video game named *Death Race* in which player-controlled cars ran down "gremlins" who screamed when hit and turned into tombstones to be avoided later on. The "gremlins" looked like stick figures, and although Exidy denied the purpose of the game was to run people down, the fact that the game's working title was *Pedestrians* suggested otherwise. The controversy was covered in the news media, including a *60 Minutes* special on violence in video games, and Exidy released only 500 consoles.[32]

The Entertainment Software Association (ESA), as part of its government affairs mandate, has several primary advocacy and outreach goals, including stopping bills seeking to regulate the sale of video games and developing positive relationships with governmental leaders.[33] The ESA also created and supports the Entertainment Software Rating Board (ESRB), an independent, self-regulatory body established in 1994 that applies and enforces ratings, guidelines for advertising, and industry online privacy principles.

Violent first-person-shooter video games hit the spotlight in the aftermath of the Columbine tragedy, resulting in congressional examination of the industry. The battle is far from over as game makers continue to push the violence envelope. During 2007–2008, 75 bills in 27 states, the District of Columbia and Puerto Rico sought to regulate the sale or distribution of video games.[34] An example: The New York assembly in June 2008 passed a bill that creates an advisory council on interactive media and youth violence and requires game consoles to have a control to allow owners to prevent the display of violent or indecent video games. The bill permits injunctions to be issued without requiring proof that anyone has actually been injured.[35]

However, as ESA points out, public perception may not match reality when it comes to kids, parents, and video games: 94% of the time parents are present at the time games are purchased or rented, and 83% of the time children receive their parents' permission before purchasing or renting a game. Parents also report always or sometimes monitoring the games their children play 88% of the time.[36]

Piracy Prevention

Video game piracy is also an issue of concern for video game companies. ESA estimates that the industry loses about $3.5 billion every year due to the illegal sale of "modded" machines, where the console's copyright protection is disabled, and cracked software is preloaded before sale.[37] But the larger problem—online piracy—cannot be as easily measured.

ESA is particularly concerned about online file sharing through Bittorrent and other sites and about cracked "warez" sites in both the United States and abroad. In its 2008 annual report, ESA reported that its outside monitoring service detected more than 700,000 infringements per month on average of the 200 titles monitored, resulting in more than six million takedown notices to Internet service providers in response to these violations.[38]

Gaming Addiction

Parents who watch their children (or spouses) spend hours on their PCs or Wiis may fear that they are addicted. Some may shrug off the concern as just overprotective parenting, but WebMD reports that an addiction treatment center in Amsterdam treats video game addicts, both children and adults. [39] Symptoms of game addiction are playing for increasing amounts of time, thinking about gaming during other activities, lying to others about gaming, and using gaming to escape other problems. The Amsterdam center treats video game addicts as it would alcoholics or drug addicts: cold turkey.[40]

Employment Opportunities

Video games are one of the fastest-growing industries in the United States. Analyst PricewaterhouseCoopers reported that the industry will remain "one of the above-average growth segments of the global entertainment industries through 2011."[41] According to ESA, the states of California, Washington, Texas, New York, and Massachusetts currently have the highest concentration of video game jobs and, collectively, directly employ over 16,000 workers.[42] ESA also puts the average salary of an entertainment software industry employee at $92,300.[43]

Game Designer / Programmer / Artist

The heart of a gaming company is design, artwork, and programming, whether hardware or software. Expect to learn Flash and C++ programming as well as a range of specialized software packages for animation, sound, and more.

There is a significant need for individuals with the kind of training offered in video game design and production courses. Bing Gordon, chief creative officer for Electronic Arts, lamented the lack of personnel for video game production: "Just imagine that a movie studio showed up at a cinema school and said, 'You know, we need three times as many directors and screenwriters as we are able to get now.' That's where we are."[44]

Quality Assurance (game testing)

Game testers are needed to make sure that games ship with as few bugs as possible. While it sounds like a dream job to play video games and get paid for doing it, in reality the job may require "playing" the same level, scene or section over and over to replicate errors or test fixes. During the "crunch time" before release, testers may work the same long hours that programmers and designers do, testing last-minute features or bug fixes.

Testers may work in-house as employees, but some companies outsource their testing to outside organizations.

However, quality assurance is one area that doesn't require advanced degrees or specialized training beyond computer literacy and good communication skills. As one game industry veteran put it, being a tester is a good way to get a foot in the door at a gaming company and to learn about the gaming industry or a particular company and watch the process from start to finish.[45] Average salaries are $10–$12/hour for testers, more for lead testers and testing managers. Game publishers may also release the game to a limited audience as a "beta" before the final launch; beta testers are usually unpaid volunteers.

Consumer Liaison/Advocate

More than just a public relations professional but requiring some of the same skills, a consumer liaison is the public face of the gaming company to its players and subscribers. Most often seen in MMORPG games, the liaison communicates game news, including problems, to the players, answers their questions, and communicates player concerns to the company. Some MMORPGs have "Game Masters," or GMs, who resolve player issues in the game. A player submits a complaint using the in-game system, and a GM contacts that player in the game to discuss the problem and offer resolution. Liaisons need excellent written and verbal communication skills and a willingness to work with the public.

Other Careers

Video game designing and publishing companies require many of the same kinds of positions that other businesses need: public relations professionals, advertising and marketing personnel, human resources, IT managers and workers, accountants, risk managers, legal staff, and more. Video games are usually shipped with game guides and manuals, so technical and creative writers may find employment here as well as Web designers and programmers for the company's online presence.

Education and Training

More than 200 colleges and universities have digital arts programs that offer training in video game design and programming. For example, DigiPen Institute of Technology in Redmond, WA, offers bachelor's degrees in Art and Animation and in Real-Time Interactive Simulation, Game Design and Computer Engineering as well as a master's degree in Computer Science. Full Sail University, based in Winter Park, FL, is known for its 24-hour class schedule and its degrees in Computer Animation, Game Art, and Game Development, among others.

Traditional universities also offer programs in game design and programming. The University of Southern California, for example, features an Interactive Media Division offering undergraduate and graduate degrees in Interactive Entertainment, Interactive Media, Computer Science Games, and Computer Science with Specialization in Games.

DANIEL SUAREZ

Executive Producer
Activision
www.activision.com

Every kid who lives on Daniel Suarez's block knows hanging out near Daniel's house around the holidays can result in a new video game. That's because Suarez is an executive producer of video games for Activision and often has multiple copies of new games at his home. Producing video games is a "lifelong dream" for Suarez. He is currently working on the *Call of Duty* and *Transformer* franchises for Activision.

Suarez's first job after graduating from California State University, Northridge, with a degree in business was working for a television production company that produced the *Power Rangers* programs. He later worked for Disney Interactive on computer games for the *Tarzan, Aladdin,* and *Atlantis* franchises and for Universal Interactive on the *Spyro* Playstation games.

After starting up his own company, which produced mobile phone games, Suarez took a job at Activision where he loves his work as an executive producer, especially the creative challenge of being in charge of everything dealing with the game. "As an executive producer, I am in the middle of the hub of the wheel in charge of public relations, legal, creative, technology, etc," he said. While Suarez doesn't have time at work to play video games, he loves playing at home and seeing the work he's done during the day. "It's fun to see all the changes," he said.

Suarez admitted the industry is very competitive. When he is hiring in his department, he looks for individuals who are articulate and proactive and who write well. But, he also said a job candidate must do something extraordinary to stand out from the crowd, not in a crazy way but in a way that tells Suarez he is hiring a person who will get the job done no matter what.

His number one piece of advice for both job candidates as well as experienced employees who want to be promoted is to "become a vital asset to whomever you work for."

» » »

Game Career Guide's website (http://www.gamecareerguide.com) features a full list of schools offering training in game design, art, programming, and more.

Future Outlook

Given the continued growth and popularity of the video game industry, publishers and designers will be looking for new ways to engage an increasingly sophisticated gaming population, but the public and government organizations will continue to take long, hard looks at content that pushes the sex and violence envelope.

Content Issues

Despite the best efforts of the ESA and ESRB, it is likely that legislation for state and federal regulations on the sale of violent and sexual video games to minors will eventually pass—and will be quickly challenged in the courts. The video game industry has had success so far in fighting off regulations that impinge on sales and development, but time will tell if legislation can be crafted to withstand judicial scrutiny and First Amendment concerns. Concern for the well-being of children is often cited by critics of video games; however, the ESA points out that 85% of all games sold in 2007 were rated "E" for Everyone, "T" for Teen, or "E10+" for Everyone 10+.[46]

Another issue potentially facing video gamers comes from the Internal Revenue Service. Some gamers have profited from selling game products, particularly in MMORPGs. Who owns the "property" in the game? Is it the players and their avatars or the gaming company? Can the IRS tax income made from the sale of virtual assets?[47]

Technology Issues

Video gamers, particularly MMORPG players, have always talked about their gaming experiences in online forums and websites. But as online trends move more toward user-generated content (Web 2.0), video games are likely to follow. More than just posting a high score or creating a home for an online avatar, players will be looking to affect their game play in significant and substantial ways. *Second Life* provides that level of interaction and customizability. Game participants don't just "play" the game—they create it.

Second Life players (called "Residents") are responsible for the creation of their entire online experiences, from housing and clothing to entertainment and economy. They create the look of their own avatars and, as in traditional MMORPGs, control the interactions of those avatars with the game environment and other Residents. However, unlike most other online games, Residents own the intellectual property rights in their virtual creations.

Linden Labs released *Second Life* in 2003. The environment is described as "an online, 3D virtual world imagined and created by its Residents." The currency of the game, Linden Dollars, can be exchanged for real-life currency between Residents.

It is somewhat of a mistake to call *Second Life* a game, although games can be played within it. More than just entertainment, *Second Life* has become a venue for creativity, business transactions, and more. "Brick-and-mortar" companies such as Dell[48] and Starwood Hotels[49] have set up virtual branches inside *Second Life,* and some countries (the Maldives and Sweden, among others) have set up virtual embassies. Reuters has a *Second Life* bureau to cover news that happens in this online world.

Other Uses for Video Games

Education

While kids are playing with their online Webkinz and learning their letters and numbers, higher education is also taking notice of the potential of video games as pedagogical tools. Many universities have presences in *Second Life,* but educators are making use of video games in other venues as well.

As part of the Institute for New Media Studies at the University of Minnesota, faculty members modified a fantasy MMORPG called *Neverwinter Nights* into a small town called Harperville and used the setting to teach journalism students how to research and write a story. There is a news library, dozens of Harperville citizens to interview, and a virtual "reporter's notebook" to keep track of information.[50] A course at Trinity University called "Games for the Web" requires students to have an account for *Everquest II,* an MMORPG, in which to conduct ethnographic research for a final paper.[51]

Exercise

Active arcade games like *Dance Dance Revolution* got gamers off their couches and moving, and now combating the stereotype of the overweight, inactive gamer, the Wii Fit debuted in the U.S. in 2008 to wild acclaim. The Wii Fit Balance Board is an additional piece of hardware that measures a user's weight and center of gravity. Users can assess their current fitness levels and then improve their health through a series of exercises and games using the board. There are exercises for strength training, balance improvement, aerobics and yoga. Progress is charted over time so users can see how they've improved. Users can set goals and monitor their activity logs.

Downloading and Watching Television and Movies

The Big Three console game companies are striving to be the one source for all entertainment needs. In 2008, Sony announced that owners of PlayStation 3 and PlayStation Portable would be able to download full-length movies, TV shows, and original programming from the PlayStation Network.[52] Sony's library currently includes nearly 300 movies and 1,200 TV episodes. For one price, players can experience the content on several devices. As Sony boasted in its press release, "The connectivity between PS3 and PSP platforms provides a seamless solution for those looking for entertainment experiences on their own terms—on the go or in their living room—all with a new-found freedom of not having to worry about TV schedules, movie listings or viewing on a desktop PC."[53]

Research

As mentioned earlier, some universities have courses that use video games as resources for students to do ethnographic research or practice professional skills. However, MMORPGs offer opportunities to study situations that would be difficult or dangerous to simulate in the real world. In what became known as the "Corrupted Blood" plague, researchers got a chance to see how a virus might quickly spread from isolated to populated areas.

In 2005, in a *World of Warcraft* "instance" (individual game dungeon), one of the monsters that players battled would infect the players with a disease upon its death. Called Corrupted Blood, the disease caused damage to the infected players over time. For the high-level players fighting the monster, the damage could be easily controlled, but it could quickly kill a lower-level player. The disease was not supposed to be able to leave the instance, but a bug in the game permitted it to travel. Within days the Corrupted Blood plague had wiped out major cities, and players were trying to remain in isolated areas to avoid contact with infected avatars.

The plague caught the attention of the media,[54] and several university professors later published papers that used the in-game plague as an analog for what might happen if a real epidemic started and how individuals would react to the outbreak.[55] *Second Life* was also suggested as an excellent venue for experiments in epidemiology.

Summary

From their earliest incarnations to their most current versions, video games have found devotees in both youth and adult markets and are not "just for boys." The industry has enjoyed tremendous growth and is expected to continue those gains as gaming companies tap into the family gaming market and other niches.

Public concern about sexual and violent content will continue to be an issue that the industry will need to address, and gaming companies have responded with an activist industry organization and a voluntary game-rating system to keep inappropriate content away from children. Gaming addiction and piracy are also topics that video game companies will watch in the coming years. More content will be generated for handheld and wireless devices as these forms of gaming garner more market share.

The video game industry is in need of programmers, designers, and artists to envision new games and bring them to fruition. Specialized degree programs and colleges cater to this type of training, but even those without degrees in game design or programming can enter the industry as testers or consumer liaisons.

As the online world becomes increasingly user generated, expect video games to follow suit. *Second Life* has already begun the trend of allowing players to control and design their own virtual world. Other uses for video games will also continue to be found, from education to exercise and beyond, making an already hugely popular pastime even more a part of our everyday lives.

ADDITIONAL RESOURCES

Associations/Organizations

Academy of Interactive Arts and Sciences: www.interactive.org

E3: www.e3expo.com

Entertainment Software Association (ESA): www.theESA.com

Entertainment Software Rating Board (ESRB): www.esrb.org

Gamasutra: www.gamasutra.com

Game Developers' Map: gamedevmap.com

International Game Developers Association (IGDA): www.igda.org

Video Game Voters Network: www.videogamevoters.org

WomenGamers: www.womengamers.com

Job-Hunting Resources

Game Career Guide: www.gamecareerguide.com

Game Jobs: www.gamejobs.com

Books

Burnham, Van. *Supercade: A Visual History of the Video Game Age 1971–1984*. Cambridge, MA: MIT Press, 2001.

Kent, Steven L. *The Ultimate History of Video Games: From Pong to Pokemon and Beyond—the Story Behind the Craze That Touched Our Lives and Changed the World*. New York: Random House, Inc., 2001.

Salen, Katie, and Eric Zimmerman. *Rules of Play: Game Design Fundamentals*. Cambridge, MA: MIT Press, 2003.

Wardrip-Fruin, Noah, and Pat Harrigan (eds.). *First Person: New Media as Story, Performance, and Game*. Cambridge, MA: MIT Press, 2006.

Wolf, Mark J. P., and Bernard Perron. *The Video Game Theory Reader*. New York: Routledge, 2003.

Magazines and Trade Publications

Computer and Video Games: www.computerandvideogames.com

Electronic Gaming Monthly: www.1up.com

Escapist: www.escapistmagazine.com

Gamasutra: www.gamasutra.com

Game Developer: www.gdmag.com

Game Informer: www.gameinformer.com

Game Industry News: www.gameindustry.com

Games First: www.gamesfirst.com

Websites

GamePro: www.gamepro.com

Game Revolution: www.gamerevolution.com

Gamers.com: en.gamers.com

Games Radar: www.gamesradar.com

GameSpot: www.gamespot.com

GameSpy: www.gamespy.com

Inside Mac Games: www.imgmagazine.com

Blogs

Joystiq: www.joystiq.com

Kotaku: www.kotaku.com

ENDNOTES

1. "World of Warcraft® Surpasses 9 Million Subscribers Worldwide," www.blizzard.com/us/press/070724.html.

2. Entertainment Software Association, "Industry Facts," www.theesa.com/facts/index.asp.

3. Ben Kuchera, "May Sales: GTA IV #1 with a Bullet; Nintendo Rules the Rest," *Ars Technica,* June 13, 2008, arstechnica.com/news.ars/post/20080613-may-sales-gta-iv-1-with-a-bullet-nintendo-rules-the-rest.html

4. Jonathan D. Glater, "Hidden Sex Scenes Draw Ho-Hum, Except from Lawyers," *New York Times,* 25 June 2008, p. C1.

5. See Webkinz, www.webkinz.com.

6. "Analysis: Worldwide Wii Sales," *Edge Online,* www.edge-online.com/features/analysis-worldwide-wii-sales.

7. "What Is Wii?" Nintendo.com, www.nintendo.com/wii/what.

8. Van Burnham, *Supercade: A Visual History of the Video Game Age 1971–1984,* Cambridge, MA: MIT Press, 2001.

9. "The 25 Greatest PCs of All Time," *PC World,* Aug. 11, 2006, www.pcworld.com/article/126692–10/the_25_greatest_pcs_of_all_time.html.

10. Gamespot, "The History of Video Games: The Golden Age 1978–1981," http://www.gamespot.com/gamespot/features/video/hov/p4_02.html.

11. See "The Dragon's Lair Project," http://www.dragons-lair-project.com/.

12. Gamespot, "The History of Video Games: The Great Crash 1982–1984," http://www.gamespot.com/gamespot/features/video/hov/p5_02.html.

13. For more details on the crash, see Steven L. Kent, *The Ultimate History of Video Games: From Pong to Pokemon and Beyond—the Story Behind the Craze That Touched Our Lives and Changed the World,* New York: Random House, Inc., 2001.

14. "Nintendo Wii Seventh Generation Video Game System Console," www.encyclocentral.com/22405-Nintendo_Wii_Seventh_Generation_Video_Game_System_Console.html.

15. Steward Brand, "Spacewar: Fanatic Life and Symbolic Death Among the Computer Bums," *Rolling Stone,* December 7, 1972, www.wheels.org/spacewar/stone/rolling_stone.html.

16. About.com: Inventors, inventors.about.com/library/weekly/aa090198.htm.

17. *Tetris,* www.tetris.com.

18. Bruce Woodcock, "Total MMOG Active Subscriptions," www.MMOGChart.com.

19. "Vivendi and Activision Complete Transaction to Create Activision Blizzard," http://www.blizzard.com/us/press/080710.html. Blizzard Had Already Acquired Activision, Makers of *Guitar Hero* and the Tony Hawk Skateboarding Titles, in December 2007; see Jessica Hall and Scott Hillis, "On Top of Their Game," *Orange County Register,* 3 December 2007, A1.

20. Ryan Kim, "E3: Nintendo Wii pulls ahead of Xbox 360 in Console Sales," *San Francisco Chronicle,* 17 July 2008, www.sfgate.com/cgi-bin/blogs/sfgate/detail?blogid=19&entry_id=28286.

21. "Console Wars," *The Economist,* March 24, 2007, 82.

22. Matt Vella, "A New Front in the Console Wars," *BusinessWeek Online,* January 15, 2008, www.businessweek.com/innovate/content/jan2008/id20080114_737476.htm?campaign_id=rss_innovate

23. Ibid.

24. Thatgamecompany, "flOw," www.thatgamecompany.com/flow.html.

25. Plunkett Research, Ltd., *Plunkett's Sports Industry Almanac 2008,* 18, www.plunkettresearchonline.com.

26. Entertainment Software Association, "Industry Facts," www.theesa.com/facts/index.asp.

27. Beth Snyder Bulik, "Video Games Unveil Feminine Side," *Advertising Age,* October 30, 2006, S10.

28. Ibid.

29. Ibid.

30. Entertainment Software Association, "Sales and Genre Data," www.theesa.com/facts/salesandgenre.asp.

31. Entertainment Software Association, "Essential Facts About the Computer and Video Game Industry 2008," www.theesa.com/facts/pdfs/ESA_EF_2008.pdf, 9.

32. Wisconsin Historical Society, "Historical Museum to Host Vintage Game Arcade," www.wisconsinhistory.org/highlights/archives/2007/03/retro_arcade.asp.

33. Entertainment Software Association, "2008 Annual Report," www.theesa.com/about/ESA_2008_AR.pdf, p. 5.

34. Entertainment Software Association, "2008 Annual Report," www.theesa.com/about/ESA_2008_AR.pdf, p. 5.

35. New York Assembly Bill A11717, assembly.state.ny.us/leg/?bn=A11717&sh=t.

36. Entertainment Software Association, "Essential Facts About the Computer and Video Game Industry 2008," www.theesa.com/facts/pdfs/ESA_EF_2008.pdf, 7.

37. Kristin Kalning, "Game Piracy Runs Rampant on the Internet," MSNBC, May 14, 2007, www.msnbc.msn.com/id/18665162/.

38. Entertainment Software Association, "2008 Annual Report," www.theesa.com/about/ESA_2008_AR.pdf, 7.

39. Sherry Rauh, "Video Game Addiction No Fun," WebMD, www.webmd.com/content/Article/124/115554.htm?pagenumber=1.

40. Ibid.

41. Entertainment Software Association, "Video Games and the Economy," www.theesa.com/games-indailylife/economy.pdf.

42. Ibid.

43. Ibid.

44. Seth Schiesel, "It's No Fantasy—More Schools are Taking on Gaming World," *Orange County Register,* 28 November 2005, 15.

45. Sloperama Productions, "Testers—The Unsung Heroes of Games," www.sloperama.com/advice/lesson5.htm.

46. Entertainment Software Association, "Industry Facts," http://www.theesa.com/facts/index.asp.

47. Plunkett Research, Ltd., *Plunkett's Sports Industry Almanac 2008,* 18, www.plunkettresearchonline.com.

48. "Dell Island in Second Life," www.dell.com/html/global/topics/sl/index.html.

49. "Aloft in Second Life," www.virtualaloft.com.

50. "Playing to Learn," *The Murphy Reporter,* Winter 2005–06, www.sjmc.umn.edu/mreporter/winter2005/neverwinter.html.

51. Aaron Delwich, "Games for the Web," www.trinity.edu/adelwich/worlds/index.html.

52. "PLAYSTATION®Network's Video Delivery Service to Offer Movies and TV Shows for Purchase and TV Shows for Purchase and Rental Through PLAYSTATION®3 and PSP®," www.us.playstation.com/News/PressReleases/480.

53. Ibid.

54. Mark Ward, "Deadly Plague Hits Warcraft World," *BBC News,* September 22, 2005, news.bbc.co.uk/2/hi/technology/4272418.stm.

55. Laura Blue, "World of Warcraft: A Pandemic Lab?" *Time,* August 22, 2007, www.time.com/time/health/article/0,8599,1655109,00.html.

Communication as Entertainment

14

Publishing

TOM CLANIN

Business could not have been better at Rueben Martinez's Libreria Martinez Books and Art Gallery in October of 2004. Martinez had two bookstores, one in Lynwood, a bedroom community south of Los Angeles, and his main store in the largely Hispanic community of Santa Ana in nearby Orange County. The MacArthur Foundation had just announced that the former barber with no college degree had been awarded a $500,000 grant, often called a "genius grant," for his work in promoting literacy in both Spanish and English.[1] Martinez said he planned to use the grant money, distributed over five years, to create a nonprofit organization that would offer tutoring and after-school classes.[2]

Libreria Martinez Books and Art Gallery started as a shelf in Martinez's barbershop. He shared his love of literature by lending books to his customers. The barbershop eventually became one of the nation's biggest sellers of Spanish-language books. Martinez was more than a bookseller. His store in Santa Ana was "a destination for leading bilingual and Latino authors," the MacArthur Foundation stated in announcing the grant. Martinez hosted famous Hispanic authors such as literary historian Carlos Fuentes and novelist Isabel Allende as well as Costa Rican President Oscar Arias, a Nobel Peace Prize laureate.[3] He also taught reading to children at his two stores, at local schools, and on a nationally televised Spanish-language television show.

Less than four years later, in the spring of 2008, Martinez, now 68, did not know if he would be able to keep his store open through the end of the year. Sales had dropped drastically, and his landlord wanted to put the building to another use. Martinez, like many other independent-bookstore owners, had become a victim of changing purchasing habits and changing land use.

Dutton Books, a landmark bookstore in the upscale Los Angeles neighborhood of Brentwood for more than 20 years, closed in the same spring because of heavy debts. Around the same time, Acres of Books, another longtime popular bookstore in the Los Angeles area, fell victim to land redevelopment.[4] In Berkeley, CA, the famous Cody's Books went out of business in June 2008.[5]

This is not a West Coast phenomenon. Paperbacks Plus, the last independent bookstore in the New York borough of the Bronx, closed at the end of June 2008 after 38 years of serving customers.[6] "Big box" stores like Barnes & Noble and Borders and online booksellers offer books at a deep discount that independents cannot match. Consumers are shopping where they can get the best value.

Magazines and newspapers also are suffering from changing reading habits. In the San Francisco Bay area community of Oakland, the 101-year-old De Lauer's newsstand, which sold newspapers and magazines from around the world, announced that it was going out of business because of poor sales. De Lauer's accountant, Joe Churchward, told the *San Francisco Chronicle* that the newsstand's time had passed "because everybody has a computer. Your news is at the click of a button."[7] The newspaper industry is also caught in this sea of change and is facing challenges on two fronts: declining circulation (the number of papers sold each day) and disappearing advertisers.

This chapter will examine how the publishing industry—books, magazines, and newspapers—functions; the job opportunities in each sector; and how the industry is adapting to new challenges.

History and Background

Origins of Publishing

The publishing industry—in fact, all mass media—originated in Germany around 1430 when Johann Gutenberg developed moveable type.[8] Books were a rarity prior to Gutenberg. They were found only in the libraries of the wealthiest Europeans and in monasteries, where monks laboriously handcopied the pages of the Bible and other books.

Gutenberg is credited with devising a way to arrange lines of individual raised letters (think miniaturized children's alphabet blocks) by hand to create columns of text.[9] Whole pages were created this way, one letter at a time. When the page was complete, it was placed on a flat-bed press that was similar to a wine or olive press, and the raised type was coated with a thin layer of ink. A sheet of paper was placed over the type, and pressure was placed above it, as if squeezing the oil out of olives, to transfer the ink to the paper. Once all the copies of one page were printed, the letters were reused to create the next page. Though the process of setting up the pages was slow, once all the type was in place for the page, a printer could make as many copies as needed.

Gutenberg's press was literally revolutionary. The printing press unleashed the power of ideas to a mass audience. Over the next few centuries, an informed middle class would take the reins of power from the aristocracy. Gutenberg made the Bible available to the general public, which allowed people to read and discuss it on their own rather than rely on Roman Catholic priests to interpret it. The printing press made it possible for scientists to publish and share their findings and theories.

Gutenberg's invention also made it feasible to republish and widely circulate the works of ancient Greek and Roman philosophers, which led to the Renaissance. The widely circulated works of later philosophers sparked the Age of Enlightenment, where reason, not the edicts of monarchs, was considered the basis of authority. These "enlightened" ideals are embedded in the U.S. Declaration of Independence and the Bill of Rights.[10]

In 1999, on the eve of the twenty-first century, the Arts and Entertainment network aired a program describing the accomplishments of the 100 most influential people of the millennium. The program's producers surveyed scientists, journalists, scholars, artists, and even TV viewers. Their consensus was that Johann Gutenberg was the No. 1 person of the millennium.[11]

The program's host, CBS's Harry Smith, said everyone on the list born after Gutenberg's press had been invented—from medical pioneers Margaret Sanger and William Harvey to Charles Darwin and Bill Gates—owed their success and fame to this invention. Smith noted that 20 million books and pamphlets were printed in the first 50 years after the printing press was introduced.

Establishment of the Penny Press

Books, pamphlets, newspapers, fliers, and other publications were produced with handset type and flat-bed presses for the next four centuries. An innovation in the 1830s helped launch the era of the newspaper "penny press" in the United States. Rather than print one page at a time, huge spools of paper were rolled over the page on the flat-bed press. This greatly speeded the printing process and allowed newspapers to increase the number of papers printed each day, the paper's "circulation." This innovation, as well as using advertising to subsidize overhead, brought the cost of newspapers down to a penny, and for the first time newspapers were available to the masses. Newspapers, for the most part, were more politically independent than in the past—paid advertising had replaced the subsidies from political factions—and they emphasized crime, local news, and human interest stories.[12]

Advances in Printing Technology

Printing technology took a giant leap forward in 1890 when Ottmar Mergenthaler, a watchmaker from Germany living in the United States, invented the linotype machine, which set type mechanically rather than by hand.[13] The machine could create four to seven lines a minute; one typesetter sitting at a linotype machine replaced five people setting type by hand.[14] Thomas Edison called it "the eighth wonder of the world."[15]

If Ottmar Mergenthaler were to visit a print shop in the 1970s, he would have had little trouble using or repairing one of his machines; they had changed little over those 80 years and were still vital to the printing industry. However, by the end of the decade, these sturdy, dependable machines were being sold to scrap-metal buyers. The computer age had overtaken printing.

Impact of Computers

By the mid-1970s technology had advanced to the point where it was financially feasible to use computers to type and print text into columns for books, magazine or newspapers. Full pagination became the norm in the '90s. This allowed the person designing the publication to use a computer to place everything exactly as he or she wanted it on the page, eliminating the composing room staff that for centuries had created the pages. Today, one person, working on a desktop computer, can create an entire book, magazine or newspaper, convert it into a PDF (portable document format), and electronically send it to his or her publisher.

The publishing industry today can be broken into three segments—books, magazines, and newspapers.

Book Publishing

The Association of American Publishers sorts books into 10 categories:

Trade Books

These are the books consumers will likely find in libraries and retail outlets. They include fiction and nonfiction adult and juvenile hardbound and paperback books. More than a third of all books sold are trade books, giving them the highest market share of any category of books.

Mass Market Paperbacks

These books cover the same topics as trade books but are produced with cheaper materials. They can be found in grocery stores, drug stores, and other non-traditional book outlets.

Book Clubs and Mail Order

Books offered by book clubs also cover the same topics as trade books, but they, too, are produced with cheaper materials. The most successful book club, Book of the Month Club, was founded in 1926 and still operates today. However, The Association of American Publishers reports sales in this category have been steadily dropping for the last few years.[16]

Mail-Order Books

Mail-order books, however, are a growing business. These are trade books purchased from a catalog or website. Big box retailers, such as Barnes & Noble and Borders, offer mail-order trade books via their websites and catalogs. Other retailers, such as Abe Books, offer rare books and other collectibles.

Amazon.com is by far the largest trade book online retailer. Formed in 1994 by hedge fund analyst Jeffrey P. Bezos, the company had nearly $15 billion in annual sales in 2007.[17] The company did not make a profit until 2002, and today has partnered with other retailers to offer jewelry, toys and even groceries.[18]

Religious Books

These include Bibles and related books as well as other religious writing and books about religions. Religious books account for only about 3% of the book sales in the United States.[19] Sales of the Bible, Quran, and books about Islam rose dramatically after the September 11, 2001, attacks, as Americans sought solace in religion or tried to understand the attackers' motives.[20]

Audio Books

Audio books have been around for some time, first as cassette tapes and now as CDs. In February 2008, Amazon.com acquired the company Audible, which sells audio digital books that can be downloaded in computers and transferred to iPods and other digital media players.[21] Audio books are growing in popularity. The Association of American Publishers reports that audio book sales increased 8.8% in 2007 compared to 2002. This is the second-highest growth in any category.

E-Books

E-books, or electronic books, had the highest sales growth, at 55.7%, from 2002 through 2007, according to the Association of American Publishers. This is because the phenomenon is fairly new, and few e-books were produced in 2002. In 2007, e-books' market share was less than 1%. E-books are downloaded on desktop or laptop computers or portable readers. Amazon's portable reader, Kindle, has a six-inch-diagonal screen and was priced at $359 on Amazon.com in July 2008. Sony and Palm have similar products. Many traditional book publishers, including McGraw-Hill and Simon & Schuster, offer e-books.

Professional

Professional books have four categories: business, law, medicine, and technical/scientific. Professional books have the second-highest market share, nearly 14%.

El–Hi

These are books published for elementary and high schools, i.e., kindergarten through 12th grade. They include classroom textbooks and school reference books. This is the second-most-lucrative category of books, with a 25% market share, and it has a steady growth.

Higher Education

These are college textbooks. Sales have been dwindling from 2005 through 2007. The National Association of College Stores estimates that on average students spent $702 for required course materials during the 2006–07 academic year.[22] Colleges also offer used textbooks for a discounted price; publishers and authors derive no income from used books. Some colleges also rent textbooks for about one-third the cost of a new book.

Magazine Publishing

Magazine readership and the number of individual magazines published in North America are steadily growing. According to the Magazine Publishers of America, from 2002 through 2007, the number of people who read magazines grew about 6%, while the number of magazines read each month also increased about 6%. Eighty-five percent of adults read magazines.[23] The number of magazines published in North America rose from 18,047 in 1997 to 19,532 in 2007. The number of magazines with websites also is growing, from 9,355 in 2004 to 13,247 in 2008.

This growth can be attributed to the huge diversity in magazine topics. Every special interest—from surfing, snowboarding, and cycling to model trains, computers, and health—has one or more magazines dedicated to it. These types of magazines usually are published monthly.

There are also weekly news magazines. *Time* is the oldest and has the highest readership of the weekly news magazines. *Newsweek* and *US News & World Report* also have large readerships, followed by *New Yorker* and *Vanity Fair,* which focus more on in-depth reporting rather than on the summary of the week's news that the top three news magazines traditionally provide.

Trade magazines are published for people working in a particular industry or business, such as construction, manufacturing, or retail sales. They provide detailed information about the specific industries they serve and are heavily supported by advertisements pertaining to those industries. These publications are generally not available on newsstands and can only be obtained through paid subscriptions.

Newspaper Publishing

Newspapers are the only business singled out for protection in the Bill of Rights (*Congress shall make no law...abridging the freedom of the press....*). The Constitution's framers understood that the news media and the free flow of information and ideas were

BARBARA GRONDIN FRANCELLA

Senior Editor
Convenience Store News

www.csn.com

Barbara Grondin Francella has spent more than 20 years as a writer and editor for *Convenience Store News.* She loves her job but didn't always plan on writing for a trade publication. In high school, she knew she wanted to work for a magazine. Back then, she thought she would be working for *Cosmopolitan.* While she didn't get to *Cosmo,* she couldn't be happier with the direction her career has taken her.

Convenience Store News is a "must-read" publication for anyone in the convenience store business. The magazine covers everything that is important to people in that business, from new product innovations to how-to articles aimed at increasing sales. Francella admitted the job isn't as high profile as editor positions with some of the more well-known magazines, but she wouldn't trade her job for anything. "Trade magazines pay relatively well—especially for beginners—but are not glamorous. However, your work can help or make a difference in the industry you are covering," she said.

Francella got her start in journalism while attending Michigan State University. While in school, she landed a non-paid internship at a small Michigan community weekly newspaper. After graduating with a degree in journalism, she moved to San Francisco and worked as an assistant editor at *California Farmer* magazine.

Two years later, she took a managing editor position with a jewelry trade magazine. When that magazine was sold to a large publishing firm, Francella moved to New York City where the new publisher's headquarters were located. Just a year later, she landed at *Convenience Store News* and is still there more than two decades later.

She said the best part about working for a trade publication is helping people in the industry she is covering. She also loves taking story ideas from "successful consumer magazines and 'trade magazine-izing' the idea."

Francella said the best advice she can give to others interested in journalism is to diversify. "With advertising revenue down, be able to write news, features, personality profiles and be a jack of all trades."

» » »

essential to the health of a democracy. That free flow of information is as essential today as it was in 1789.

Though newspapers' revenue came mostly from subscription fees in the early days of this nation, today, newspapers rely on advertising for the vast majority of their revenue. Advertising rates are determined by the number of papers sold—rates go up as more people see the ad, the size of the ad, whether the ad is black and white or color, and the placement of the ad; advertisers pay a premium to be on Page One or the first page of a section.

Newspapers traditionally were family owned and were envied for their huge profits, often more than 30%. In bad economic times, when advertising revenues dropped, the owners knew that once they rode out the economic storm, the high profits would return as the economy improved. Starting in the 1960s, however, many newspapers wanted an infusion of cash for expansion and started selling shares of their companies to the public through the New York Stock Exchange and other stock exchanges. Investors, people looking to expand their wealth or savings for their retirement through their 401(k)s, now own the newspapers.

Investors don't care about the ups and downs of the economy or about the unique role newspapers play in an informed democratic society. They expect a steady return on their investments, and they expect the media companies they invest in to take steps to ensure profits even when ad revenues are down. They expect newspapers to cut overhead by laying off employees, as other businesses do, to ensure steady profits.

Challenges and Trends

Making a Profit in Book Publishing

Nearly all of the income in book publishing comes from sales of the books, though some novels include paid product placements.[24] Writers receive royalties, which are a percentage of the profits of each book sold. Royalties vary depending on the type of the book and number of copies sold.

Few trade book publishers accept unsolicited manuscripts, so writers need literary agents to present their work to publishers and to negotiate any advance payment on the book's royalties. Their fees are 10%–15% of their clients' royalties.

For trade books, advances on royalties typically range from $2,000 to $20,000. J.K. Rowling received a £1,500 (about $3,000) advance from her British publisher for her first book, *Harry Potter and the Philosopher's Stone*. Based on the book's success in Great Britain, her American publisher—Scholastic Inc., which publishes children's books—outbid other U.S. publishers and offered her a $100,000 advance. Scholastic changed the name of the book to *Harry Potter and the Sorcerer's Stone* because the publisher believed "sorcerer" was a more marketable word in the United States than "philosopher."

Regardless of the size of the advance, the author receives no royalties until the publisher recoups its advance. If the book doesn't do well and the publisher doesn't recoup the cost of the advance and the costs of publishing and promoting the book, the publisher takes the loss. This means publishers have to be careful about what projects they invest in. They consider the quality of the writing, popularity of the genre, and the reputation and demeanor of the writer as well as how the author will relate to audiences on book tours and in TV and radio interviews promoting the book.

Rowling's wildly popular Harry Potter books have made her the most financially successful writer of modern times. According to *Forbes* magazine, more than 1 million copies of the seventh, and final, book in the series, *Harry Potter and the Deathly Hallows,* were sold in the first 24 hours after the book was released. In May 2008, *Forbes* listed Rowling as the richest woman in Great Britain, with a net worth of $1 billion; she is the only billionaire author on *Forbes'* list.[25]

Book sales represent only a portion of the Harry Potter financial empire. The highly successful movies (the filmmaker purchased the rights from Rowling) helped fuel sales of myriad Harry Potter-related products, including clothing, "flying" brooms, dolls and a bust of Harry, a Hogwarts school banner, posters, and even Harry Potter glasses. An online retailer, alivas.com, named for the shop in Diagon Alley in *The Sorcerer's Stone* where Harry purchased his magic wand, offers wands at $75 or more. PlayStation fans can play quidditch, the game that Hogwarts students played in midair on broomsticks. All of these products add to Rowling's wealth.

Using Vertical Integration for Financial Success

Major multimedia companies use vertical integration, where various media companies have the same owner. Time Warner Co., for example, could use one of its U.S. publishing companies—Little, Brown and Company, for example—to publish a book in the United States but use Time Warner Book Group UK to publish it in Great Britain. Time Warner Audio Books could also offer it.

If the book's a hit, Warner Bros. Studio could make the movie, and the author and principal actors in the movie could be featured in Time Warner's *People* or *Entertainment Weekly* magazines or on *Larry King Live* on CNN, which is also owned by Time Warner. Later, the movie could be offered as pay-per-view on Time Warner Cable or on Time Warner-owned HBO pay-per-view. HBO could later add it to its free lineup of movies. The movie might later turn up on Turner Classic Movies, which is also owned by Time Warner.[26]

Generating Magazine Revenues

Unlike books, which rely on product sales to generate income, magazines and newspapers rely on advertising. The content of most magazines is roughly evenly split between advertising and articles, which are referred to as editorial content. A magazine's advertising rate depends on the size of the ad, the publication's circulation (publications with larger circulations have higher ad rates), reader demographics (wealthier people with more disposable income are more valuable to advertisers), whether the ad is in color, and placement of the ad in the magazine.

A magazine's subscription price barely pays for mailing, and sometimes doesn't even pay for that. Thirty-two percent of magazine sales are single sales, e.g., magazines sold at newsstands, airports, and other retail outlets.[27] The remaining 68% of readership are subscribers who pay annually at a deeply discounted subscription rate. Magazine publishers are almost willing to give their products away because paid subscriptions help guarantee their circulation to advertisers.

Golf Digest, for example, costs $4 for a single copy, but the subscription price for 12 issues is only $12—$1 per issue. The *New Yorker,* which publishes 47 times a year (some editions of the weekly magazine cover two weeks) costs $4.50 for a single copy, but the subscription rate is $45 a year, a little less than $1 per issue. The advertisements in magazines pay for the salaries, printing, and other overhead.

While more than 19,000 magazines exist in North America, they are owned by only a handful of companies. The three largest companies—Time Warner Inc., Advance Publications and Hearst Corp—each had revenues exceeding $2 billion in 2007.[28]

Coping with Change in the Newspaper Industry

Online Media

A big change for newspapers began in the early 1990s when papers started putting their content online because, as one media economist explained, they were afraid of being left behind from the information-technology bandwagon.[29] They may have come to regret that decision. Today, more and more people are clicking onto their favorite websites for news whenever it's convenient rather than spreading their home-delivered newspaper on the kitchen table each morning. And they see no reason to have to pay for the news they read.

This steady migration of readers to the Internet, along with investors' demand for profits, has caused tremendous upheaval in the newspaper industry. According to the Newspaper Association of America, total paid newspaper circulation, the basis for setting advertising rates, peaked at 62,650,000 in 1990. In 2006, the last year for which numbers are available, paid circulation was 53,179,000.[30]

Declining Advertising

Newspapers are also dealing with declining advertising. Craigslist, the free online classified ads website, is considered the largest and most popular website of its kind.[31] Created in the late 1990s, it has decimated newspapers' classified advertising revenues throughout the country.

Major department store and supermarket mergers and closures also have eliminated advertising as have airline mergers. Wal-Mart, the nation's largest retailer, is adding to newspapers' woes by refusing to advertise in the publications. Also, as advertisers are looking for a large audience, they are following readers to the Web. Many of those ads are placed on newspaper websites, but their revenue is pennies compared to the hundreds of dollars that newspapers generate.

Reconfigured Priorities

This economic "perfect storm" has forced newspapers to lay off hundreds of people in recent years as they try to stem the tide of falling profits. Papers such as the *Boston Globe* and *Philadelphia Inquirer,* which once had bureaus scattered across the globe, have laid off those reporters or ordered them to return home. The number of pages in newspapers and the pages' size have both shrunk.

As bad as it sounds, it is not all doom and gloom in the newspaper industry. Small newspapers, those under 50,000 circulation, are doing well.[32] Their circulation is holding steady and even growing in some areas because they are the only source for local news, which many readers want. Small papers' overhead is much less than larger papers.' They don't pay as well as their larger brethren, especially those with circulations above 100,000. Smaller papers, unlike their larger counterparts, don't have reporters based at their state capitals or in Washington, D.C. They also don't have bureaus around the nation and world.

Even the larger newspapers aren't faring as badly as some headlines indicate. McClatchy Co., which owns the well-respected *Miami Herald* and *Sacramento Bee,* saw its revenues fall 44% in the second-quarter of 2008 but still had a $17.3 million profit for the quarter; while Ford Motor Co. reported an $8.7 billion *loss* for the same quarter.

The irony for the larger newspapers is that they remain wildly successful while their profits are plummeting as a result of reduced circulation and advertising. Although paid circulation is falling, website readership is soaring. The *Los Angeles Times,* for example, has seen sales of the paper drop from over one million in 2001[33] to under 800,000 in 2008.[34] At the same time, the paper's website in mid-2008 was getting about 15 million individual page views (visitors to the Web page) each month.[35] More people are reading the *Times,* and many other newspapers, than ever before. Newspapers are responding to this new readership by adding multimedia stories, reader interactive features, and additional information on their websites. This has created a demand for new skills and has created job opportunities for those who have those skills.

Employment Opportunities

Book Publishing

The book publishing industry offers jobs to people with vastly different skills. It needs people who know how to keep a publishing house functioning smoothly, how to spot potential best sellers and work with writers, how to design books and their covers, and how to promote and market books.

Administrative employees manage daily operations. Among other tasks, they take care of daily correspondence, make authors' travel arrangements when they are on tour promoting their books, and ensure that communication is maintained among the writer, agent, and publishing house.

Editorial employees review and select books, negotiate with agents or authors, and often help edit the book. They work closely with writers and their agents and with booksellers. They also are involved in the design, marketing, and promotion of the books they are assigned.

Graphic designers create the cover and the look of each book. A well-designed cover can have a huge impact on sales; designers stay in close contact with the book editor and marketing director. When everyone is happy with the design, people in the prepress department prepare the pages for the printer.

Promotions personnel work with the marketing and publicity teams to create effective advertising and publicity campaigns. They also oversee point-of-purchase displays, catalog presentations, and other promotional materials.

Publicists are responsible for promoting the book and author without spending money for advertising. They write news releases about the book and the author and send the releases, along with a copy of the book and the author's touring schedule, to the producers of TV and radio programs that interview authors. The public relations department also deals with queries from the public, including the news media, handles any in-house publications, and creates and promotes public service campaigns like the Association of American Publishers' "Get Caught Reading" campaign.

People in marketing create the advertising strategies, including online ad strategies, for the book and author. They also determine the pricing strategies and release date. (Will the book sell better in the fall, when people are holiday shopping, or the late spring, when people are looking for light summer reading?)

Publishing companies also have a financial department to handle expenses and income, a human relations department to take care of employee-related issues, a team to take care of the website—this includes the company's home page and links to each book's page and online promotions—and an information technology department to keep the computers and phones working.

Publishing houses also have a legal department to deal with contracts and other legal issues and perhaps an audio department in charge of having the books recorded onto CDs. Some companies might also have their own prepress and printing department, but they are more likely to farm out this work. Smaller companies also often hire independent contractors to edit the books and use outside attorneys.

Magazine Publishing

The magazine's publisher is in charge of all operations, including marketing, advertising sales, and content. Since almost all magazines are intended to make money for their owners or shareholders, most publishers have backgrounds in marketing or sales, rather than in editorial, because coming from the "money side" provides insight on how the business operates.

Other business-side jobs include advertising representatives, who solicit advertising for the magazine and work with the advertisers; online sales staff, who handle advertising on the magazine's website; marketing personnel, who work on promoting magazine sales; and the art director, who oversees the overall look of the magazine. Most magazines also have public relations departments that deal with queries from the public, including the news media; perhaps produce an in-house publication for the company; and create and promote any public service campaigns.

Most writers for magazines are freelancers, meaning that they are not salaried employees but rather contract workers paid by the article. However, many other editorial department jobs are full time. These include the editor-in-chief, who is in charge of the magazine's editorial content; researchers, who work with reporters and editors in gathering information; copyeditors, who edit the articles for grammar, punctuation, word usage, clarity, and the magazine's style; fact checkers, who double check the accuracy of information in the articles; photo editors, who work with photographers and photo libraries to select photos for the magazine; and Web producers, who oversee the content of the magazine's website.

Like book publishers, magazine companies also have a financial department; a human relations department; an information technology department; and a legal department to deal with contracts and other legal issues, including possible libel and First Amendment issues.

Newspaper Publishing

Newspapers also have publishers who oversee all aspects of the business and editorial sides of the paper. The sales department includes people who sell ads for the paper and its website, determine where the ads will go in the paper, and place the ads on the electronic version of the paper.

The editorial department, also called the newsroom, handles all aspects of gathering and presenting the news. One person, the editor, is in charge of the newsroom. One or more managing editors oversee the paper's day-to-day operations. Editors for each section—typically news, business, sports, local news, and features and entertainment—report to the managing editors. Reporters gather information and write the stories.

Photographers and graphic artists provide the photos and informational graphics, called infographics, which accompany the stories or sometimes serve as the stories. Copyeditors edit articles for grammar, punctuation, word usage, clarity, and the paper's style and write headlines or other text that accompanies stories. Layout editors determine the appearance of each page and "build" the pages on a computer.

As papers move away from emphasizing one print edition each day to updating news on their websites 24 hours a day, they are looking for reporters with multiple skills who can take advantage of the multimedia platforms available on their websites. Newspapers expect reporters and photographers to be able to shoot and edit video, create audio slide shows, and post them all on the Web. Editors also need to know how to edit audio and video and post them on the Web. While these skills are essential for today's journalists, editors and Web producers say they still expect reporters to have high writing and critical thinking skills and to understand the ethics of their profession.

Production and press room employees prepare the pages to go on the presses and operate the presses. The circulation department is in charge of delivering the paper and promoting sales of the paper. Like book publishing and magazines, newspapers also have a financial department, a human relations department, an information technology department, and a legal department or outside attorneys.

Future Outlook

Expanding Electronic Book Publishing

While we may not yet live in a paperless world, the book publishing world is rapidly moving toward electronic books and Internet promotions. More books will be available for reading on Kindle, Sony Reader, and Palm Reader formats, although their sales will continue to be far below traditional book sales for the next few years.[36] (Remember the 55.7% sales growth from 2002 through 2007.) Libraries also are expected to increase their number of e-book titles.

More people will be publishing their own books. New software and websites such as www.lulu.com now allow would-be writers to create limited editions of books. Apple offers software that allows amateur photographers to create their own picture books. People can publish limited-edition cookbooks, so they can share their favorite recipes with friends and family. Or they might print a photo book of their Alaskan cruise or road trip across America. Budding writers and poets who can't find a conventional publisher or a literary agent who appreciates their work can publish and promote their work online.

Retailers will also be doing more online promotions. As more people go to the Internet looking for information, publishers are moving their promotion resources to the Internet.

Developing New Methods of Magazine Delivery

The future of the magazine industry in North America is bright although changes are taking place. Magazine readers are no longer willing to wait a month, or even a week, to read about events taking place. They are going to the Internet to find out what is happening rather than waiting for their magazine delivery. Magazines are responding by putting breaking news—stories happening right now—on their websites as soon as they can. *Golf*

RUKMINI DAHANUKAR

Owner and Graphic Designer
The Nirmiti Company

"The profession caught me by surprise," said Rukmini Dahanukar about the business of graphic design. "I never thought of myself as an artist." She may not think of herself as an artist, but Dahanukar has made a successful career for herself and her business partner by focusing her talents on designing logos, layouts, and other creative materials for publication. Her company, Nirmiti, is based in India. However, Dahanukar can be found designing from just about every corner of the world as she travels the globe pursuing her hobby of running marathons.

Dahanukar caught the design bug in college when she was asked to develop a cosmetics catalog. She believes one of the best ways to figure out if you like a particular career is to try it while still in college. "While you are still a student, you can afford to make mistakes," she said. Dahanukar attended universities in India as well as the United States.

Business is booming for Dahanukar. "It's a strange time in India, a lot more jobs, and the economy is up." She designs everything from print ads for newspapers to music store catalogs to visuals for counter displays.

One of the most frustrating parts of the job for Dahanukar is when clients are not clear on what they want since a lot of time is wasted on figuring out what the client doesn't like. The best part of the job is taking a vision or an idea and turning it into something real, something tangible. "When I see 10,000 catalogs all stacked up, and it's my design, I get the biggest kick out of it," she said.

The best advice Dahanukar can give to students wanting a career in the graphic design aspect of publishing is to be flexible. "You can't stick to one medium anymore. You have to be prepared and train yourself across the board," she said. The successful designer of tomorrow, she added, will need to feel as comfortable working with web design as with print design.

» » »

Digest, for example, had an Associated Press story about Padraig Harrington's victory at the British Open on July 20, 2008, on its website that same day.

Time magazine is also responding to readers' demand for instant news. It has begun posting major stories on its website as soon as possible and using the magazine to provide analysis and interpretation of the news.[37] For example, *Time* will report on its website the daily, or sometimes hourly, activities of the president's tour of Europe, and the print version of the magazine will later try to explain the significance and meaning of what occurred. This shift is requiring more articles and more Web producers to continually update the websites.

Rethinking the Traditional Newspaper Model

A glance at the newspaper industry as it has functioned for the past 180 years tells us it's a dinosaur with a huge carbon footprint that does not meet the needs of twenty-first century information consumers. More than 4,000 metric tons (8 million pounds) of newsprint are produced from trees each month to feed huge, energy-consuming presses.[38]

Once the papers are printed, they are bundled and trucked to central locations, where workers put bundles in their vehicles and drive throughout the community, throwing papers on driveways and porches, dropping copies off at businesses, and stopping to fill news racks throughout the area. The next day, the paper is either at the bottom of a birdcage, in a recycling bin, or on its way to a landfill dump. The traditional way of consuming the information newspapers provide is a huge waste of materials and energy.

Creating a New Economic Model

An electronic platform for delivering in-depth information is both ecologically and economically more efficient, but the newspaper industry still needs to create an economic model for the Web. A study by the Pew Research Center's Project for Excellence in Journalism in 2008 agreed, stating that "…somewhere, a key exists that can unlock the secret to monetizing Web content." The study also found that most newspaper editors are optimistic about their papers' futures. They believe their publications will find that key, adapt, and survive.[39]

Russ Stanton, the *Los Angeles Times* editor, is also optimistic. Speaking at an Orange County Press Club dinner in July 2008, Stanton said he expects there will always be some print version of the paper, but probably much smaller than it is today. People hungry for news will also be able get *LA Times* stories via the Internet; through the *Times'* partnerships with radio and TV outlets; and via cell phones, personal digital assistants, and other mobile devices. The *Times* editor said newspapers need to take full advantage of new technology, giving as an example a subscription service sending cell phone messages to LA Dodgers fans every time the team scored a run.

Refining the Role of the Internet

The Internet will continue to influence how newspapers evolve. People want to be involved with their newspapers. Many papers are allowing readers to make comments at the end of articles on their Web pages. Important stories posted in the morning are sometimes rewritten for the printed newspaper to include information taken from readers' comments once that information is confirmed.

Some papers are letting readers become "citizen journalists" and are encouraging them to post photos and videos and share information with other readers. This has proved vital during disasters, such as floods, when readers can report on the conditions around their homes and which roads are open.

The Internet also gives papers the opportunity to offer information that the print edition of the paper can't, such as a full grand jury report about a local political leader indicted on corruption charges, a recording of a 911 emergency call to police, or a video tour of a new exhibit at a local zoo.

Given all these changes, the day may come when newspaper presses are as quaint as linotype machines, and people will be reading newspapers on wireless notebooks.

Summary

The publishing industry is nearly 600 years old and continues to evolve. The book and magazine industries, both of which offer a vast variety of subjects for readers, continue to thrive, and their outlook is bright. Electronic books and magazines will become more common in the future. Magazines are posting breaking news on their websites and offering analysis in their print editions. This helps them to keep their subscribers from looking elsewhere for information.

Newspapers are experiencing a paradigm shift that might revolutionize how people consume information. Newspapers, through their websites, have become multimedia, offering video, audio slide shows, and reader-interactive elements.

Jobs are plentiful in book and magazine publishing. Although newspapers are laying off people, they also are looking for younger reporters with good multimedia skills.

ADDITIONAL RESOURCES

Book Publishing Industry

Associations and Organizations

American Book Producers Association: www.abpaonline.org
American Booksellers Organization: www.bookweb.org/index.html
Association of American Publishers: www.publishers.org

Book Industry Study Group: www.bisg.org

Book Industry Trends: www.bisg.org/publications/index.html

BookWire: www.bookwire.com

Independent Book Publishers Association: www.pma-online.org.

Job-Hunting Resources

Booksjobs.com: www.bookjobs.com

Books

Camenson, Blythe, Robert A. Carter, and S. William Pattis. *Opportunities in Publishing Careers.* New York: McGraw-Hill, 2000.

Greco, Albert N. *The Book Publishing Industry,* 2nd ed. Mahwah, NJ: Lawrence Erlbaum Associates, 2004.

Hupalo, Peter I. *How to Start and Run a Small Book Publishing Company: A Small Business Guide to Self-Publishing and Independent Publishing.* West St. Paul, MN: HCM Publishing, 2002.

Magazines and Trade Publications

Publishers Weekly: www.publishersweekly.com

Magazine Industry

Associations and Organizations

American Society of Magazine Editors: www.magazine.org/asme

Magazine Publishers of America: www.magazine.org

Society of National Association Publications: www.snaponline.org

Job-Hunting Resources

Magazine Publishing Jobs: www.mediabistro.com/Magazine-Publishing-jobs.html

Books

Harris, Carol. *Producing Successful Magazines, Newsletters and E-Zines.* Oxford, England: How-to Books, 2005.

Johnson, Sammye, and Patricia Prijatel, *The Magazine from Cover to Cover,* 2nd ed., Oxford, England: Oxford University Press, 2006.

Sumner, David E., and Shirrel Rhoades. *Magazines: A Complete Guide to the Industry.* New York: Peter Lang Publishing, 2006.

Magazines and Trade Publications

Association Publishing: www.snaponline.org

Publishing Executive: www.pubexec.com

Websites

Who Owns What: www.cjr.org/resources

Newspaper Industry

Associations and Organizations

American Society of Newspaper Editors: www.asne.org

Freedom Forum: www.freedomforum.org

Newspaper Association of America: www.naa.org

Project for Excellence in Journalism: journalism.org

Society of Professional Journalist: www.spj.org

Job-Hunting Resources

J-Jobs Database: journalism.berkeley.edu/jobs

JournalismJobs.Com: journalismjobs.com

Books

Bradlee, Ben. *A Good Life: Newspapering and Other Adventures.* New York: Simon & Schuster, 1996.

Burns, Jennnifer Bobrow, and Janice Castro. *Career Opportunities in Journalism.* Checkmark Books, 2007.

Cronkite, Walter. *Reporter's Life.* New York: Ballantine Books, 1997.

Goldberg, Jan. *Careers in Journalism,* 3rd ed. New York: McGraw-Hill, 2005.

Magazines and Trade Publications

American Journalism Review: www.ajr.org

Columbia Journalism Review: www.cjr.org/resources

Editor & Publisher: www.editorandpublisher.com

Quill: www.spj.org/quill

ENDNOTES

1. Ben Fox, "Hispanic Bookseller Honored with Prize," *Associated Press,* 3 October 2004.
2. Tony Barboza, "Is Story Ending for Cultural Icon? Like Many Other Independent Bookstores, Libreria Martinez in Santa Ana Fights to Stay Open," *Los Angeles Times,* 6 May 2008, B1.
3. Ibid.
4. "The Plight of Libreria Martinez," *Los Angeles Times,* 13 May 2008, A16.

5. Charles Burress, "101-year-old Oakland Newsstand to Close Tonight," *San Francisco Chronicle,* 25 June 2008, B1.

6. Tanyanika Samuels, "Bronx's Last Independent Bookstore to Close," *New York Daily News,* 4 June 2008, 45.

7. Burress, B1.

8. William Sloan and James Stovall, *The Media in America: A History,* Worthington, OH: Publishing Horizons Inc., 1989: 16

9. Ibid.

10. See Gregory Rawlins, "The New Publishing: Technology's Impact on the Publishing Industry Over the Next Decade," Indiana University, November 1991, www.cs.indiana.edu/pub/techreports/ TR340.pdf.

11. "Biography of the Millennium: 100 People—1,000 Years," A&E Home Video, 1999.

12. Sloan, 123–124.

13. Ibid, 221.

14. "Words on a Page," London Museum, www.digitalhistory.uwo.ca/i2i/artefact%20pages/linotype. html.

15. American Society of Newspaper Editors, www.asnenews.org/archives/backissues/aug05/ features/805lmark.html.

16. "Association of American Publishers 2007 S1 Report," Association of American Publishers, www. publishers.org/main/IndustryStats/documents/S12007Final.pdf.

17. Brad Stone, "Amazon.com Inc.," *The New York Times,* 28 March 2008, topics.nytimes.com/top/ news/business/companies/amazon_inc/index.html?scp=1-spot&sq=amazon.com&st=cse.

18. Ibid.

19. "Association of American Publishers 2007 S1 Report," Association of American Publishers, www. publishers.org/main/IndustryStats/documents/S12007Final.pdf.

20. "Seeking Answers Through Books," *Pittsburgh Post-Gazette,* 7 October 2001.

21. Brad Stone, topics.nytimes.com/top/news/business/companies/amazon_inc/index.html?scp=1-spot&sq=amazon.com&st=cse.spot&sq=amazon.com&st=cse

22. National Association of College Stores, www.nacs.org

23. Magazine Publishers of America, www.magazine.org.

24. Motoko Rich, "Product Placement Deals Make Leap From Film to Books," *New York Times,* 12 June 2006, C1.

25. Andrew Farrell, "Meet Britain's Billionaires," *Forbes.com,* May 15, 2008, www.forbes.com/busi-nessbillionaires/2008/05/14/billionaires-united-kingdom-biz-billies-cx_af_0514britbillies_slide_35. html?thisSpeed=15000.

26. *Columbia Journalism Review,* www.cjr.org.

27. *The Magazine Handbook,* Magazine Publishers of America, magazine.org.

28. "Magazine Ownership," Project for Excellence in Journalism, journalism.org/node/433.

29. Conversation with Robert Picard, 1993, www.robertpicard.net.

30. Newspaper Association of America, www.naa.org.

31. Andrew McAfee, "The Impact of Information Technology (IT) on Businesses and Their Leaders," Harvard Business School, June 2006, blog.hbs.edu/faculty/amcafee/index.php/faculty_amcafee_v3/ comments/the_practice_yields_the_process.

32. Frank Ahrens, "Big Profits in Small Packages," *Washington Post,* 8 March 2007, D1.

33. "Tribune Co.: Ad Slump? What Ad Slump?" *Business Week,* 12 March 2001.

34. Richard Perez-Pena, "For Publisher in Los Angeles, Cuts and Worse," *New York Times*, 19 February 2008, A1.

35. Conversation with *Los Angeles Times* Editor Russ Stanton, July 2008.

36. "Fifteen Trends to Watch in 2008," *Publishers Weekly*, 7 January 2008, www.publishersweekly.com/article/CA6516743.html.

37. Project for Excellence in Journalism, journalism.org/node/433.

38. Newspaper Association of America, www.naa.org.

39. Project for Excellence in Journalism, journalism.org.

15

Event Planning ANDI STEIN

The U.S. arrival of Pope Benedict XVI in April 2008 was heralded with great fanfare by both the public and the press. The trip was the Pope's first visit to the United States since assuming the Catholic Church's highest position in 2005. As such, it was a three-day frenzy of activity, which included a meeting with President George W. Bush on the White House lawn; a visit to a synagogue, St. Patrick's Cathedral, and Ground Zero in New York City; and two public masses—one at Nationals Stadium in Washington, DC, and the other at Yankee Stadium in New York.

Overall, the visit was deemed a success, and thousands of people were able to catch a glimpse of the pontiff during his whirlwind tour. What most of those in attendance were unaware of, however, were the thousands of hours logged by those who planned the three-day event and made it a success.

Every movement, every activity, and every detail was carefully planned by a core group of professional event planners, whose jobs encompass orchestrating everything from intimate, private birthday parties to large-scale public concerts on a day-to-day basis. The skills and expertise of these individuals enabled the Pope's visit to unfold as smoothly as it did.[1]

Event planning is a lucrative business within the entertainment industry and can be an ideal career for those who thrive on details. Putting together a program or event is not unlike assembling the pieces of a giant jigsaw puzzle, as it requires great care and deliberation. Every day, large and small-scale events are routine parts of people's lives, and someone is ultimately responsible for coordinating all the details to ensure the success of these events.

For those who enjoy organizing people and activities, the opportunities within the event planning field are vast, as events come in all shapes and sizes. Personal events can include milestones such as weddings, bar mitzvahs, confirmations, and anniversary celebrations. Public events may consist of outdoor concerts or large-scale fundraisers such as races or golf tournaments. Company events can encompass annual meetings, product launches, grand openings, and employee retreats, to name just a few.

The challenges of planning an event can include organizing hundreds of small details to create one large, picture-perfect final product; working within a predetermined budget; troubleshooting and dealing with unexpected problems; and working to attract both the public and the media to the event itself. For those who enjoy the prospect of mastering these challenges, the end results can be very rewarding.

This chapter will look at what it takes to become an event planner by exploring some of the day-to-day activities involved in the business of entertaining the public by putting on events.

History and Background

Unlike other topics covered in this book, there is no definitive history of event planning. Special events have likely long been part of people's lives, and the process of planning and organizing them has gradually expanded from an informal to formal activity as events have become more complicated and sophisticated over time. However, background information about the field can provide those interested in the subject with details about the different types of events that may require the services of professional planners.

Event planning can encompass the organization of a variety of activities from small, social celebrations to large-scale corporate meetings and conventions. According to the U.S. Department of Labor, which classifies event planning under the heading "meeting and convention planners," those in the industry

> ...held about 51,000 jobs in 2006. About 27 percent worked for religious, grantmaking, civic, professional, and similar organizations; 17 percent worked in accommodation, including hotels and motels; 8 percent worked for educational services, public and private; 3 percent worked for government; and 6 percent were self-employed The rest were employed by convention and trade show organizing firms and in other industries as corporate meeting and convention planners.[2]

Events themselves can be classified into several different categories. These include social, fundraising, public, and company events.

Social Events

Social events are often those activities that mark the milestones of people's lives. Weddings, anniversaries, graduations, and religious celebrations are only a few of the events that might require the services of a professional event planner. According to Jill S. Moran,

> For those who are completely overwhelmed by the thought of inviting six people to a dinner party, let alone organizing an event for a hundred, an event planner becomes an indispensable partner—not only by imparting a knowledge of the planning process, but by juggling the many traditions, vendors, and details as well as offering advice with the often overwhelming decisions the social client will have to make.[3]

Social events are relatively constant, as people routinely celebrate milestones like birthdays and anniversaries. An event planner can be essential for taking care of the details for these types of events, so that the clients are free to enjoy the celebrations without the hassle of worrying about the details of making them happen. The organization of a social event can be a challenge because part of the event planner's job is to tailor the event to the individual tastes and preferences of the person having the celebration. This can involve working closely with one or perhaps a handful of people to find out their likes and dislikes and determine how to make the event something the celebrant will cherish and those in attendance will remember.

Fundraising Events

Nonprofit organizations often rely on special events as a means of raising money for their causes. Fundraising events can be a good source of revenue for a nonprofit, as the money raised can be put toward the mission of the organization or the services it provides to the public.

Races such as the American Cancer Society's "Relay for Life"[4] or the Susan G. Komen Breast Cancer Foundation's "Race for the Cure"[5] are popular types of fundraising events. Individuals pay a fee to participate in the race, and part of this money goes toward the cause of the organization.

Nonprofits such as the Muscular Dystrophy Association and the Children's Miracle Network use telethons as a means of raising money. This involves broadcasting a series of entertainment acts on television over an extended period of hours or days. Viewers are encouraged to call in and pledge their support by making donations to the cause. Sometimes nonprofits will retain the services of celebrities as part of their fundraising efforts. The inclusion of a celebrity at a fundraiser can generate media attention and help draw bigger crowds to the event.

Benefit concerts have been used to raise money for broader social causes. The Live Earth concert series, spearheaded by former vice president Al Gore in 2007, for example, brought together dozens of performers to raise awareness of and money for the protection of the environment.[6] Other types of events used to raise money for charitable causes include golf tournaments, fashion shows, celebrity auctions, and black-tie galas. These may be tailored toward specific groups, such as established donors, or open to the general public.

RHONDA ALLEN

Wedding Planner
Owner, New Beginnings Weddings
www.newbeginningsweddings.com

Rhonda Allen turned a hobby into a busy career as an event planner specializing in weddings. Before she started her own business in Atlanta in 2001, she helped several friends plan their weddings. Allen's husband suggested she might think about getting paid as an event planner since she was spending so much time doing it. With that suggestion, New Beginnings Weddings and Allen Signature Events was born. Today, New Beginnings has five employees and plans 20 weddings and another 25–30 parties a year. Most of her clients are referrals.

The key to thriving in the event planning business, Allen explained, is to "love people, no in-between." She also said, "You must be a problem-solver because something is going to go amiss, and you have to be prepared." Allen has seen her share of near-disasters, like the time a wedding was delayed because the limo driver couldn't find the bride's mother at her hotel. Allen said she was talking to both the mother and the driver on the phone but couldn't seem to get them together. The bride was so upset she was ready to call off the wedding. So Allen jumped into her car and drove over to the hotel to get the mother. It was the best solution at the time. The wedding eventually went off without another hitch.

Allen admitted the hardest part of her job isn't making brides' dreams come true. Instead, she said, it's explaining why wedding planners cost approximately 10% of the price of the wedding. "Wedding planning is a service. It's an intangible thing. It's hard to explain the fees associated with the planning," she said.

Internships are one of the best ways to figure out if the business is for you, according to Allen. Being successful in the wedding planning business takes more than a love of weddings. It takes someone who is creative and can focus both on the big picture and the smallest of details at the same time. Allen offers an apprentice program through her company. The fee-based program allows applicants to become an assistant event planner for at least one wedding and to see firsthand what the business is all about.

» » »

Public Events

Some events are intended to bring together large numbers of people in a public setting. The U.S. visit of Pope Benedict was an example of such an event. Public events can be particularly challenging for event planners as they can be multi-part affairs and may require the accommodation of hundreds and sometimes thousands of participants.

County fairs, which are a popular summertime pastime, are examples of public events. Featuring displays, performances, contests, and amusement rides, they can provide attendees with hours of entertainment in a contained setting—often a park or fairground specifically designated for the event. Political rallies, street fairs, outdoor concerts, and festivals are other examples of events that may be open to the general public.

The Gilroy Garlic Festival in Northern California, for instance, attracts more than 100,000 people each summer and features food, crafts, cooking demonstrations, and live entertainment.[7] One of the most famous public events in history was the Woodstock Festival, a three-day outdoor rock concert that was held on a farm in upstate New York in 1969 and drew half a million people.[8]

Some public events generate international interest and attendance. The Olympics, for example, attract both athletes and spectators from all over the world. Planning for each Olympics begins years in advance of the actual events because of the vast number of details that must be coordinated.

Company Events

Organizations such as corporations, trade associations, and universities routinely rely on events to bring together members of their various internal and external publics—employees, shareholders, and customers, to name just a few. Some of these events may be part of the company's regular activities, while others may be used to denote special occasions—product launches or open houses, for example.

Meetings are a big part of corporate life and may encompass monthly board meetings, employee training sessions, annual shareholder meetings, etc. The organization of these meetings can be one part of the job of an administrative assistant or human resources staff member or, if the meetings are frequent enough, they may be the primary responsibility of an in-house event planner. Some meetings are held on-site at the organization's headquarters, while others may be held off-site, requiring additional attention to detail from the individual planning the event.

Conventions and trade shows are types of corporate events that may last for several days and can require months or even years of planning, depending on the nature of the event and where it is taking place. According to the *California Occupational Guide,*

> The massive logistical operation of a large convention, trade show or exposition often starts as many as five years before the event. The first step, booking space in halls and hotels, often must be done years in advance. Then, one or two years before the event, meeting planners begin developing topics, choosing featured speakers and creating agendas. Much of the work also involves coordinating who will present programs and set up booths. Sometimes hundreds of vendors will exhibit their services or products.[9]

One example of a trade show that requires significant advanced planning is the annual National Association of Broadcasters (NAB) show. Held in Las Vegas each spring, the event attracts approximately 100,000 attendees from around the globe who come to see the latest trends in broadcasting products and equipment.[10]

Some events, like new product launches or grand openings, may be designed for an organization's customers, while others may be geared toward a company's employees. Holiday parties, company picnics, and team-building seminars fall into this category. Although these may not necessarily be as complicated to organize as an annual convention, they still require the skills and expertise of someone to plan and execute them.

Like individuals, organizations can also celebrate milestone events such as anniversary celebrations, which may be widely broadcast to the general public. When Disneyland celebrated its 50th anniversary in 2005, for example, advertisements for the celebration began appearing nearly six months before the actual date of the park's anniversary event.[11]

The many types of events discussed above offer opportunities and benefits for those who are detail oriented and enjoy putting together many individual pieces to create one successful big picture of an event.

Figure 25: Types of Events

Social
    Anniversaries
    Baby Showers
    Bachelor/Bachelorette Parties
    Birthday Parties
    Dinner Parties
    Engagement Parties
    Graduation Parties
    Housewarmings
    Religious Celebrations

Fundraising
    Benefit Concerts
    Fashion Shows
    Galas
    Golf Tournaments
    Telethons
    Walk-a-thons

Public
    County and State Fairs
    Marathons
    Outdoor Concerts
    Political Rallies
    Street Fairs

Company
    Annual Meetings
    Awards Banquets
    Company Picnics

Conventions
Employee Retreats
Grand Openings
Open Houses
Product Launches
Retirement Parties

Challenges and Trends

Getting Organized

Whether it be planning a dinner party for 10 or a conference for 10,000, one of the biggest challenges for an event planner is organization. As mentioned earlier, event planning may require the coordination and management of numerous details. Having an understanding of the key elements of organization needed to plan an event can help those working in the field stay in control and manage these details efficiently and effectively.

Identifying Purpose and Audience

The first step in planning an event is to have a clear sense of its purpose and audience. Knowing exactly why the event is being held and who will be likely to attend can help facilitate the planning process.

The Special Events and Protocol Department at the University of California, Los Angeles (UCLA) is responsible for managing and overseeing a variety of campus events and activities. The department recommends that event planners begin by asking several questions: "What are the key goals/objectives of this event? Specifically, what is the desired outcome, and what do you want your guests to take away from this experience?"[12]

For some events such as anniversary celebrations or holiday parties, the purpose may be fairly clear-cut. Other events may require some assessment of the purpose before beginning the planning process. Putting together an employee retreat, for instance, may require some deliberation to determine what employees will want and need to get out of the experience so that appropriate activities can be scheduled for those who attend.

Understanding the intended audience for an event is also essential, so that the right people can be invited, and the activities planned for the event will be likely to appeal to them. According to event planners Paulette and Jodi Wolf, in assessing the audience, it's important to consider a variety of factors. These may include the age of the attendees; whether the event is designed for singles, couples, families, or a mixture of each; where participants will be coming from; and, in some cases, whether attendees are likely to know each other. "The demographics of your guests are very important to the event process. The tone, tempo, and design of your event will be decided on in part by who your guests are."[13]

Managing Time

As noted earlier in the chapter, organizing an event often requires a long lead time. Consequently, it is to the benefit of the event planner to build in enough time to adequately address all the details that will need to be attended to as the planning process unfolds.

One way to accomplish this is to set up a timeline that can be used as a framework for the event. Start by setting the date of the event. Then, make a list of all the things that are likely to need to be done by this date. Working backwards, assign the various tasks to dates along the timeline, so it becomes clear which tasks will need to be completed by which dates. Planner Jill Moran advises,

> Start with a month-by-month plan of activities, then shorten the time increments as the event date draws near. Outline the tasks involved and the parties responsible for them. This allows you to monitor progress and identify expectations. It will also help you budget your time.[14]

By putting some advanced thought into developing the timeline and following it closely, in an ideal world, everything should be ready to go by the actual date of the event.

Managing Money

While keeping tabs on time is crucial to the success of an event, keeping tabs on the budget is even more so. It is rare for an event planner to be given free rein to spend as much money as needed to put on an event. In most situations, the planner will be presented with a set budget ahead of time and will be expected to cover all the expenses of the event within the parameters of this budget.

To keep within a set budget, it is necessary to take steps that will help manage expenses prudently, according to Kevin Waters:

> A budget spreadsheet that enables you to project expenditures and revenues should be drawn up. If your event has taken place in previous years, you are at a distinct advantage. Looking at an event's history is a good way to get a sense of the breakdown of associated costs.
>
> However, if you are starting from scratch, what should you include? The short answer is everything. Divide your spreadsheet into two distinct sections—Income and Expenditures—and take time to think through every element of revenue and costs associated with your event.... The more meticulous you are at this stage, the more realistic your budget will be.[15]

Even after putting together the initial budget, it is wise to monitor it closely to ensure that spending is staying within the allotted funds. It's a good idea to compare money spent with money available on a regular basis throughout the planning process to make sure you don't exceed what you originally budgeted to spend on the event.

Putting the Pieces Together

Once the purpose, timeline, and budget have been determined, it's time to get down to the business of organizing the details of the event. These are likely to vary depending on the type of event. However, some general topics may apply across the board.

Negotiating with vendors, for instance, is often a routine part of planning many different types of events. Vendors provide products or services for the event such as food, tables and chairs, audiovisual equipment, lighting, flowers, table linens, etc. In some cases, particularly when putting together corporate events, planners may be instructed to use specific vendors, while in others, they may want to request bids from several potential vendors and then choose the best ones for the job.

Deciding on a program for the event can be done early in the planning process. If the event is a conference or seminar, decisions will need to be made about who the speakers or presenters will be. If the event's purpose is to entertain—a concert or play, for instance—performers will need to be booked well in advance of the event date. If audiovisual equipment will be needed for the event, it's advisable for the planner to arrange to have it tested well ahead of the event's start time and to have a back up plan in place if, by chance, the equipment doesn't work as expected.

Food is often a key part of an event, and planning may include deciding on a menu, arranging for catering, and hiring servers. Making arrangements for setup and cleanup on the day of the event should be factored into the planning process ahead of time as well to avoid any unwelcome, last minute "surprises."

While the details of putting together an event may at times seem overwhelming, a little bit of upfront organization can go a long way. Making a detailed checklist at the onset of the planning process and following it closely can offer planners the security of knowing what needs to be done when. This can serve as a road map that can help keep everyone on track toward making the event a success.

Promoting and Publicizing the Event

Communicating information about an event to the public and media is essential to help attract the intended audience. If an event is fairly small or targeted to a specific group of people—a wedding or holiday party, for instance—all that may be needed is some sort of formal invitation or a more informal "evite," or electronic invitation. For larger events such as conventions or trade shows, or for public events like outdoor concerts or street fairs, a more structured marketing approach may be needed to promote the event.

A number of options exist for promoting public or fundraising events. Both print and online newspapers frequently publish community calendars and encourage members of the community to submit newsworthy event listings that may be of interest to the general public. Event organizers can also place paid advertisements in a variety of media outlets—radio, television, newspapers, websites, trade magazines, etc.

If an event is targeted at a specific group such as members of a trade association, direct mail pieces or articles in the organization's print or electronic publications can be used to make potential attendees aware of the upcoming event.

In today's age of technology when people get their information from a number of different sources, it's worthwhile to use a variety of methods to reach a potential event audience. As members of the Sydney Convention and Visitors Board suggest,

> Use an integrated marketing approach that includes postal mail, email, telemarketing, your website, buying advertisements in the newsletters your customers and prospects read, press

releases and posting event information to online calendars and industry or relevant business publications.[16]

While many events are designed to be private affairs aimed at self-contained audiences, some events may have newsworthy elements and therefore be of interest to the media. These might include events promoting a specific cause or those that feature a celebrity as part of the festivities. For these types of events, it is worthwhile to identify those media outlets that may be interested in covering the event and to provide them with information well ahead of time. This information can be distributed in the form of a press release, press kit, email alert, or, in some cases, a personal phone call to the appropriate media contact. Sufficient details need to be provided, including specifics about date, time, and location as well as contact information.

On the day of the event, it's advisable to designate one person to work with any media who might show up to cover the event. It's also a good idea to have plenty of publicity materials on hand and to make sure that the media have access to speakers and special guests who might be of interest from a newsworthiness perspective.

Dealing with the Unexpected

No matter how well orchestrated an event might appear to be, event planners need to be prepared for that last-minute glitch—large or small—that can throw everything into disarray. Although most people don't like to dwell on the possibility of a crisis, those who plan events need to be aware that sometimes things can go wrong at the last minute.

In some cases, the crisis may have nothing to do with the event itself. Earthquakes, weather, and even acts of terrorism are all examples of external forces that can have an impact on an event. These can lead to the sudden unavailability of the venue where the event was to be held or the abrupt cancellation of attendees.

Sometimes the crisis can be directly related to the event itself—when a caterer delivers the wrong food, the audio/visual equipment won't work properly, or an attendee suddenly becomes ill, for instance. For those working in the business, the need to remain calm and collected and to be flexible and quick thinking is imperative.

Planning can help stave off some potential last-minute incidents. Researching vendors thoroughly before hiring them can enhance the potential for quality control and reduce the chances of delivery surprises. Making sure the event has adequate security and an exit plan in place in case there is a need to evacuate people from the building can anticipate problems caused by potential power losses or weather-related problems. Purchasing ample liability insurance can cover situations that might involve injuries to attendees.

Finally, if something does go wrong, maintaining a calm demeanor can go a long way to enable an event planner to remain levelheaded and make the kinds of quick decisions that may be needed under the circumstances.

Employment Opportunities

Event planning careers have traditionally attracted more women than men. Meeting Professionals International (MPI), the world's largest association of meeting and event planners, reports that 75% of its membership is female. This is attributed to the fact that some of the key elements of the job—multitasking and communicating, for example—draw on strengths that studies show are typically associated with females.[17] According to a survey conducted by *Money* magazine and Salary.com, event planning also ranked among the top 20 jobs for young people in 2007.[18]

In-House Event Planners

As noted earlier in the chapter, event planning can sometimes be one part of a larger job within an organization—often the responsibility of an administrative assistant or someone who works in public relations or marketing. In the corporate world or in some large universities and trade associations where events are produced on a regular schedule, organizations may employ one person or team to be responsible solely for the coordination and management of events.

Event Planning Agencies

Some companies prefer to outsource their event planning activities to firms that specialize in putting on special events. These can be ideal work environments for those who enjoy the opportunity to work on different types of events for several clients at once. Event planning can also be a good career for those who prefer to work independently and may wish to specialize in one type of event such as weddings or parties.

Education and Training

Unlike other jobs in the entertainment industry that often require a certain level of technical expertise or training, event planning does not. What it does require is a set of skills that are compatible with the nature of the work involved. Good organization, communication, and time management skills are essential. The ability to multi-task, meet deadlines, and work well under pressure is also critical. An understanding of public relations and/or marketing is helpful, as day-to-day activities may involve interacting with the public and media.

While specialized training is not necessarily required to be an event planner, because of the growing popularity of the field, a variety of certificate and degree programs have been developed in recent years for those interested in pursuing careers in the business. According to Blythe Camenson in *Opportunities in Event Planning Careers,*

> There are just a few universities that offer degree programs. Some focus on undergraduate degrees, and others offer graduate programs. Learning can take place in a classroom or, with

PATRICIA HYMES

Events and Promotions Coordinator
California State University, Fullerton
Career Center
www.fullerton.edu/career

For Patricia Hymes, multi-tasking is a key part of her day-to-day job. As the Events and Promotions Coordinator for the Career Center at the California State University, Fullerton, Hymes is responsible for coordinating, promoting, and managing 10–15 large-scale events hosted by the center each year.

Each event involves keeping track of a variety of details such as, "promoting the events to participants and attendees, securing event sites, negotiating costs with and securing vendors, planning and organizing all aspects of the events, troubleshooting the day of the event, and fiscal management," she explained.

"The most challenging part is being able to juggle and manage several events at one time. Our events sometimes happen within days of each other, so making sure that every detail for each event has been checked can sometimes be tricky."

Hymes is well acquainted with the Fullerton campus, as she got her B.A. in Communications and Afro Ethnic Studies from the school. She also holds certificates in Event Planning and Meeting Management. Prior to her current job, she coordinated events for the university's Office of the Vice President for Student Affairs.

"What I enjoy most about my job is seeing something the staff has worked on for months actually come to fruition. Seeing the event participants and attendees benefiting from the hard work we all put in is a very rewarding feeling," she said.

"I would encourage anyone thinking about going into this industry to meet as many people in as many different areas as possible. Conduct informational interviews with professionals in all areas of event planning. Volunteer to work on as many different types of events as possible. This will give you the opportunity to see the many areas and determine which area you would like to focus on," she said.

Hymes believes the field of event planning holds a lot of potential for people with varied backgrounds. "One of the most important things to note is that sometimes there is no clear and direct path to event planning. Employers are now looking more at related experience rather than major or degree. This is why it's key to gain hands-on or related experience regardless of your educational background."

» » »

the advent of online learning, from the comfort of a home office. Also, the professional associations in this field play a large role in training and certifying event planners.[19]

One such association is the Convention Industry Council, which sponsors a Certified Meeting Professional (CMP) program for industry workers who want to expand their skills (www.conventionindustry.org/cmp).

George Washington University in Washington, DC, offers both an on-site and online certification program in meeting and event management (www.gwu.edu). The school also offers a B.A. in business administration with an emphasis in tourism and hospitality management. The University of Nevada, Las Vegas, offers a major in Meetings and Events Management within its Harrah College of Hotel Administration. The Meeting Professionals International website provides a list of additional schools that offer training, certification, and degrees in event planning (www.mpiweb.org).

Future Outlook

The event planning industry is expected to continue on an even pace, according to a study conducted by Meeting Professionals International (MPI).[20] However, the industry is expected to feel the effects of general societal trends that will have their impact on the business of event planning.

Going Green

One of these pertains to the protection of the environment. As individuals are becoming more environmentally aware, event planners are expected to follow suit in upcoming years with a focus on "green planning." According to Shannon Kilkenny, this means "doing business that consciously includes energy conservation, minimizing consumption of natural resources, reducing waste, reusing resources, recycling and using Earth-friendly products. Green meetings and events are not mandate today but will be mandate before we know it. Times are evolving rapidly in that direction and event planners, venues, suppliers and participants are responding. They are beginning to follow ecological practices and implementing environmentally friendly processes and programs into the way they design their events."[21]

An emphasis on green planning is likely to be seen through a trend toward the recycling of paper, metal, plastic, and glass products during an event; an increased reliance on electronic vs. paper promotional materials; and a focused effort to conserve energy by trying to reduce the overuse of air conditioning, lights, and audio/visual equipment.

Going Global

Just as the word "green" has become a popular buzzword within the event planning industry, the term "globalization" is making its mark as well. According to an article in the *San Diego Business Journal,* event planners are expanding the range of their event venues to growing international markets such as the Middle East and the Far East. As a result, planners will need to learn more about different cultures to prepare themselves for work with vendors, customers, and members of the media in these new global markets.[22]

Expanding Technology

As with many of the topics covered in this book, technology is expected to play more of a role in event planning over time. An MPI study determined changes in technology to be the "number-one ranked trend for corporate and industry planners."[23] Electronic planning tools such as online registrations for meetings and conventions are likely to proliferate, along with "sophisticated technology that allows participants to custom design their schedules, make meal selections, contact exhibitors, and meet other participants online prior to an event," noted Stephanie Ash in *Northern Ontario Business.*[24]

Outsourcing Events

Finally, a trend toward outsourcing is beginning to emerge, as more and more companies are finding it cost effective to farm out their events to independent firms rather than try to put them on themselves. This could ultimately mean an increase in the number of these firms and additional job opportunities for those interested in working for event planning companies rather than as in-house event planners.[25]

Summary

Event planning is an important part of the entertainment business, as it provides an opportunity to bring people together to socialize, interact, and network. Events can range from social celebrations such as parties and milestone events to company activities such as conventions and trade shows.

The challenges of planning an event involve coordinating activities, managing money, working with diverse groups of people, developing promotional strategies, and dealing with unexpected crises. These challenges are a good match for those who possess strong organizational skills and excellent attention to detail.

Employment opportunities within the field are good, as the nature of the business offers a variety of work environments for those interested in pursuing careers in the industry. A specific educational background is less crucial than skills and abilities in order to succeed in the industry, although degree programs are available for those who want to obtain credentials in the field.

In the future, general societal trends are likely to have an increase on how the industry develops. These include a commitment to environmental conservation, a focus on globalization, and an increased reliance on technology.

Event planning is a field that provides steady employment and a multitude of opportunities for those who enjoy pulling together many diverse pieces to create one dazzling final product.

ADDITIONAL RESOURCES

Associations and Organizations

Alliance of Meeting Management Consultants: www.ammc.org

Association for Convention Operations Management: www.acomonline.org

Convention Industry Council: www.conventionindustry.org

Meeting Professionals International: www.mpiweb.org

Professional Convention Management Association: www.pcma.org

Society of Corporate Meeting Professionals: www.scmprof.com

Job-Hunting Resources

The Meeting Connection: www.meetingconnection.com

Meeting Jobs: www.meetingjobs.com

Books

Boehme, Ann J. *Planning Successful Meetings and Events*. New York: American Management Association: 1999.

Camenson, Blythe. *Opportunities in Event Planning Careers*. New York: VGM Career Books: 2003.

Friedman, Susan. *Meeting and Event Planning for Dummies*. Hoboken, NJ: Wiley Publishing, Inc.: 2003.

Moran, Jill S. *How to Start a Home-Based Event Planning Business*. Guilford, CT: Globe Pequot Press: 2004.

Wolf, Paulette, and Jodi Wolf. *Event Planning Made Easy*. New York: McGraw-Hill: 2005.

Magazines and Trade Publications

Association Meetings: www.meetingsnet.com

Corporate Meetings & Incentives: www.meetingsnet.com

Convene: www.pcma.org

Meeting News: www.meetingnews.com

Special Events: www.specialevents.com

Successful Meetings: www.mimegasite.com

ENDNOTES

1. See Sewell Chan, "Candles, Clergy, and Communion for 57,000, *New York Times,* 12 April 2008, A1; and Jean Marbella, "Fielding the Setup for Papal Event," *Baltimore Sun,* 18 April 2008, B1.

2. U.S. Department of Labor Bureau of Labor Statistics, *Occupational Outlook Handbook,* http://www.bls.gov/oco/ocos298.htm.

3. Jill S. Moran, *How to Start a Home-Based Event Planning Business,* Guilford, CT: Globe Pe

4. See Relay for Life, www.relayforlife.org/relay/about.

5. See Susan G. Komen Foundation, www.komen.org.

6. See www.liveearth.org.

7. See Gilroy Garlic Festival, www.gilroygarlicfestival.com.

8. See Andy Bennett (ed.), *Remembering Woodstock.* Burlington, VT: Ashgate Publishing Company, 2004.

9. State of California Employment Development Department, *California Occupational Guide #553,* Sacramento: CA, 2002: 2.

10. See National Association of Broadcasters, www.nab.org.

11. See, Michele Himmelberg, "Come World Come All; Elaborate Rose Parade, Internet Ads Will Invite Planet to Celebrate 50 Years of Disneyland," *Orange County Register,* 31 December 2004, 1.

12. UCLA Special Events and Protocol, "Event Planning Strategic Questions," www.specialevents.ucla.edu/resources/eventplanning.

13. Paulette Wolf and Jodi Wolf, *Event Planning Made Easy,* New York: McGraw-Hill, 2005: 8.

14. Moran, 103.

15. Kevin Waters, "A Practical Step-by-Step Guide to Organising Successful Events," *The British Journal of Administrative Management* (December 2006/January 2007): 17.

16. Sydney Convention and Visitors Bureau, "Tips for Planning an Event," www.scvb.com.au.

17. See Ethan Bartanen, "Many Women Have a Knack for Meeting/Event Planning," *Indianapolis Business Journal* 26:9 (May 9, 2005): 29.

18. See Marshall Krantz, "It's More Than Just the Money," *Meeting News* 31:5 (April 16, 2007): 16.

19. Blythe Camenson. *Opportunities in Event Planning Careers.* New York: VGM Career Books, 2003: 25. See also, Betsy Blair and Krene Korn. "Education Gets Serious." *Financial & Insurance Meetings* 42:5 (September 2006): 24.

20. Meeting Professionals International, *Future Watch 2008,* www.mpiweb.org.

21. Shannon Kilkenny, "Going Green! Changing the Way You Plan Events," *Boulder County Business Report* (Fall 2007/Winter 2008): 10.

22. Pat Broaderick, "Meeting Planners Watch Trends More Closely Than Weather Reports," *San Diego Business Journal* 28:23 (June 4, 2007): 21.

23. Meeting Professionals International, *Future Watch 2008,* www.mpiweb.org.

24. Stephanie Ash, "Trends in Event Planning," *Northern Ontario Business* 26:10 (August 2006): 30.

25. Ibid.

Contributors

Genelle Belmas received her doctorate from the University of Minnesota and her master's degree from the University of Wisconsin. She is active in the American Bar Association and in the Society of Professional Journalists. She teaches courses in media law, media and society, computer-assisted reporting, qualitative research methods, and communications technologies, and she has developed a course about video games. Her research interests include First Amendment theory, flag display and desecration law, indecency and obscenity policy, and student speech and press rights. She is currently working on a media law textbook, which will be published in Fall 2009.

Tom Clanin is a communications professor at California State University, Fullerton. He worked in journalism for more than 25 years as a photographer, reporter, and editor. He is co-author of Copy Editor's Handbook for Newspapers, 3rd ed. (2007), and News Writing in a Multimedia World (2004). His work in journalism has been honored by the California Newspaper Publishers Association, the Society for News Design, the Society of American Business Editors and Writers, the Orange County Press Club, and the Pacific Coast Press Club. In addition, he was named the 2008 Educator of the Year for four-year colleges by the California Journalism Education Association.

Index